D1028900

In the Wake of Columbus

Louis De Vorsey, Jr., is professor of
geography at the University of Geor-
gia, Athens, and past president of The
Society for the History of Discoveries.
John Parker is curator of the James
Ford Bell Library at the University of
Minnesota in Minneapolis. He has
been both secretary and president of
The Society for the History of
Discoveries.

In the
Wake of
Columbus

Islands and
Controversy

edited by Louis De Vorsey, Jr., and John Parker

Wayne State University Press, Detroit
1985

The material in this volume was previously published as Volume XV of *Terrae Incognitae*, the official publication of The Society for the History of Discoveries. For assistance provided in the preparation and publication of that volume, the editors gratefully acknowledge the University of Georgia Research Foundation, the University of Georgia Geography Department, the Nova Albion Foundation, and the University of Georgia Cartographic Services Laboratory.

Library of Congress Cataloging in Publication Data

Main entry under title:

In the wake of Columbus.

   Previously published as v. 15 of Terrae incognitae.
   Includes bibliographies.
   Contents: The Columbus landfall problem / John Parker
— Columbus landed on Caicos / Pieter Verhoog —
Columbus's first landing place / Oliver Dunn — [etc.]
   1. Columbus, Christopher — Addresses, essays, lectures.
2. America — Discovery and exploration — Spanish — Addresses,
essays, lectures. I. De Vorsey, Louis. II. Parker,
John, 1923–   . III. Terrae incognitae.
E112.I63   1985   970.01′5   85–671
ISBN 0–8143–1786–3

Contents

Contributors   vi

Preface   vii

John Parker   The Columbus Landfall Problem:
A Historical Perspective   1

Pieter Verhoog   Columbus Landed on Caicos   29

Oliver Dunn   Columbus's First Landing Place: The Evidence
of the *Journal*   35

Robert H. Fuson   The *Diario de Colón*: A Legacy of Poor
Transcription, Translation, and Interpretation   51

James E. Kelley, Jr.   In the Wake of Columbus on a Portolan Chart   77

Arne B. Molander   A New Approach to the Columbus Landfall   113

Robert H. Power   The Discovery of Columbus's Island Passage
to Cuba, October 12–27, 1492   151

Oliver Dunn   The *Diario*, or *Journal*, of Columbus's First
Voyage: A New Transcription of the Las Casas
Manuscript for the Period October 10 through
December 6, 1492   173

Contributors

JOHN PARKER is curator of the James Ford Bell Library at the University of Minnesota. He is past secretary and past president of the Society for the History of Discoveries.

PIETER VERHOOG was a professional navigator and maritime historian. He served with the Holland America Line from 1910, beginning as an apprentice on the four-master *Nieuw Amsterdam*, until 1953, ending as commodore-captain of the *Nieuw Amsterdam II*. He published more than two dozen articles and books about Columbus, his followers, and the pre-Columbian discovery of America. Commodore Verhoog died May 16, 1984.

OLIVER DUNN is the retired associate director of libraries, Purdue University. He previously held positions at the California Institute of Technology and at Lockheed Aircraft Corporation. He is particularly interested in the Spanish voyages of discovery and colonization.

ROBERT H. FUSON is professor of geography at the University of South Florida, Tampa. His research on Columbus has taken him to both sides of the Atlantic and spans a period of more than thirty years. He is presently chairman of Florida's International Columbus Symposia, a series of annual events that will culminate in 1992.

JAMES E. KELLEY, JR., is a mathematician, computer specialist, management consultant, and writer. His historical research interests are the technology of the portolan chart, late medieval navigation, and the attending technical, social, and economic conditions of the time.

ARNE B. MOLANDER is a staff engineer with the Defense Systems Group of TRW, Inc., McLean, Virginia. He has been researching the Columbus landfall question since 1969.

ROBERT H. POWER was elected a fellow of the California Historical Society in 1982. He served as president of that society from 1977 to 1979. He is the author of several articles on the geographical discoveries of Francis Drake, the first of which appeared in 1954.

Preface

In the next few years, the approaching quincentennial of Columbus's voyage of discovery will inevitably bring the life and times of the Admiral of the Ocean Sea under increased study by professional scholars and amateurs alike. The Society for the History of Discoveries naturally and willingly assumes a leadership role in the study of the voyages of Columbus and other aspects of the beginning of the Age of Discovery as well. There is much that remains unknown and open to new interpretation with respect to Christopher Columbus. His most important writing—his journal—exists only in a later, abridged version. His personality and his motives emerge in fragments only. His appearance, so far as we know, was never recorded in a portrait from life. And of his famous voyage we remain uncertain of its most salient fact—the landfall of his little fleet in the Western Hemisphere.

That he named his landfall island San Salvador, and that an island in the Bahamas bears that name officially, might seem at a moment's reflection to be conclusive. But for nearly three centuries after 1492, the issue of precisely where Columbus landed was not a matter that concerned geographers or historians. When serious consideration of the landfall was undertaken for the first time in the nineteenth century, disagreement was the dominant theme in the discussion, and it continued well into the twentieth century. The late Admiral Samuel Eliot Morison, a member of this Society, accepted J. B. Murdock's proposal of Watlings Island as the point of landfall, and Morison's scholarship was sufficiently respected in all matters pertaining to Columbus to give Watlings a general acceptance among Columbus enthusiasts as the landfall of October 12, 1492. But calling the island San Salvador did not satisfy some close students of the problem, and an alternative landfall was offered by the late Commodore P. H. G. Verhoog in 1947 which found acceptance by other scholars in subsequent years.*

The Society for the History of Discoveries took up the problem in 1980 when Verhoog's views were presented at its annual meeting. The questions raised by Verhoog inspired others, and shortly the Society was in the center of a revisionist but friendly debate, aided by a new translation of the Las Casas abridgment of the relevant part of Columbus's journal, by a reexamination of Columbus's route

---

*We announce with deep regret the death of Commodore Verhoog on May 16, 1984.

through the Bahamas to Cuba and Hispaniola, and by new research techniques. The results of these inquiries and a restatement of Verhoog's thesis make up the contents of this volume.

As in all serious scholarship, the search here is for truth. The Society for the History of Discoveries offers a forum for this search. It does not endorse specifically the conclusions of any of the contributors, but it endorses the spirit of inquiry which is evident in all of them. We expect the search for Columbus's landfall to continue.

Louis De Vorsey
John Parker

The Columbus Landfall Problem:
A Historical Perspective

John Parker

The Columbus Landfall problem is one which invites conflicting views. There is a lack of precision in the major source, the *Journal* of Columbus, and there are many islands in the region where the landfall undoubtedly took place. Mercifully, we have been spared national rivalries which have plagued other questions of discovery. Instead we have been historian against historian, navigator against navigator. The debate, now nearly two centuries old, has brought to the problem a variety of skills and methods — as indeed future research will probably do.

From 1492 until 1731 there was no landfall problem. There was no discussion. There apparently was no interest. In the latter year the English naturalist Mark Catesby published the first volume of his great work, *The Natural History of Carolina* (London, 1731–47). Its purpose had nothing to do with Columbus, but in his concern for drawing fish in their natural state Catesby sailed out into the Bahamas. Without discernable method or source he assigned the landfall of Columbus to Cat Island. Catesby merely wrote, "Cat Island, . . . was formerly called Salvador, or Guanahani, and is yet more remarkable for being the first land discovered in America by Christ. Columbus."[1] There is no published record of a response among historians or geographers of the time.

A generation went by, and since Catesby had aroused no challengers to his opinion, it was natural enough for John Knox, publisher of voyage literature, in 1767 to footnote his account of Columbus's landing on San Salvador with these words: "Now known by the name of Cat-Island." He offered neither methodology nor source for his note.[2]

Almost another generation went by before another writer, Juan Bautista Muñoz, mentioned the landfall, and in doing so proposed a new island. Muñoz in 1779 had been commissioned by Spain's king Charles III to write a history of the New World. An intensive search of Spanish archives served him in writing the one volume that was published, *Historia del Nuevo Mundo* (Madrid, 1793). The papers Muñoz

---

[1] Mark Catesby, *The Natural History of Carolina*, 2 vols. (London: Benjamin White, 1771) 2: xxxviii. This is the third edition. I have not seen the first, but have no reason to believe there was a change in this portion of the text.
[2] *A New Collection of Voyages*, 7 vols. (London: John Knox, 1767) 2:77.

1

gathered apparently were partially dispersed subsequently and then reassembled in various places, according to Justin Winsor, and he left no record of either his reasoning or his research in stating that the landfall island was Watlings.[3] He does not take issue with Catesby or Knox, nor does he indicate that any other island had been considered. A German edition prepared by Matthias Christian Sprengel appeared in 1795, and an English translation in 1797, the translator unnamed. Notes to the English text are taken from the German translation, but neither of the translations informs us how Muñoz reached his decision for Watlings Island. The earliest proposal of Watlings as the landfall island merely states, "Es, en mi opinion la que hoy se dice de Watlin, ten dida norte sur, cercada toda de un arrecife de penas."[4]

To this point, and for another thirty years, the debate, if indeed there was one, was rootless because the major source for Columbus's voyage had not been addressed. In 1825 Martín Fernández de Navarrete put us all in his debt by publishing the *Journal* of Columbus in its only extant form, namely, the version made by Bartolomé de Las Casas, one of the early historians and commentators on Spanish discovery and conquest in the New World.[5] It is with Navarrete's edition of the Las Casas text that the problem of the landfall becomes linked to the entire cruise by Columbus through the Bahamas en route to Cuba, for it became clear that the landfall itself could not be identified except by the bearings and distances to islands visited subsequently, with Cuba as the first certain point in the entire voyage. Navarrete chose Turks Island as the landfall, and it must be stated that the landfall was not his primary concern, but rather a presentation of the entire voyage through publication of the *Journal*. And he was more transcriber than editor in any case.

Still, his point of view held sway briefly. When the first English language edition of the *Journal* appeared as the *Personal Narrative of the First Voyage of Columbus to America*, edited by Samuel Kettell (Boston, 1827), Kettell's notes offered support for Navarrete's view, which was that Columbus's voyage from the landfall through the Bahamas was basically westward, via Caicos and the Inagua islands to Nipe in Cuba. Kettell acknowledged that Cat Island had been favored as the San Salvador of Columbus, but stated that its description did not fit the *Journal's* description and that bearings and distances beyond the landfall would not produce a route to Cuba that was justified by the *Journal*. Here are all of the ingredients of the future landfall controversy, but Samuel Kettell does not do much with them. He justifies Grand Turk from the *Journal*: an island that is flat, has no peaks, is surrounded by reefs of rocks, and has a lake in the center. "The course afterwards pursued by the ships on leaving it [the landfall island] agrees also with the direction which it lies from the others" is the substance of Kettell's support for Navarrete's route from Turks Island to Cuba.[6] The intervening islands were Grand Caicos, Little Inagua, and Great Inagua. Kettell offers no detailed comparison of this proposed route or the islands

[3] Justin Winsor, *Narrative and Critical History of America*, 8 vols. (Boston: Houghton, Mifflin, 1886) 2: ii–iii.
[4] John Boyd Thacher, *The Continent of America: Its Discovery and Baptism* (New York: William Evarts Benjamin, 1896), p. 23.
[5] Martín Fernández de Navarrete, *Colección de los viages y descubrimientos que hicieron por mar los españoles desde fines del siglo quince con varios documentos ineditos*, 5 vols. (Madrid: Imprenta real, 1825–37), 2: 1–197.
[6] Samuel Kettell, ed., *Personal Narrative of the First Voyage of Columbus to America* (Boston: Thomas B. Wait & Son, 1827), p. 34.

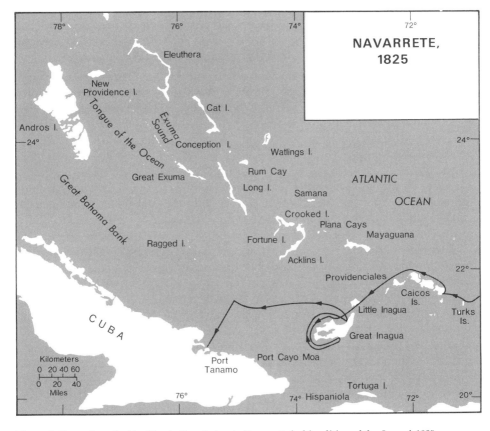

Figure 1: Route described by Martín Fernández de Navarrete in his edition of the *Journal*, 1825.

visited en route to Cuba with the descriptions given in the *Journal*. Kettell acknowledges the Watlings Island landfall of Muñoz but dismisses it since Muñoz "does not subjoin his reasons."[7]

The first challenge to Navarrete came from Washington Irving in 1828, in his *Life and Voyages of Christopher Columbus*. After a dramatic account of the landing, Irving tells us where it happened: "The island where Columbus had thus, for the first time, set his foot upon the New World was called by the natives Guanahane. It still retains the name San Salvador, which he gave to it, though called by the English Cat Island." Irving acknowledges "some dispute having arisen as to the island on which Columbus first landed," and in an appendix has a naval adviser (Alexander Siddell Mackenzie) refute Navarrete's claim for Grand Turk. Mackenzie then goes on to make a case for a route from Cat via Conception, Exuma, Crooked, Fortune, and the Sand islands on the way to Cuba. He has trouble with the *Journal* statement of October 14, that from San Salvador, "I saw so many islands that I could not decide to which I would go first. . . . Finally I sought for the largest and resolved to steer for it." At most only one island is in sight from Cat, and that is contested by some observers. It would have to be Conception Island. The distance is about right, seven leagues as called for in the *Journal*, but the size is wrong, being much less than ten leagues east-west by five north-south as Columbus described it. And clearly it is not one of a cluster of islands as Columbus seems to imply: "and of the others some are more and some are less distant, all are very flat, without mountains, and very fertile; all are inhabited and they make war upon one another." All of this Mackenzi ignores. He insists that Columbus could not have sailed westward from San Salvador because of the prevailing winds, but sends him westward from Conception to Exuma on October 16. It is obvious that Mackenzie started with Cat Island as his landfall, and he was defending it against another theory. He was not seeking a landfall from among several possibilities.[8] The issues had not yet sufficiently matured to call forth attempts at precision in its solution.

The Cat Island proponents had their greatest vogue in the 1820s and 1830s. In 1828, the same year Irving published his views, a French translation of Navarrete's transcription of the *Journal* appeared, and an accompanying note by Jean Barnard de La Roquette stated that he did not find Grand Turk conforming at all to the Guanahaní of the *Journal*. It was not fertile, did not have a large lake in the middle, as the *Journal* entry for October 13 required, and it had no harbor capable of handling "all the ships of Christendom," which Columbus described on October 14. Also it was six degrees south of the island of Hierro in the Canaries (21° 30′ against 27° 50′), whereas Columbus wrote on October 13, "this is on one line from east to west with the island of Hierro in the Canaries," the only statement of latitude reference made during the Bahamas cruise. De La Roquette brought to the argument the text of Antonio Herrera y Tordesillas, *Historia generale de los hechos de los Castellanos en las islas i tierra firme del mar oceano* (Madrid, 1601) and a map from that work to show that Cat Island conformed more nearly to the location of Guanahaní than did Grand Turk. He related Herrera's text closely to the *Journal* as presented by Navarrete,

[7] Ibid., p. 35.
[8] Washington Irving, *A History of the Life and Voyages of Christopher Columbus*, 3 vols. (New York: G. & C. Carvill, 1828), 2:156, 3:307–26.

4

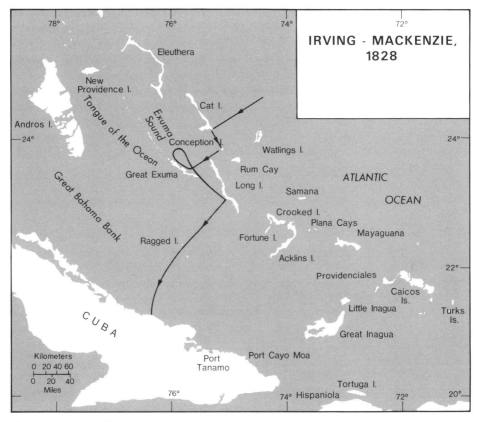

Figure 2: Route described by Washington Irving and his naval advisor Alexander Siddell Mackenzie in *A History of the Life and Voyages of Christopher Columbus*, 1828.

indicating that Herrera had access to the *Journal* or to copies of it. De La Roquette fortified his view favoring Cat Island by noting its greater fertility than Grand Turk. He cites the concurring views of Rear Admiral de Rossel, who nevertheless favored Long Island as island IV (Isabela) rather than Fortune or Crooked.[9] The Cat Island theory at this stage was not immune to modification.

Confronted with these opinions, Navarrete in 1828 held firm, maintaining that it was the westward voyage subsequent to the landfall—the islands encountered on the way to Cuba—that made his own opinion secure.[10] Also in 1828, the Baron de Montlezun wrote of Columbus's voyage through the Bahamas and got himself into an evaluation of the historians who had tackled the landfall question. After giving Muñoz's opinion verbatim, he goes on to state that Muñoz destroys his own case by making Cat Island the third island on Columbus's route after Watlings, and Conception an "astonishing confusion" en route to Long Island. The baron dismissed Nararrette's theory on the basis of latitude, which he said was the error, the source of all his subsequent errors. He also believed Grand Turk was too small to be the landfall island.[11] He offers briefly his own route: Cat, Conception, Exuma, and Long, making the clear identity of Exuma as island III (Fernandina) the major support for his case.[12]

The Cat Island landfall was also supported by Alexander von Humboldt in his *Examen critique de l'histoire de la geographie du nouveau continent* (1837), bringing for the first time Juan de la Cosa's map as an authoritative source in the landfall question.[13] The endorsement by that noted scholar was the high water mark of the Cat Island proponents.

The erosion began with a challenge from an otherwise unknown George Gibbs, the first commentator who knew the Bahamas from experience. Gibbs read a paper for the New York Historical Society on October 6, 1846, published in the *Proceedings* of that body the same year.[14] In his "Observations to show that the Grand Turk Island, and not San Salvador, was the first spot on which Columbus landed in the New World," he first undertook to destroy the case for Cat Island. He went to Cat Island and noted that "no land whatever can be seen from the highest hills, nor from the masthead of a vessel,"[15] making it impossible for Columbus to have chosen one island from among many to sail to from his landfall island. Conception, according to Gibbs, did not at all correspond to the description of Santa Maria de la Concepción as described in the *Journal*. He also noted that Cat Island could not be circumnavigated in a day. He follows Navarrete in lining up Grand Turk, Caicos, Little

---

[9] Jean Bernard Marie Alexandre Dezos de La Roquette, trans., *Relations des quatre voyages enterpris par Christophe Colomb*, 3 vols. (Paris: Treuttel & Wurtz, 1828) 2:37–88, 339–45.

[10] Ibid., p. 344.

[11] Baron de Montlezun, "Revue nautique du premier voyage de Christophe Colomb," *Nouvelles annales des voyages et sciences geographiques*, 2d ser., vols. 10, 12 (1828–29), 10:299–350; quote from Munoz, p. 85, by Montlezun, 10:317.

[12] Ibid., pp. 331–33.

[13] Alexander, freiherr von Humboldt, *Examen critique de l'histoire de la géographie du nouveau continent*, 5 vols. (Paris: Gide, 1836–39).

[14] George Gibbs, "Observations to Show That the Grand Turk Island, and Not San Salvador, Was the First Spot on Which Columbus Landed in the New World," *Proceedings of the New York Historical Society, 1846*, 137–148.

[15] Ibid., p. 138.

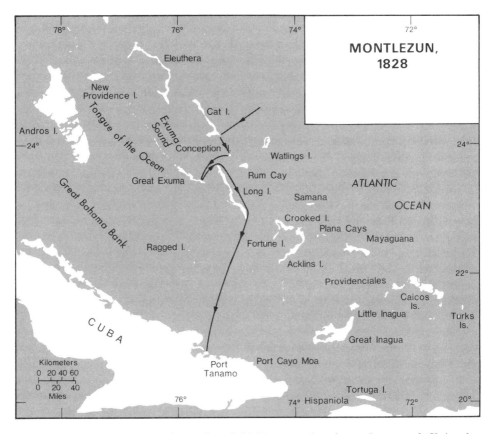

Figure 3: Route described by Baron de Montlezun in his "Revue nautique du premier voyage de Christophe Colomb," 1828.

Inagua, and Great Inagua as the route to Cuba. His arguments are somewhat redundant, but his major contribution would seem to be his attention to the *Journal's* entry for November 20, although he is in error in stating that en route to Haiti from Cuba Columbus observed that both Haiti and island IV (Isabela) were in sight.[16] Yet this entry does point to Little Inagua as Isabela, which Columbus notes is eight leagues from Guanahaní, suggesting a landfall island farther south than either Cat or Watlings. Gibbs's paper was summarized in *Athenaeum*, December 12, 1846, condensing his arguments into ten reasons why Turks was preferable to Cat as the landfall island.[17] It should be noted here that Gibbs was a resident of Turks Island. Gibbs had some influence of importance. When R. H. Major in 1847 published his *Select Letters of Christopher Columbus* through the Hakluyt Society, he favored Navarrete's view. In later years he stated that he had been reinforced in this opinion by Gibbs.[18]

To the mid-nineteenth century, therefore, only two sites, Cat and Turks islands, had any substantial advocates. The first heavyweight challenger to these points of view appeared in 1856 when British navy captain A. B. Becher published his book, *The Landfall of Columbus*. Becher's introductory statement about the landfall question declared that the problem was entirely unresolved: "When a controversy is apparently decided, it passes by and is forgotten. . . . But when it is found afterwards that the decision is unsound, and indeed all parties concerned in it are wrong, the original question becomes as unsettled as ever. . . . This is precisely the case with the Landfall of Columbus."[19] While disagreeing with Navarrete's conclusions, Becher asserts that Navarrete's transcription of the *Journal* is the only adequate authority for finding the correct answer. He proposes to prove his case by the *Journal* only. Becher's choice for the landfall is Watlings Island, and he tends to make a case less on the description of the landfall than on the subsequent cruise toward Cuba.

Becher faults Irving for not following the *Journal* closely and Navarrete for giving too much emphasis to the westward route of Columbus, not allowing sufficiently for variations north and south. But heading Columbus out from Watlings, Becher confronts the "so many islands" which Columbus reported. He attributes them to exaggeration by Columbus, stating that a little magnification of the truth was a prerogative, considering the success of the voyage to that point. He deals with the problem of Rum Cay's size by stating that Columbus was wrong in his description of it. In fact he links Rum Cay and Long Island as island II (Santa Maria de la Concepción). From Long Island he takes Columbus to Exuma, back to Long, and thence to Crooked Island. For this latter part of the voyage Becher does not compare the *Journal's* text closely with the islands. The *isleo* near island IV (Isabela) so clearly set forth in the *Journal* is identified by Becher as Bird Rock, off the north point of Crooked Island. But where the journal takes Columbus westward "twelve leagues to a cape" Becher takes him south because there is no westward coast from Becher's

---

[16] Ibid., p. 144.

[17] *Athenaeum*, December 12, 1846, p. 1274.

[18] R. H. Major, trans. and ed., *Select Letters of Christopher Columbus, With Other Original Documents, Relating to His Four Voyages to the New World*, 2d ed., Hakluyt Soc., 1st ser. 43 (London, 1870). The first edition was published by the Hakluyt Society in 1847, 1st ser. 2. The influence of Gibbs is noted on pp. liii–liv.

[19] A. B. Becher, *The Landfall of Columbus on His First Voyage to America* (London: J. D. Potter, 1856), p. xi.

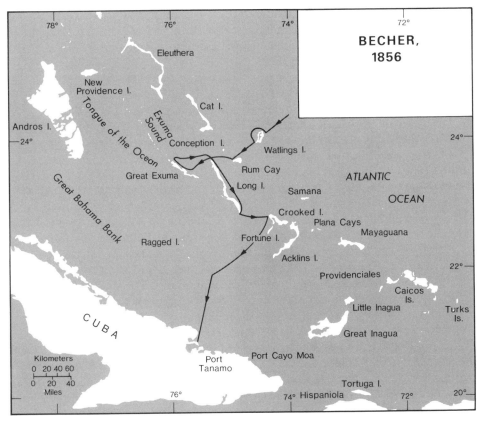

Figure 4: Route described by A. B. Becher, *The Landfall of Columbus*, 1856.

isleo. Becher used the *Journal* where he could find it corroborating what he perceived to be the route, and he ignored it at other times. At one point to make his case he had to take Columbus a hundred miles in ten hours at night in unfamiliar waters, hardly an acceptable act of seamanship.

Later scholars would trounce Becher's theories and his route, but in 1870 when the next important book on Columbus appeared, the second edition of R.H. Major's *Select Letters of Columbus*, Major recanted his earlier allegiance to the Navarrete school and took up with Becher, who reflected "a seaman's point of view." He was also strongly influenced by the map in Herrera's *Historia generale*, which he believed was made from "original manuscripts in the handwriting of Columbus and his contemporaries," possibly a loose interpretation of de La Roquette's statement about the nearness of Herrera's language to Navarrete's transcription of the *Journal*.[20] He offers no proof of Herrera's use of such sources. He pauses briefly to dismiss the most recent offering on the landfall, Francisco Adolfo de Varnhagen's "La verdadera Guanahaní de Colon" which had been communicated to the faculty of humanities at the University of Santiago de Chile in 1864. Varnhagen had proposed Mayaguana as the landfall, a proposal rejected by all later commentators.[21]

Major does not come off well as a critical student of the landfall. He moved too easily, perhaps, from Navarrete to Becher, but he did not accept Becher's point of Columbus's sighting of Watlings Island, which was the northeast point of the island. Major believed it was the southeast corner. He brought Herrera's map into use as had been suggested by de La Roquette. He lined up Herrera's place names with modern ones, and Guanahaní is clearly Watlings. At the same time he rejects Humboldt's use of the La Cosa map, contending that "the imperfectness of the Bahama group . . . renders it perfectly inadequate for settling so minute a question."[22] He notes a major error of the Cat Island advocates: it is forty-two miles long. The landfall was an "isleta." But here the critical approach ends. He does not examine Becher's reasoning or route through the islands to Cuba. Like a dory-boat he follows Becher to Long Island, Great Exuma, and Crooked Island.

Becher had no standing as historian equal to Major's, and it was probably the latter who secured the position of the former for the next twenty-six years. Becher's was the most elaborate theory advanced thus far, and an uncritical reading of it is quite convincing. But its failure to come to grips with the points in the *Journal* which did not sustain the route Becher chose made it natural prey for anyone who knew navigation and seamanship and had an interest in the problem. Such was Gustavus V. Fox, a U.S. Navy captain who had served as assistant secretary of the Navy from 1861 to 1866.

Fox's study of the landfall was published in a monograph titled "An Attempt to Solve the Problem of the First Landing Place of Columbus in the New World." It was published in the *Report of the Superintendent of the U.S. Coast and Geodetic Survey,* June 1880, which appeared in 1882. Fox begins by discounting the Cat Island theory, stating that no Spanish authority supports it. He found its origins in Joannes de

[20] Major, p. lix.
[21] Francisco Adolfo de Varnhagen, "La verdadera Guanahani de Colon," *Annales de la Universidade de Chile* 24 (Santiago: Imprenta Nacional, 1864): i–x, 1–20.
[22] Major, p. lxiii.

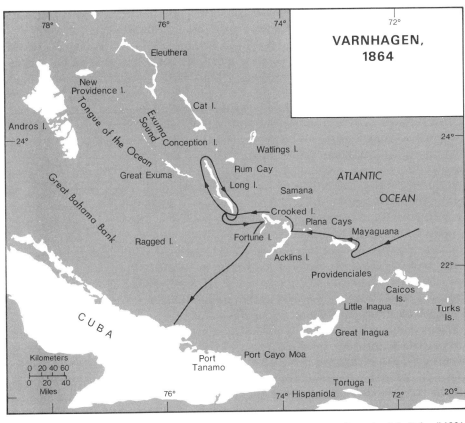

Figure 5: Route described by Francisco Adolfo de Varnhagen, "La verdadera Guanahani de Colon," 1864.

Laet's *Nieuwe wereldt* (1625) where Cat Island was represented as Guanahaní, and Fox states that later map publishers merely followed Laet's example.[23] He entirely discounts Major's identification of Watlings with Guanahaní from the Herrera map. After giving some credence to La Cosa's map, he considers maps in general as inadequate primary sources, concluding that the landfall would "never be reached by their evidence."[24]

Only the *Journal* had the answers, he believed, and he sought to bring new light from it through a new translation of the crucial period, October 12–29. In parallel columns he gives Navarrete's transcription and an English translation by H. L. Thomas of the U.S. State Department. His basic reference is a U.S. Coast and Geodetic Survey map, prepared from Admiralty surveys of 1832–36, and from "such Spanish charts as were available."[25] He first examines the four main tracks offered to that date: from Grand Turk, Cat, Watlings, Mayaguana. He finds Navarrete's route inconsistent with the *Journal*, and Navarrete's landfall too far south in comparison with the La Cosa and Herrera maps. Fox completely shatters the Cat Island landfall. He accepts Gibbs's remark that no island can be seen from Cat, eliminating the "so many islands" problem from that proposed landfall. Also, Conception, according to Fox, does not at all fit Columbus's island II (Santa Maria de la Concepción). Columbus could not have coasted east and west on Exuma, the proposed island III (Fernandina) of the Cat proponents, because it has no east-west coast, and he could not have anchored at its southern end because there is not sufficient depth of water. A route from Exuma to Long Island (island IV, Isabela) is an impossibility because of shoal water, wrote Fox, and likewise from the north coast of Long Island to Cuba. The Cat island landfall and route would never be proposed seriously again. Muñoz's Watlings theory is quickly disposed of. The route from Watlings to Conception or Rum Cay, Long, and Cat Islands involves impossible distances and directions when compared to the *Journal*. Varnhagen's Mayaguana landfall fails on many specifics of navigation, and not less on Fox's contention that Varnhagen simply omitted significant passages from the *Journal* in order to make his case. Another weakness was Varnhagen's too close adherence to Becher in the later part of the course.

But for Fox, Becher is the primary target. He contends that the *Journal* could not take Columbus around Watlings Island from the northeast landfall point given by Becher (Oct. 14: "I went along the island in a north-northeasterly direction to see the other part which lay to the east"). The size of Rum Cay is an "insurmountable obstacle" to its identification as island II (Santa Maria de la Concepción). If joined to Long Island, which Becher did, and which Fox says is ridiculous, then Exuma could not be island III (Fernandina) because it is not visible from Long, which the *Journal* says it must be ("I departed from the Islands of Santa Maria de la Concepción . . . for that of Fernandina which loomed very large to the westward"). Along the

[23] Joannes de Laet, *Nieuwe wereldt ofte beschrijvinghe van West-Indien* (Leyden: Isaack Elzevier, 1625). The map, titled "De groote ende kleyne eylanden van West-Indien," is bound at the beginning of the text.
[24] Gustavus V. Fox, "An Attempt to Solve the Problem of the First Landing Place of Columbus in the New World," *Report of the Superintendent of the U.S. Coast and Geodetic Survey*, June, 1880 (Washington: G.P.O., 1882), Appendix 18, pp. 346–417, 352.
[25] Ibid., p. 373.

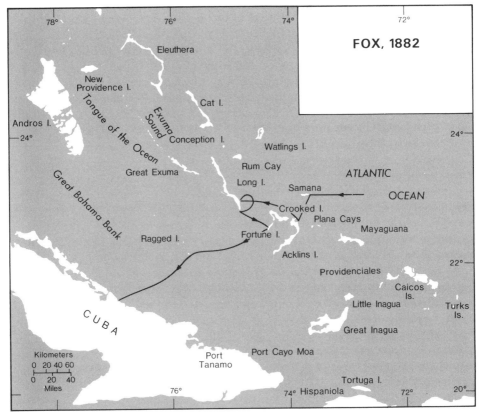

Figure 6: Route described by Gustavus V. Fox, "An Attempt to Solve the Problem of the First Landing Place of Columbus in the New World," 1880.

coast of Exuma, Becher must take Columbus 100 miles in ten hours, inventing a gale to do so, the night of October 17–18—an impossibility, according to Fox.[26]

From Exuma, Becher takes Columbus to Long Island, to its southern end, and from there to Crooked Island. At this point he meets Fox's route, and the two are in agreement on the passage to Cuba. How did Fox get Columbus there? He proposes as the landfall the small island of Samana, a name which appears on the La Cosa map along with Guanahaní. Despite his previously announced lack of faith in maps, Fox produces fourteen of them that make Samana a good candidate for the landfall.[27] The "so many islands" of the *Journal* are the hills of Plana Cays, Acklins and Crooked islands, the latter two probably connected at the time, giving it a combined dimension very close to Columbus's reckoning for Santa Maria de la Concepción (13 by 29 miles compared with Columbus's 16 by 32 miles). With great care for tides, currents, and for times of landing and times at which Columbus wrote in the *Journal*, Fox takes Columbus to Long Island (island III, Fernandina) to its southeast end on October 17. He then sends Columbus up and down its coast north-northwest and south-southeast, anchoring finally two miles from its southern cape, which Columbus called two leagues, raising the problem of Columbus's confusion of measurements. From this point Fox takes Columbus to Fortune Island, his island IV (Isabela), on October 19, finding the rocky *isleo* at the north end of Fortune, just south of Crooked Island. From here on October 24, according to Fox, Columbus sailed to the Ragged Islands and then to Cuba. Fox concludes with a summary of his findings, noting continued discrepancies between the *Journal* and his own route. This was easily the most careful analysis of the voyage thus far.

It was good enough to call forth an extended review, which was in fact a challenge, by J. B. Murdock, published in the U.S. Naval Institute *Proceedings* in April, 1884.[28] In his essay "The Cruise of Columbus in the Bahamas, 1492," Murdock begins by praising the care with which Fox went about his work, but Murdock believed the evidence led to a different conclusion. Murdock believed that all early charts were so full of errors as to make them worthless and he chose to ignore them. He read the *Journal* against the "best modern charts procurable."[29] He employed another translator, Professor Montaldo of the U.S. Naval Academy, to check the translation Thomas had made for Fox.

Despite his passion for accuracy, Murdock states at the outset that "the journal contains statements that appear to be absolutely irreconcilable with the present topography of the Bahamas."[30] This is admirable candor, but it does not imply that Murdock was trying every possible set of islands for a proper fit with the *Journal*. Rather it indicates that a likely route had been selected and it did not fit exactly with the *Journal*. He does of course confront the major writers, and their landfalls and routes. Now there are five of them: Navarrete, Varnhagen, Irving, Becher, and Fox. He dismisses the earlier ones with ease. He finds Navarrete agreeing with the *Journal*

[26] Ibid., p. 385.
[27] Ibid., p. 389.
[28] J. B. Murdock, "The Cruise of Columbus in the Bahamas, 1492," *Proceedings of the U.S. Naval Institute* (April, 1884), pp. 449–86.
[29] Ibid., p. 450.
[30] Ibid.

in "only one or two points." Varnhagen gets off the mark in the wrong direction, taking Columbus west-northwest where the *Journal* indicates a southwest course. Irving makes a similar mistake, taking Columbus south-southeast from his Cat Island landfall, and the route is flawed from there on, eventually crossing the Bahama Bank from Long Island to Cuba, which Murdock says is unnavigable. Becher presents a problem for Murdock. Agreeing with him on the Watlings Island landfall, Murdock joins Fox in finding Becher's subsequent voyage widely variant from the *Journal*, but accepting Crooked Island as island IV (Isabela).

Murdock then turns to the landfall and route proposed by Fox. He agrees that Crooked Island is a very convincing island II (Santa Maria de la Concepción), which makes Samana a fairly good landfall because the *Journal* is sufficiently vague on the landfall island to make almost any small island fit it. But Fox's route, in Murdock's judgment, breaks down at island III (Fernandina), which the *Journal* notes was a larger one, seen to the west. Fox's Fernandina was Long Island, which cannot be seen from Crooked, and Fox had acknowledged this, allowing the possibility that over-hanging clouds had indicated its presence below.[31] Murdock does however accept the southeast point of Long as Columbus's departure point for island IV (Isabela). But there were further troubles in getting to island IV. Crooked had already been used as island II, so to conform to the south-southeast and east-southeast direction required in the *Journal* it had to be Fortune Island, sending Columbus between Crooked and Fortune, a passage only a mile wide which Columbus did not mention. These problems and some later ones on the route to the Ragged Islands made Fox's landfall invalid, in Murdock's view.

So Murdock advanced his own theory, and a new methodology. Starting at Puerto Padre, the generally accepted landfall on Cuba, he worked backward to the Ragged Islands (Islas de Arena) which had the correct distance and bearing, seventy-eight miles north-northeast–south-southwest. Back from there to island IV (Isabela) took him about sixty-five miles on an east-northeast–west-southwest bearing to Crooked and Fortune islands, with Bird Rock as the "rocky islet" of Columbus. Long Island is the next step back, as island III (Fernandina), a six-hour voyage with the southeast cape of Long being about twenty-five miles west of the rocky islet (Bird Rock) and Long's dimension, over twenty leagues, corresponding closely with the *Journal*. Now if he is right so far, Murdock's island II (Santa Maria de la Concepción) will have to be one from which III is in sight and very large to the west. This is the first major problem for Murdock, for Rum Cay is the only possibility, but Long Island is not visible from Rum Cay. But the *Journal* itself presents a problem here, for Columbus's distance between II and III being twenty-six miles would seem to preclude the visibility which the *Journal* calls for. Murdock writes, "the fact of visibility cannot be reconciled with the distance given."[32] No one else, Murdock notes, has come up with a III that is visible from II either. Murdock's next problem was the dimensions of Rum Cay. Columbus calls for about ten leagues east-west, and five north-south. Those numbers converted to miles make it about right. Murdock accepts Fox's suggestion made in another context that Columbus must have sometimes confused

[31] Ibid., p. 470.
[32] Ibid., p. 476.

15

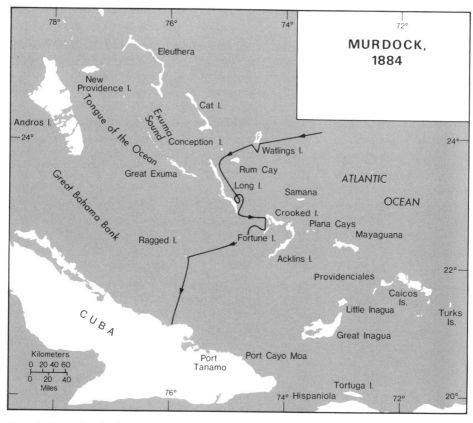

Figure 7: Route described by J. B. Murdock, "The Cruise of Columbus in the Bahamas, 1492," 1884.

the two measurements. From Rum Cay back one step leads only to Watlings Island, and the distance is about right. But when he got to Watlings Island, Murdock had the old problem of "so many islands" seen from there in the direction of island II (Santa Maria de la Concepción). Only one place, he wrote, Caicos, could supply the cluster of islands required in this part of the *Journal*, and Murdock states that there is no route from that locale that "agrees with any of the subsequent record."[33] The last major landfall theorist of the nineteenth century may have unwittingly pointed to some new directions for theorists of the twentieth.

Regrettably, the giants in the field of discovery history in the last years of the nineteenth century steered clear of the problem. Justin Winsor's second volume of the *Narrative and Critical History* was too early to take note of Murdock. He did acknowledge Fox's contribution but stayed out of the argument.[34] Clements R. Markham in editing the *Journal* for the Hakluyt Society let R. H. Major do his arguing for him.[35] John Boyd Thacher is more expressive, championing the Watlings landfall. He cites Fox and all who preceded him, but not Murdock. My own reading of Thacher indicates he had read Murdock and used his work, but did not bring up the problems Murdock had raised with his own most-favored route.[36] He was bolstered in his conclusions by the *Chicago Herald* expedition of 1891, the first expedition ever mounted to seek a solution to the landfall question. Thus ended the nineteenth century, with Watlings Island having the greatest acceptance of the various landfalls that had been proposed, thanks more to Murdock than to Becher or Muñoz, its earlier advocates. Yet there were problems with islands II, III, and IV on the Murdock route. Rum Cay was not the largest among "so many islands"; Long Island did not loom "very large to the westward" from Rum Cay; and from Bird Rock no coast "ran from that islet to the west" and extended "for twelve leagues to a cape."

If the nineteenth century had not completely solved the problem, the first generation of the twentieth did no more than confirm the fact. The next major writer on the subject was R. T. Gould, a British naval officer, who in 1927 reviewed the whole discussion of the previous hundred years for the Royal Geographical Society and stated that after a century of research it remained "a problem . . . which cannot even now be said to have been absolutely resolved"; further, "to speak in mathematical language, a rigorous solution of the problem is impossible."[37] But he went forward with a somewhat mathematical methodology: "If one accepts the principle of assessing the value of the various solutions by the percentage of evidence which one is compelled to disregard in each case, it is not difficult to pick out one solution to which there attaches a very high degree of probability." The common failing among

[33] Ibid., p. 485.
[34] Winsor, 2: 52–56.
[35] Clements R. Markham, *The Journal of Christopher Columbus* (during his first voyage, 1492–93) (London: Hakluyt Society, 1983). Citing Major only, Markham takes Columbus to Rum Cay, Long Island, and Crooked Island.
[36] Thacher, pp. 23–26. It is most unlikely that Thacher could have read Fox without being aware of Murdock's review of Fox's work. Thacher works back from Cuba, Murdock-style. Also, he mentions the *Chicago Herald* expedition and "subsequent researches carried on by government authority" as supporters of the Watlings landfall theory (p. 26).
[37] R. T. Gould, "The Landfall of Columbus: An Old Problem Re-stated," *Geographical Journal* 49 (1927): 403–29.

landfall proponents, he wrote, with the exception of Murdock, was "a decided lack of impartiality and balanced judgment." He very much favored Watlings, but he believed that more evidence in the form of a complete Columbus *Journal* or a map by Columbus would be needed to find a final answer. But Murdock earned his highest praise: "The world owes [to Murdock] the first clear and impartial statement, unshaken in its essentials by later criticism, of the reasons which go to show that in all probability Watling Island is the true Guanahaní." In combing through the works of his predecessors, Gould found only Herrera's map to provide worthwhile carto-graphic evidence, and even with other maps offered, only Cat and Watlings were landfall possibilities, with the latter clearly superior. Gould's major problem with the Watlings landfall was the "so many islands" question at island II (Santa Maria de la Concepción). He suggests that a southwest direction need not be assumed (which would not help since there are no other islands closer to Watlings) and he ventures the theory that numbers of clouds might have led Columbus to a presumption that islands lay beneath them. Also, he had a problem with the discrepancy in the size of Rum Cay and Columbus's Santa Maria de la Concepción. While examining all currently extant theories closely, Gould does not indicate any original research of his own into the possibilities of still other potential landfall islands.

In 1930 the Argonaut Press published Cecil Jane's edition of the *Journal*, where incredibly the landfall question is not even mentioned.[38] Jane's distrust of Las Casas as a historian was not applied to the Las Casas transcription of the *Journal*. The following year Glenn Stewart wrote of sailing the route from Watlings to Cuba, and he had no trouble identifying the islands set forth by Murdock. He wrote in the *Geographical Review* that the "so many islands" seen from Watlings were separate headlands of Rum Cay, and the wrong dimensions of that island are attributed to Las Casas's use of leagues instead of miles in making his transcription.[39]

A new approach to the landfall question was offered by John W. McElroy in the July, 1941, issue of the *American Neptune*. Beginning with Watlings as the assumed landfall, because "authoritative opinion is now unanimous" on that point, McElroy attempted further proof by studying the dead reckoning methods of Columbus during his ocean voyage. This brought him to a landfall at 23° 47' .4N, "about nine miles south of San Salvador [Watlings], at 2:00 A.M. 12 October 1492." [40] In this work McElroy had the collaboration of Samuel Eliot Morison who had already begun his translation of the *Journal*, a version which was not published until 1963.[41] In the meantime his great biography of Columbus, *Admiral of the Ocean Sea* (Boston, 1942) made clear his case for the Watlings Island landfall.

In the preface to his edition of the *Journal*, Morison criticizes all previous transla-tions but does not take note of the translations of the landfall-to-Cuba episode made for Fox and Murdock. Morison effectivley takes himself out of the argument by stating that "almost everyone by 1900 accepted the identification of Guanahaní with

[38] Cecil Jane, *The Voyage of Christopher Columbus* (London: Argonaut Press, 1930).
[39] Glenn Stewart, "San Salvador Island to Cuba," *Geographical Review* (1931), pp. 124–30.
[40] John W. McElroy, "The Ocean Navigation of Columbus on His First Voyage," *American Neptune* 1:209–40.
[41] Samuel Eliot Morison, *Journals and Other Documents on the Life and Voyages of Christopher Columbus* (New York: Limited Editions Club, 1963).

the island that the English call Watlings."[42] But in his brief review of the landfall controversy Morison does not cite either Muñoz or Becher, the earliest Watlings advocates. Nor does he advance a methodology of his own. He endorses McElroy's study of dead reckoning which led to Watlings, and from there he largely endorses Murdock's route. His mission with respect to the landfall is to defend Watlings's claim, not to explore for other possibilities. One finds some problems in his defense. For example, the October 13 entry in Morison's translation of the *Journal* states that the landfall island was very level—"no mountains." In his earlier *Admiral of the Ocean Sea* Morison's map shows a mountain—Kerr Mountain— and its height, 140 feet. In his edition of the *Journal* the map does not name the mountain or indicate its height. On the "so many islands" problem, Morison accepts the view that the cays below the horizon looked like many islands, and he observed this himself from a point ten miles out from Watlings. He does not say that Columbus was ten miles out when he saw them, or that the people of Guanahaní who named them were unaware that this group of cays was really one island. He does not discount the importance of the Indian's statement, nor does he suggest that the many islands they knew might refer to others beyond the horizon to the southwest, apparently accepting the *Journal*'s following statement about the islands Columbus mentioned: "Finally I looked for the biggest [island] and decided to go there, and so I did, and it is probably distant from this island of San Salvador five leagues, and some of them more and some less. All are very level without mountains, and very fertile, and all inhabited, and they make war on one another." He does discount the views of historians who accept this statement as an indication that Columbus was sailing through "an archipelago like Turks Islands." As for Rum Cay's dimensions, five by ten leagues, Morison has Columbus change to a new measurement: "This is the first instance of Columbus using a different league, equivalent to between 1 and 1.5 nautical miles for distance along shore." Morison does not suggest that Columbus consistently used one type of league for shoreline and another for sea measurement. When Columbus sees island III (Fernandina) "large to the west," Morison states that he could not see Long Island from a point three miles south of the western tip of Rum Cay. Yet what the *Journal* says is that Columbus sighted an island, "a bigger one to the west," upon his arrival at island II (Santa Maria de la Concepcion) and that he then "made sail to navigate all that day until nightfall" to reach its western end. Morison does not admit the problem: he writes, "But he could not have sighted Long Island until he reached the western end of Rum Cay." Columbus quite simply (or Las Casas) was wrong. When Columbus sails westward for Fernandina on October 16, he refers to his "departure from the islands of Santa Maria" (again the implied archipelago). Describing Fernandina, Columbus says the island was "level," yet Morison notes on Long Island hills and bold headlands. Now if island III is "8 leagues on a parallel" from island II, then it must have been an island of some height to have been seen from island II, and Morison does not attribute that height to Long Island, and clearly it does not have it, or it would be visible from Rum Cay. But if it is level, as Columbus says, then to see it from eight leagues plus ten leagues more, the east end of island II, would seem impossible. Thus there are problems in islands II and III

42 Ibid., p. 66, n. 5.

19

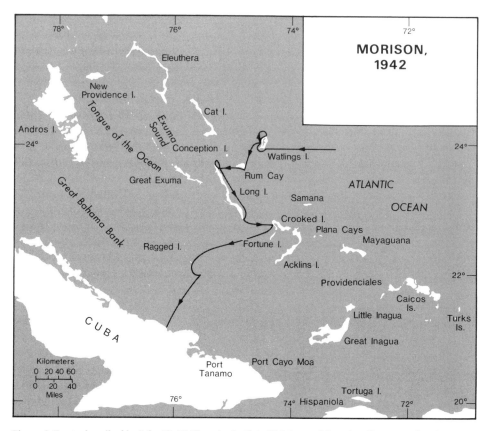

Figure 8: Route described by John W. McElroy in the July 1941 issue of *American Neptune* and endorsed by Samuel Eliot Morison, *Admiral of the Ocean Sea*, 1942.

which Morison does not address, nor admit with Murdock that they are problems.

Island IV (Isabela) also presents a problem, alluded to earlier. Arriving at the "rocky islet" at the north end of island IV (Bird Rock according to Morison and others), Columbus says, "then we ran along the coast from the islet to the west, and made 12 leagues to a cape which I call Cabo Hermoso which is on the western side." Bird Rock is the obvious "rocky islet" on the Watlings, Rum Cay, Long, Crooked islands route. But there is no coast of any length leading westward from it. The nearest coast on Crooked Island actually tends south-southeast. To this problem Morison responds, "the only way to make sense out of this passage is to read *sueste* for *gueste* and to reduce the distance." Making sense of a passage of text implies that the route is set and the text must be adjusted, not the reverse.

So in effect, there is some problem with all three of the islands following the landfall in the Murdock-Morison route, just as there was with the routes of Fox, Becher, Varnhagen, Irving and Navarrete. And while the Watlings landfall received general acceptance from most students of discovery, there were some who demurred. R. T. Gould, who had favored the Watlings landfall in 1927, in reviewing Morison's *Admiral of the Ocean Sea* in 1943 had second thoughts, clearly preferring Conception Cay as the landfall site.[43] There was a serious challenge to Watlings launched in 1947 by Pieter Verhoog in a small book titled *Guanahaní Again*. Verhoog's views were sufficiently credible to initiate some debate in the public press in the United States, and to get a hearing for Verhoog in the *Proceedings of the U.S. Naval Institute* in 1954.[44]

Verhoog, like Murdock and Fox, was a man of the sea by profession, with a record of distinguished service with the Holland-American Line. His interest in navigational problems and in the Spanish language brought him to a study of the landfall question. He states that he began his studies without any particular landfall in mind, but collected everything he could find in the sources that might be called a sailing direction. He disdained the use of early maps. His method was to create a plotting map in which one millimeter represented one Columbian mile, and he entered the data from the *Journal* on it. He incorporated into his theory the proposition that the forest growth in the Bahamas was much taller in 1492 than at present, making visibility possible from twice the present distance. He also found errors in the extant translations of the *Journal* for the Bahamas period. Verhoog rejected the notion that Columbus confused leagues and miles, or that he used miles for some land measurements. Verhoog insisted that Columbus used a league that is the equivalent of four miles, and a nautical mile that is about twenty percent shorter than the present nautical mile.

Thus Verhoog's plotting chart, an entirely new methodology in the landfall question, produced an entirely new landfall proposal: South Caicos Island. The chart included the following features from the *Journal*: from thirty to forty miles east of the landfall island there should be an island that was the source of a light seen by

[43] G. H. T. Kimble and R. T. Gould, Review article in *Geographical Journal* 101 (May 1943): 260–65. Gould's case for the landfall on Conception is expounded at greater length in his *Enigmas* (London, 1945; reprinted New Hyde Park, N.Y.: University Books, 1965), pp. 66–94.

[44] Pieter Verhoog, *Guanahaní Again* (Amsterdam, 1947); idem, "Columbus Landed on Caicos," *Proceedings of the U.S. Naval Institute* 80 (1954):1101–11.

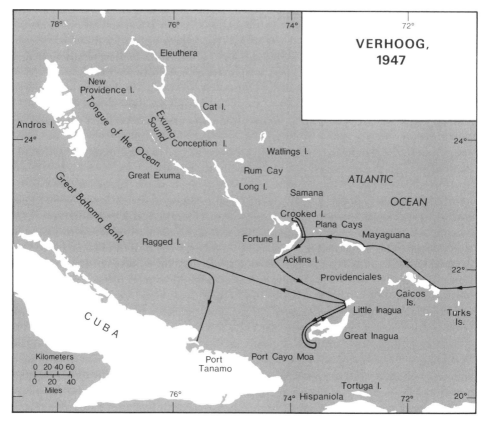

Figure 9: Route described by Pieter Verhoog in *Guanahaní Again*, 1947.

Columbus on the night before the landfall. The landfall island (San Salvador) must be about forty-eight to eighty present nautical miles in length, and from it there must be many other islands in sight. The island must have a large inner harbor surrounded by a belt of reefs. At its northern end it must have a narrow entrance where a fort could be built on a peninsula resembling an island. Island II (Santa Maria de la Concepcion) should be about twenty-eight miles from San Salvador. The island should have an east coast about twenty miles in length, and a north coast at least forty miles long. Island III (Fernandina) must be from thirty-two to thirty-six miles west of Santa Maria and should have a length of at least seventy-two miles. It should have a large harbor with an *isleo* at its mouth about eight miles from its northeast point, and a cape at its southwest end deserving Columbus's appellation *Cabo Verde*. Island IV (Isabela) should have a northern coast about forty miles long and have an *isleo* off its northern cape. The northwest part of the island should be a beautiful cape, with a beach and anchorage near by. The southwest part of the island should have a cape with a lagoon nearby. The southern coast should be rocky. This distance between island III and the rocky islet off island IV should be twenty-five miles, and it should be about thirty Columbian nautical miles from San Salvador. Placing these data on a chart, Captain Verhoog produced a course that was somewhat circular, from South Caicos to Mayaguana, Acklins, and Great Inagua, with Little Inagua the "rocky islet" off the coast of island IV.

More than anyone else in this century, Captain Verhoog inspired a revived interest in the landfall problem. His landfall and route were warmly approved by Capt. P. V. H. Weems, who in writing in the *Proceedings of the U.S. Naval Institute*, in May 1955, concluded, "I am fully convinced that he has finally determined the identity of 'San Salvador' to be the Caicos Island group."[45] In the same issue of the *Proceedings* John Lyman analyzed the McElroy justification of the Watlings landfall, called into question the effects of leeway and current upon Columbus's transatlantic bearing, and noted that they would tend to pull him to the south of what he believed to be his true bearing. Thus a more southerly landfall than Watlings was likely. He concluded "the odds thus are . . . 3 to 2 that Commodore Verhoog is correct."[46]

The appeal of this landfall led to an expedition by Edwin and Marion Link in 1955, the results of which were published by the Smithsonian Institution in 1958.[47] Captain Weems and Lt. Cmdr. Mendel L. Petersen of the Smithsonian Institution accompanied the expedition. By airplane and in a sixty-five-foot boat the Link party explored the "possible courses" Columbus might have followed through the Bahamas. These turned out to be the Verhoog and Morison routes, to give them the names of their advocates, plus the Links' route, which partook of both of the others. The expedition retained Armando Alvarez Pedroso, a Cuban biographer of Columbus, to read crucial passages in the *Journal*. Accepting the Caicos landfall, the Links departed from Verhoog's route at island II (Santa Maria de la Concepcion). Their reading of the *Journal* had Columbus sailing past one major island before coming to anchor at Santa Maria. To the Links this meant sailing past Mayaguana

45 *Proceedings of the U.S. Naval Institute* 81 (1955): 587.
46 Ibid., p. 586.
47 Edwin A. Link and Marion C. Link, *A New Theory on Columbus's Voyage through the Bahamas*, Smithsonian Miscellaneous Collections 135 (Washington: Smithsonian Institution, 1958).

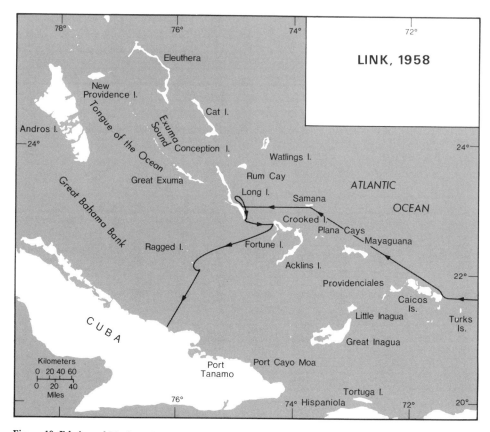

Figure 10: Edwin and Marion Link, accompanied by P. V. H. Weems, followed this route on an expedition through the Bahamas in 1955 and believed it to be the route taken by Columbus in 1492.

and stopping at Samana. Westward from there to island III (Fernandina), the Links took Columbus to Long Island and there joined the Morison route to island IV (Isabela), which was Crooked Island, en route to the ragged Islands and Cuba.

The Links expedition's most original contribution to methodology was in giving less attention to distances than to sailing time elapsed according to the *Journal*. They are distrustful of Columbus's estimates of distances, they doubt that he actually "saw" islands in the distance before sailing to them. Specifically, they could not see Mayaguana from Caicos, and they doubted that Columbus could have seen Rum Cay from Watlings. This, plus the uncertainty as to the distance of a league or a nautical mile in the *Journal*, made elapsed time of sailing appear a more solid form of evidence. They were not, of course, confident of the speed of Columbus's ships, but, accepting known distances and sailing time between points, they came up with speeds from two and one half to seven knots. Using such speeds they justified the route via Caicos, Samana, Long, and Crooked islands. Then with fine impartiality they advanced eleven reasons based on their own observations why Watlings could not be the landfall island and thirteen to prove that Verhoog's route after the correct landfall was not valid. Whatever the merits of its conclusions, this private expedition stands as an open-minded approach to both northern and southern landfalls.

The controversy as it has continued has not often been characterized by generosity on the part of the participants, often being attack upon and defense of Verhoog and Morison. E. Roukema, in the *American Neptune*, 1959, announced his purpose: "to prove that Professor Morison's view was and is correct," and observed, "on the whole I am afraid that the case for the Caicos Islands is even worse than those for some of the other islands."[48] Robert Fuson in the *Professional Geographer*, March, 1961, examined Verhoog's theory and was completely convinced of its correctness, exhibiting an anti-Morison tone in the process.[49] Two issues later of the same journal, July, 1961, contained a review of Fuson's paper, and there Edwin Doran pointed out six errors in Fuson's reasoning, defending Morison's theory along the way. In his article Doran makes no mention of Verhoog's book and article that started the controversy.[50] Similarly Ruth G. Durlacher Wolper, the director of the New World Museum on San Salvador (Watlings) undertook an expedition in 1959 to show that Columbus had indeed landed there. But she makes no effort to carry the voyage further. In her description of the expedition, published by the Smithsonian Institution, she omits Captain Verhoog's writings from her bibliography and his name from the list of scholars who had addressed the landfall problem.[51] Less openly partisan were Ramón J. Didiez Burgos in advocating in 1974 a landfall at the Plana Cays with a subsequent route via Acklins, Long and Fortune islands, and Arne Molander in 1981 favoring Egg Island off the north cape of Eleuthera.[52]

[48] E. Roukema, "Columbus Landed on Watlings Island," *American Neptune* 19 (April, 1959):79–113. Quotes from pp. 79 and 88.

[49] Robert H. Fuson, "Caicos: Site of Columbus' Landfall," *Professional Geographer* 13 (March, 1961):6–9.

[50] Edwin Doran, Jr., "This Columbus-Caicos Confusion," *Professional Geographer* 13 (July, 1961):32–34.

[51] Ruth G. Durlacher Wolper, *A New Theory Identifying the Locale of Columbus's Light, Landfall, and Landing*, Smithsonian Miscellaneous Collections 148, no. 1 (Washington: Smithsonian Institution, 1964), pp. 1–41.

[52] Ramón J. Didiez Burgos, *Guanahani y Mayaguan*, Sociedad Dominicana de Geografia, vol. 6 (Santo Domingo: Editoria Cultural Dominicana SA, 1974). Arne B. Molander, "Columbus Landed Here—Or Did He?" *Américas* 33 (October, 1981):3–7.

Figure 11: Route described by Ramón J. Didiez Burgos in *Guanahani y Mayaguan*, 1974.

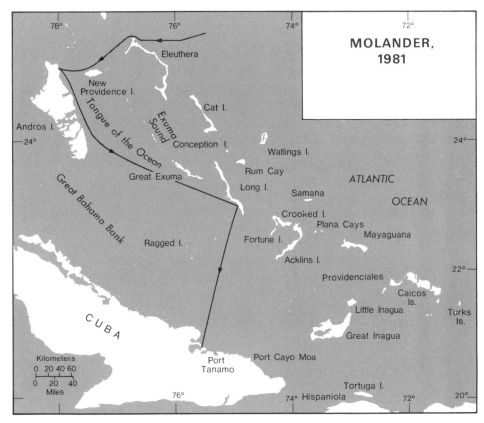

Figure 12: Route described by Arne B. Molander. See his article in this volume.

It was in the hope of reopening to a scholarly audience all points of view on the landfall issue that the Society for the History of Discoveries accepted a paper by Captain Verhoog for its annual meeting in 1980. Hearing his arguments convinced some members that they should have another try at determining the landfall. They have gone back to the *Journal* as their primary source. The history of its transcription and translation have been reexamined. The crucial passages of the *Journal* have been retranscribed for this issue of *Terrae Incognitae*. New techniques have been applied to research. New landfalls have emerged in the minds of some of our authors. Uncertainties remain for others. The papers which follow were presented in earlier drafts at the Society's annual meeting in 1981. It is expected that they will stimulate further research and comment which will appear in future issues.

Columbus Landed on Caicos

Pieter Verhoog

Attention to the exact landfall of Columbus in the Bahamas did not start before the middle of the eighteenth century. About two dozen historians have worked on this subject since, most of them non-navigators and non-hispanologists. The original texts dealing with the subject are mainly in old Spanish, and correct translations are very scarce. The historians have suggested a series of islands: Cat Island, Watlings, Grand Turk, Mayaguana, and others. Most of them finally preferred Watlings Island. R. H. Major in 1870 shifted from Grand Turk to Watlings. J. B. Murdock in 1884, Markham in 1893, and finally Admiral Morison all favored Watlings, Morison trying to fix the landfall on Watlings forever in 1942. But Commander R. T. Gould published "The Landfall of Columbus" in his *Enigmas* (London, 1945) to prove that the Watlings Island landfall is no longer tenable, which is not difficult to prove, as I will show here.

To begin with I will present some passages from Columbus's *Journal* so that my arguments may be more easily followed. October 11: "They took in all sail, remaining with the mainsail, waiting for day, a Friday, on which they reached the small island of the Lucayos, which is called in the language of the Indians 'Guanahani'." October 13: "This island is fairly large and very flat. . . . In the center of it there is a very large lake." October 14: "[In the ship's boat] I went along the island in a north-northeasterly direction, to see the other part, which lay to the east. . . . A great reef of rocks . . . encircled the whole of that island, while within there is deep water and a harbor large enough for all the ships of Christendom, the entrance to which is very narrow. It is true that inside the reef there are some shoals, but the sea is no more disturbed than the water in a well. . . .I examined the whole of that harbor, and afterward returned to the ship and set sail. I saw so many islands that I could not decide to which I would go first. . . .Finally I sought for the largest and resolved to steer for it. It is five leagues from this island of San Salvador. [The next day Columbus revised this distance.] The island was more than five leagues distant, being rather about seven. . . . The side which lies low toward the island of San Salvador runs north and south for a distance of five leagues. The other side, which I followed, runs east and west for more than ten leagues. . . . From this island I saw another and larger to the west. To this island I gave the name Santa Maria de la

29

Concepcion. . . . After that I set sail to go to the other large island which I saw to the west. . . . From this island of Santa Maria to the other was some nine leagues from east to west. . . . This large island . . . I gave the name Fernandina." October 16: "This island is very large, and I am resolved to round it . . . . And all this coast runs north-northwest and south-southeast; I saw quite twenty leagues of it, but it did not end there."

October 19: "At dawn I weighed anchor and . . . presently before we had sailed for three hours we saw an island to the east, toward which we steered, and all three vessels reached it before midday at its northern point, where there is an islet and a reef of rocks on its seaward side to the north and another between it and the main island. . . . I named it Isabela. . . . The said islet lay on the course from the island Fernandina, from which I had navigated, from east to west. The coast ran from that islet to the west and extends for twelve leagues to a cape, which I named Hermoso." October 20: "Today at sunrise I weighed anchor from the place where I was with the ship, anchored off the southwest point of this island of Samoet-Isabela, in order to steer to the northeast and east." October 21: "At ten o'clock I arrived here at this Cape del Isleo and anchored. I shall presently set out to go round the island. . . . After that I wish to leave for another very large island, which I believe must be Cipangu. . . . These Indians . . . call it Colba."

In advocating the Watlings Island landfall, Clements R. Markham made or used a translation of the famous *Journal* of Columbus of 1492 which is wrong in several places, and he also tried to tinker with or bend the many discrepancies inherent in a Watlings landfall. He invented the cloud hoax, namely, that the many islands seen from Guanahaní (island I) were clouds. The result: Columbus sailed to the largest cloud he saw, and found it to be an island forty by twenty Columbian *millas*. All this became necessary because from Watlings only one small island can be seen: Rum Cay. Next, Markham tried to make the small and dangerous space between the rocks north of Watlings, where the surf from the Atlantic often spouts more than 100 feet high, the tremendous inner harbor of Guanahaní, a harbor which the Columbus *Journal* says is large enough for all the ships of Christendom, and where the water is quiet as a well. Moreover, Markham simply left out dimensions and distances that did not tally with his interpretations, or eventually declared these to be "mistakes by scribes." Which scribes? Only one copy of the *Journal* survived, the abridged copy from the pen of Las Casas. Morison flatly accepted this complete Markham interpretation. He added only one more trick: Columbus sometimes used two kinds of miles. And from then on Morison took a Watlings landfall as fixed—no more questions, the discussion was finished: Columbus landed on Watlings Island.

In 1947 I published a booklet, *Guanahaní Again* (long out of print), in which I proved that Columbus in 1492 landed in the Caicos group of islands. Caicos as the landfall had never before been suggested. From contemporary sources (Las Casas, Fernando Colón, Oviedo, Martyr) and later ones (Navarrete, Thacher, and others), I had sifted out a considerable number of texts that could be used as "sailing directions." It had struck me how historians had so far used only some of these precious notations and left the rest unread or unused. Being a professional navigator, I used them all to sketch a map of this part of the Bahamas. My map, compared with the modern sea charts, showed clearly that island I (Guanahaní) was Caicos,

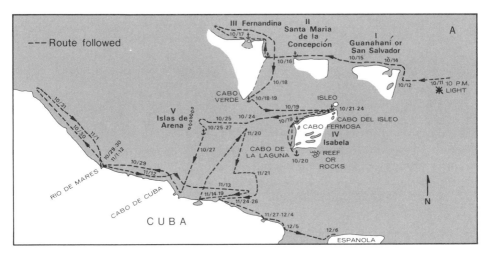

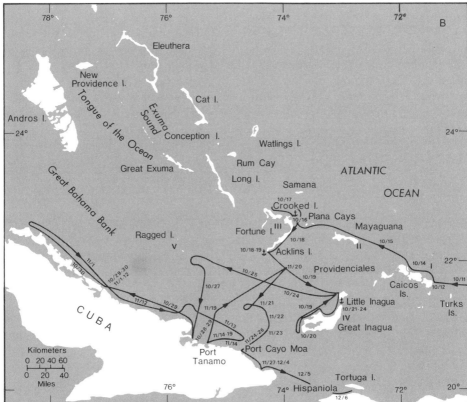

Figures 1 & 2: The route sketched on the upper map was plotted on a blank sheet of paper, using all sailing directions mentioned in the *Journal*. The lower map shows the same route transferred to a modern map of the region, Caicos Island appearing as the site of Columbus's first landfall. (These maps are adapted from versions first published in *Proceedings of the U.S. Naval Institute* 80 [1954]: 1102–3.)

island II (Santa Maria de la Concepción) was Mayaguana, island III (Fernandina) was Acklins, and island IV (Isabela) was Inagua, with Little Inagua in the northeast as the *isleo*. After that, Columbus sailed to Cuba, a name given by the "Indians" he had on board. Columbus believed Cuba to be a part of the Asiatic continent, that he was not far from "India."

Several newspapers published articles about Caicos-versus-Watlings, including the *New York Times*, *Chicago Sunday Tribune*, *Miami Herald*, and others. The *New York Times* received an angry note from Morison. He called me a crackpot. The *New York Times* responded in the same spirit. They had studied *Guanahaní Again*. Earlier a publicity manager in New York had sent Morison a letter about *Guanahaní Again*. Morison had answered with a few lines: "I didn't think it would serve any good purpose for me to read Captain Verhoog's book," signed at Seal Cove, 4 August 1947. This shows *à parti pris* a closed mind.

In October, 1954, I published a paper, "Columbus Landed on Caicos," in the *Proceedings of the U.S. Naval Institute* (vol. 80, no. 10, pp. 1101–11). The end of this paper gives ten outstanding points in condensed form to show why Caicos and not Watlings was Columbus's "San Salvador." In that period I was told the *Proceedings of the U.S. Naval Institute* had asked Morison to write a critique of my article for them. He never did. In a private letter his colleague John W. McElroy wrote to a friend, "Morison wants me to write an article to rebut Verhoog, but there is nothing to rebut him with." Because Morison kept delaying, the *Proceedings* (vol. 81, no. 5, May 1955) published a review by P. V. H. Weems which concluded, "I am fully convinced that he [Verhoog] has finally determined the identity of "San Salvador" to be the Caicos Island group."

As far as I know the only comment against a Caicos landfall Morison ever published personally was in his last work, *The European Discovery of America: The Southern Voyages* (New York, 1974), p. 65. In this passage he makes some serious mistakes. In the "backtrack" from Cuba he lets Columbus sail on 19 November 1492 from Baracoa. It is remarkable that in his *Admiral of the Ocean Sea* (Boston, 1946) Morison let Columbus sail for this backtrack from Port Tanamo. This last is correct: from 14 until 19 November, Columbus anchored in the Cuban Port Tanamo. Columbus called it Puerto del Principe, and his description of this harbor is perfect. But why this radical switch from Tanamo to Baracoa? I have an inkling this is a maneuver of the same kind as the wrong translation used by the talented painter Björn Landström in his picture book *Columbus* (New York, 1967). Landström got his complete navigational material from Morison, "whose work was of inestimable value" to him. After the backtrack date from Cuba on 19 November, Landström let Columbus steer north-northwest for two days (p. 82). The Spanish text gives northeast by north ("Nordeste quarto del Norte"). Why this wrong translation? Because north-northwest leads to Watlings, and northeast by north to Inagua and Caicos", all more or less.

Another bold mistake of Morison here is his statement about the immense inner harbor of Guanahaní. He writes, "Caicos has an immense lagoon, very shallow and full of coral heads; the island does not in the least correspond to Columbus's description of San Salvador." It does, exactly! Shallow spots is exactly what Columbus tells us—and the whole lagoon not even so very shallow for ships of that period. In the eighteenth and nineteenth centuries, men-of-war were chasing pirates in that immense lagoon of Caicos (*West Indies Pilot 3* [London, 1933], p. 168). To top it off, Morison makes a remark about "another Dutch captain, Edzar Roukema . . . demolishing . . . Caicos."

Roukema phoned me in the summer of 1956 as a "colleague-captain" who solicited my advice for his study of Amerigo Vespucci. I did not even know his name. I gave him an afternoon. Soon I noticed that he knew next to nothing about Vespucci and his times. He avoided all the texts I had ready for him; he hardly knew names like Navarrete and Las Casas, never had heard of Varnhagen, Fiske, Thacher, Joseph Fisher, Damião Peres, Costa Brochado. In this historical field he was an ignoramus. Instead, he constantly tried to talk about big tankers and modern navigation. Before leaving he casually remarked that he intended to study the landfall of Columbus. I told him to buy *Guanahaní Again*. He already had it. Next he started to write letters to me, not about Vespucci, but about the 1492 landfall of Columbus, letters with muddled navigational remarks and hairsplitting arguments about the Spanish word *isleo*. After his second letter I answered shortly but politely because my time was precious to me.

In April 1959 Roukema published an article, "Columbus Landed on Watlings Island," in the *American Neptune*, a periodical in which Morison had much influence. In this article Roukema stated that R. T. Gould also took Watlings Island for Guanahaní. This, after Commander Gould had proved the opposite in his book, *Enigmas* (London, 1945, pp. 66–94), as I remarked above. Roukema had mainly one authority: Morison. Not a single new aspect or argument was presented. It was the same whirligig: cloud-hoax, scribe's mistake, Columbus sometimes using two different miles — the same dull ignoring of important data. And this was supposed to "demolish" the Caicos theory.

Because we have so much direct contemporary information, a historian might soon get lost in the forest of notices, mostly in old Spanish. That is why a few hard data, often forgotten or simply left out, may help. We must always remember that Columbus in 1492 visited four islands, none of them very small, before reaching Cuba, the name given to the largest island by the "Indians" he had on board.

These are the geographical pillars, indestructable by chicaneries:

(1) According to the *Journal*, 20 November 1492 during the "backtrack" from Cuba toward Guanahaní, Columbus noted that the landfall island, Guanahaní, was distant from island IV (Samoet or Isabela) only eight leagues or thirty-two Columbus miles, equal to about twenty-six present nautical miles. "Guanahaní . . . que estaba ocho leguas de aquella Isabela." How did he know this distance? Columbus must have estimated this by eyesight when his ships were anchored near the *isleo* off the northeast cape of island IV from October 20 to 24, 1492 (see the *Journal* for those dates). The very high trees of that period — "canoas" with eighteen "bancos" — could certainly be seen at a distance of twenty-six nautical miles. And the Indian guides from Guanahaní accompanying Columbus on board would have pointed that all out. The distance from island I (Caicos) to island IV (Inagua and Little Inagua) is about twenty-six nautical miles.

(2) The north coast of island IV (Samoet or Isabela) runs about east-west, and it is

about forty nautical miles long (12 leguas = 48 millas). The north-*east* cape has an *isleo* nearby. The north-*west* cape is round and clean of rocks outside, and was called by Columbus "Cabo Hermoso" ("beautiful cape"). All of this information is mainly from the 19 October entry in the *Journal*, but some is also drawn from 21–24 October. This description from Columbus's *Journal* suits exactly Great Inagua as island IV, with Little Inagua as the *isleo*. In fact, nowhere else in the Bahamas does one find an island that does tally. Navarrete must have seen this, and so took Inagua for island IV. But he started with Turks Island as island I, and that makes the scheme flop. For the text of the *Journal* see Navarrete, or Carlos Sanz, *Diario de Colón* with its complete facsimile of the Las Casas manuscript. For *isleo* take the definition of Las Casas (*Historia*, vol. 1, chap. 27): "Isleo o isla pequeña que estaba junto con la tierra firma" ("small island near to the mainland"). Columbus calls a very small island *isleta*.

(3) Island I, the landfall, must be about forty-eight of our present nautical miles, or sixty Columbus *millas* over all (see Las Casas, *Historia*, vol. 1, chap. 40; Fernán Colón, *Historia*, chap. 22). From island I many islands were to be seen. Columbus sailed to the largest island he saw, and called it Santa Maria de la Concepción. Island I must have an immense inner harbor, "large enough for all the ships of Christendom," in which the water is as quiet as in a water well ("pozo"). In the north of the island is a narrow entrance (Lorimer Creek on Caicos), on which a fort could be made on a peninsula that looks like an island. The east coast leading to this entrance runs north-northeast. All around the island runs a girdle of rocks. All of these descriptive notices about island I are in the *Journal* for October 12–14 (Las Casas manuscript, fols. 10–11 in Sanz, *Diario*).

The above points (1–3) are a part of the ten points I present at the end of my paper in the *Proceedings of the U.S. Naval Institute*, which, together with the others made up the "Sailing Directions" for a plotting map. They all tally with the Caicos Islands as the Columbus landfall. Since publishing these views, I have never found a single serious objection against Caicos as the landfall of Columbus in 1492. The Watlings Island landfall fails on almost every point by comparison.

Of late a few Latin American historians have tried again to drag Cat Island into the limelight as the landfall of Columbus. Size and islands to be seen from it tally with the *Journal* indeed; and the large bight behind this Isla de Gato makes an immense harbor, more or less, if one skips a few notices in Columbus's description. But that is all. Starting with Cat Island as island I, one soon finds the remaining route impossible. This "landfall" has been argued by several competent historians in the course of years.

In the January 16, 1978, newsletter of the Society for the History of Discoveries, I wrote, "it seems that this long mooted landfall of Columbus will be elucidated at last." I am pleased that the society has had the courage to investigate this part of the most important discovery of all times, a discovery that changed the world we live in. As for Admiral Professor S. E. Morison, he has been recognized as a great historian, especially for World War II at sea and the part the United States had in it. Let us leave him on his historical pedestal. But with a mistake. *Errare humanum est.*

Columbus's First Landing Place:
The Evidence of the Journal

Oliver Dunn

In the United States and in other English-speaking countries, informed popular knowledge of Columbus's life and his voyages of discovery probably derives more from Samuel E. Morison's *Admiral of the Ocean Sea* than from any other source.[1] Morison's wide-ranging command of the documentary evidence and his first-hand acquaintance with the areas through which Columbus sailed provide the basis for what may be called the prevailing and "standard" view of Columbus's origins and early life, as well as his later accomplishments and difficulties. Not so well known is Morison's later book, *Journals and Other Documents on the Life and Voyages of Christopher Columbus*, which includes his translation of the *Libro de la primera navegación*, that is, the *Journal* of Columbus's first transatlantic crossings.[2]

It is this *Journal* that provides most of the information we have about these voyages, although additional bits are included in works by Ferdinand Columbus and by the historian Oviedo. In the form in which it survives, the *Journal* is a day-by-day series of abstracts and excerpts made by Bartolomé de Las Casas from a copy of a more complete account of the voyages, now lost. The Las Casas manuscript itself was unknown until 1790, when Martín Fernández de Navarrete discovered it in the library of the duke of Infantado. Today it is in the National Library, Madrid. Important printed editions of the Spanish text include Navarrete's own, published as part of his *Colección de los viajes y descubrimientos*[3]; Cesare de Lollis's for the Italian government's monumental commemorative publication, the *Raccolta di documenti e studi* (in vol. 1, pt. 1)[4]; Guillén y Tato's, with valuable notes and illustrations, published by the Instituto Histórico de Marina, Madrid[5]; Carlos Sanz's line-by-line

[1] Samuel Eliot Morison, *Admiral of the Ocean Sea: A Life of Christopher Columbus*, 2 vols. (Boston: Little, Brown, 1942).

[2] Morison, ed., *Journals and Other Documents on the Life and Voyages of Christopher Columbus* (New York: Heritage Press, 1963).

[3] Martín Fernández de Navarrete, ed., *Colección de los viajes y descubrimientos que hicieron por mar los españoles desde fines del siglo quince*, 5 vols. (Madrid: Imprenta real, 1825–37), vol. 1.

[4] R. Commissione Colombina, *Raccolta di documenti et studi*, 14 vols. (Rome: Ministero della pubblica istruzione, 1892–96).

[5] Julio F. Guillén y Tato, *El primer viaje de Cristóbal Colón* (Madrid: Instituto histórico de marina, 1943).

edition paralleling a facsimile of the Las Casas manuscript[6]; and that of Arce and Gil Esteve[7].

All of the printed Spanish editions alter the manuscript text to some degree, some more, some less, by expanding contractions, modernizing the spelling, or by adding capitals and punctuation. Although Morison writes that the Sanz edition is the best, this is by no means the case; since it appeared too late for Morison to use in preparing his translation, he actually relied on the much more accurate de Lollis edition and on a photostatic copy of the manuscript itself. In regard to English translations, Morison is critical of all prior to his own, although he fails to mention L.A. Vigneras's revision of the Cecil Jane version published in 1960 by the Hakluyt Society. We may presume that this corrected many of the errors pointed out by Morison in reviewing the original Jane publication of 1930.

The present paper takes a generally supportive view of Morison's work but stops short of agreeing that, as he asserts, the place of the first landing "may be considered settled."[8] Morison argues that Columbus landed on the island in the Bahamas now officially named "San Salvador or Watlings," the first half, of course, being the name Columbus gave to his first West Indian landfall. And in Morison's view, Columbus, after sailing from this island, called at three others before reaching the north coast of Cuba. Columbus named the three islands "Santa María de la Concepción," "Fernandina," and "Isabela." Morison identifies them as the modern Rum Cay, Long Island, and the Crooked-Fortune-Acklins islands group. To establish his views, Morison relies on three main lines of argument. The first is that a plot of Columbus's westward ocean crossing on a modern chart points to Watlings as his landing place. The second is that the physical characteristics of Watlings, "alone of any island in the Bahamas, Turks or Caicos groups fits Columbus's description" of the island in the *Journal*. The third is that "the position of San Salvador [i.e. Watlings] and of no other island fits the course laid down in the *Journal* if we work it backwards from Cuba."[9] It should be interesting to examine these arguments in the light of the *Journal* text to see if they do, or do not, support Morison's views.

Columbus's *Journal* divides naturally into three main parts: first, the westward crossing, beginning with the departure from the Canaries on September 6 and continuing to the landfall on October 12; second, the landfall and the subsequent voyage through the West Indies to Cuba and Española, beginning October 12 and lasting until the departure for Spain January 16; third, the homeward crossing, January 16 to March 15, 1493. The first part of the *Journal* contains an almost complete account of the courses sailed and distances made good each day of the crossing. The second part is not so complete in navigation data, but does supply some information about each island called at, and about the courses and distances sailed to reach them. The third part, like the first, includes a daily record of the return voyage to Spain.

Several investigators have tried to determine whether a plot of the courses sailed

[6] Carlos Sanz, ed., *Diario de Colón: Libro de la primera navegación y descubrimiento de las Indias*, 2 vols. (Madrid: Gráficas Yagües, 1962).
[7] Joaquín Arce and Manuel Gil Esteve, eds., *Diario de a bordo de Cristóbal Colón* (Turin: A. Tallone, 1971).
[8] Morison, *Journals*, p. 66, n. 5.
[9] Morison, *Admiral*, 1:300.

and distances gained each day on the westward voyage might lead to a specific island as the one on which Columbus first landed. One such investigator is J.W. McElroy, who served as navigating officer on Morison's Harvard Columbus expedition of 1939–40. McElroy's study, published in the inaugural volume of the *American Neptune*, shows that, with certain corrections to the *Journal* data, a plot of the voyage takes Columbus's fleet to a position very close to the actual location of Watlings Island.[10] McElroy's principal correction is to the record of distances made good. These are stated in the *Journal* in terms of leagues and miles, four miles equalling one league. Basing his own view on Morison's, McElroy asserts that Columbus's mile is the equivalent of about 4,840 English feet. The league, therefore, is about 19,360 such feet, or about 3.18 modern nautical miles. So the sum of the daily distances recorded, amounting to 1,090 leagues, converts to 3,466 nautical miles.

This distance, plotted on a modern chart or map, puts Columbus's landing in the Gulf of Mexico, 300 miles or so west of Watlings. To account for such a discrepancy, McElroy and Morison hypothesize that Columbus habitually overestimated *Santa María's* speed, with the result that the 1,090 leagues he thought he had sailed was really a shorter distance. Then, to calculate the actual extent of Columbus's error, McElroy first assumes that Watlings was the landing place, then determines the Mercator distance between Watlings and Columbus's point of departure in the Canaries. The figure calculated is 3,116 nautical miles. Next, allowing for an estimated one percent slippage in keeping the fleet on course, and for the distance of eight miles between Gomera harbor and the approximate point of actual departure, McElroy calculates that Columbus's fleet sailed 3,155 nautical miles to reach its destination. This figure, compared with the 3,466 miles (1,090 leagues) Columbus thought he had sailed, gives an overrun of 311 miles, which, expressed as a fraction of 3,466, is nine percent. So, in McElroy's tabulation of daily distances covered, and in the chart of the crossing based upon them, each of the recorded figures is reduced by nine percent.

Another series of corrections is to the compass courses of the *Journal* to take account of compass variation, the angular difference between true north and the magnetic north indicated by the compass needle. Although, apparently, Columbus and other mariners of his time were familiar with the phenomenon, they were just beginning to progress towards the knowledge that variation itself changed with a change of location on the earth's surface. McElroy and Morison believe that Columbus did not compensate for such changes during the voyage. Relying on an 1899 publication of the Royal Magnetical and Meteorological Observatory of Batavia in which compass variations in the Atlantic for the period around 1500 were calculated, McElroy adjusts Columbus's generally westward course in accordance with the compass variations presumed to obtain at the time of the voyage.[11] Their effect overall is to bend Columbus's true headings somewhat south even when his compass indicated that he was sailing due west. Other possible causes of deviation from the

[10] John W. McElroy, "The Ocean Navigation of Columbus on His First Voyage," *American Neptune* 1 (1941):209–40.

[11] McElroy cites an appendix ("Isogonen–Karten für die Epochen 1500 etc.") to W. Van Bemmelen, "Die Abweichung der Magnetnadel," *Observations of the Royal Magnetical and Meteorological Observatory at Batavia*, supplement to vol. 21 (1899).

course that Columbus thought he was following are mentioned, but then dismissed as either too inconsiderable or indeterminate to be taken into the account. McElroy and Morison both specifically deny that ocean currents could have affected the course of the crossing. Morison writes that, "fortunately for Columbus, all his Atlantic crossings except the outward passage of the Third Voyage were in regions of the ocean where the current was negligible."[12]

With the two modifications described above, McElroy's chart of the voyage locates Columbus's fleet at the time of the landfall in 23° 47.4' N, 74° 29' W, "about nine miles S of San Salvador," instead of in his "true" position about six miles distant and somewhat south of its center: the latter position deduced by McElroy from the *Journal* and from other documents. This very small difference, McElroy writes, "proves that Columbus kept his dead-reckoning with uncommon care; and that within the framework of his knowledge and the very slight development of celestial observations in 1492, he was really a great navigator."[13] In view of the corrections that have had to be made to produce this happy result, McElroy's remarks seem ironic. Can the data, thus "corrected," prove that Columbus's first landfall was Watlings Island? It seems clear that they cannot, since, in order to determine the amount by which Columbus's estimates of distance must be reduced to make things come out right, McElroy assumes that Watlings was in fact his destination. The argument is circular.

Why did Columbus overestimate his distances? McElroy and Morison find the explanation in presumed habitual optimism on Columbus's part in estimating *Santa María*'s speed. Morison says that Columbus simply estimated "by eye, by watching the bubbles or the gulfweed float by," and that "he never knew exactly how fast his ship was moving because he had no fixed standard and no check."[14] Whatever the method Columbus employed to judge his vessel's speed, it must have been very similar to the way or ways used by his own pilot and the pilots of *Pinta* and *Niña*, since their comparison of computed positions after sailing twelve days put them within 20 leagues of one another. The "pilot of Niña found himself 440 leagues from the Canaries; he of the Pinta 420."[15] If the distances recorded by Columbus for those same eleven days are added up, they total 436. The average of the three distances is 432, from which none of the three differs by more than 12 leagues, or three percent. However, the *Journal* also says that, according to the *Santa María*'s pilot, his ship had covered only 400 leagues. This figure, McElroy writes in a note to Morison's edition of the *Journal*, was the "phony" reckoning published to the crew to diminish uneasiness over the length of the voyage, but actually "closer to the truth" than the figures Columbus recorded.[16]

The similarity of computed positions leads to a question concerning Morison's and McElroy's view of the lengths of Columbus's mile and league. It may be that Columbus's alleged overestimate of speed is nothing but an inference made necessary by the length of the mile that McElroy and Morison assume without argument

---

[12] Morison, *Admiral*, 1:255.
[13] McElroy, p. 217.
[14] Morison, *Admiral*, 1:248.
[15] Morison, *Journals*, p. 55.
[16] Ibid., p. 55, n. 3.

that Columbus used. If Columbus actually reckoned his distances in shorter miles, the overestimate of distance and speed would be lessened or disappear and Columbus's dead reckoning ability would be given a better foundation than McElroy can provide.

James E. Kelley, author of another paper in this volume, argues convincingly that Columbus measured distances at sea in miles of about 4,060 English feet, a unit of 5,000 "palms" instead of 5,000 "neo-Roman feet," Morison's equivalent. With the shorter mile, the league is equal to about 2.67 nautical miles and Columbus's recorded 1,090 leagues become 2,910 nautical miles in place of 3,466. Plotted on a chart, this distance would put Columbus's landing where in fact there are no islands and about 245 miles short of Watlings. Kelley believes, and modern pilot charts clearly show that, in spite of McElroy's and Morison's statements to the contrary, westward-flowing ocean currents do exist in the regions of the Atlantic traversed by Columbus's fleet. Kelley estimates that they could have given Columbus a free ride of up to 300 miles. In this case, and although Kelley does not commit himself as to the landing place, it well might have been Watlings. Instead of overestimating, Columbus was underestimating the distances made good daily, but for a reason that he could not detect, and his estimates of his ship's speed through the water can stand as recorded. But is should now be clear that whatever the length of Columbus's mile the bare *Journal* data do not in themselves lead to a specific island with any precision. To get Columbus to his landing, other extraneous information must be brought to bear on the problem, including information about currents, compass variation, and other factors, all difficult or impossible to quantify.

It is worth noting that Morison, although he cites McElroy's study with approval, does not claim that it amounts to a proof of the Watlings landfall. For him, greater certainty arises from his other two lines of argument: the fit of Watlings to the *Journal*'s description of San Salvador; and the fit of the course of the interisland voyage to the locations and characteristics of Rum Cay, Long Island, and Crooked-Fortune and Acklins islands. What does the *Journal* tell us about San Salvador, and how does the information compare with the characteristics of Watlings Island? On Thursday, October 11, Columbus's fleet sailed 27 leagues west-southwest between dawn and sunset, and a farther 22.5 leagues west between sunset and 2 am Friday, October 12. It was then that land was sighted, two leagues distant. The ships lay to, waiting for daylight, before approaching an island more closely. Although it seems likely that the first view of the island was of its eastern shore, the *Journal* does not explicitly say so, or state on which side of the island the landing took place. Nor does it say, if the landing was on the western side, whether the fleet rounded the island by a northern or southern route. It says only (and this is Las Casas, not Columbus), "they arrived at a small island of the Lucayos [i.e., the Bahamas] which was called Guanahaní in the language of the Indians.... The admiral went ashore in the armed boat and Martín Alonso Pinzón and Vicente Yañez his brother, who was captain of the Niña."[17]

Morison infers from the rough seas ("mucha mar") and the distances made good on the 11th that there was still a stiff breeze blowing on the 12th; he believes that

---

[17] Arce and Gil Esteve, Oct. 12 (my translation).

Columbus would not have tried to land on the exposed and reef-ringed eastern shore of Watlings, but searched for and found a sheltered anchorage on the western side. And from the fact that he later went in one of the ship's boats to the north-northeast to see what there was in the eastern part of the island, Morison infers that the fleet first rounded the island by its southern end.[18] While such inferences seem likely, they are not completely certain, and other students of the voyage have reached different conclusions. With the entry for October 12, Las Casas begins to quote Columbus's actual words ("palabras formales"). Columbus wrote that San Salvador was quite big ("bien grande"), level, and without mountains. There was a large lake or lagoon ("laguna") in the middle, and elsewhere there were many other bodies of water ("muchas aguas"). At least one coast ran north-northeast. The island was encircled by a reef. Inside the reef at some unspecified point there was a harbor big enough to hold many ships. In some parts the harbor was deep, in others shallow. Its entrance was very narrow. At one point there was a small peninsula that Columbus thought with two day's work could be cut off from the rest of the island to make a good site for a fortress. It took from dawn until afternoon on October 14 to leave the anchorage in the ships' boats, to explore the north-northeast trending coast and the harbor, and to return to the fleet. The island was heavily populated ("mucha gente") and was green all over, with many trees and fruits of different kinds.

A map of Watlings does reveal a general correspondence with the physical features of San Salvador described by Columbus. Both east and west coasts run roughly north-northeast south-southwest. There is a large lake or lagoon in the middle of the island as well as many other smaller bodies of water. At the north end of Watlings, Graham's Harbor forms a large open bay within the reefs, and it has a narrow entrance. Projecting into the harbor on its eastern side is a point of land, formerly connected with, but now separated from the island. Morison's belief that the landing took place on the western shore of the island is supported by the fact that the only real break in the surrounding reef is on that side, about eight nautical miles from the southwest point of Watlings. Although Columbus provides only a subjective or qualitative indication of the island's size, Watlings is in fact about fifteen nautical miles in length north-south by about eight miles east-west. As can be seen from Columbus's rather sketchy account of San Salvador, hardly enough information is given to establish the identity of the island with much confidence. Those who maintain that Columbus landed elsewhere find at least most, if not all of the features mentioned in the *Journal* on *their* islands or find difficulties in fitting Watlings to Columbus's description.

One such difficulty centers on the "light" seen four hours before the landfall. To the east of Watlings there is no land on which a light could have been seen, and Watlings itself, it is objected, was still too far distant for a light on shore to have been visible. And a light on a conjectural Indian fishing canoe an estimated thirty miles from the island, particularly at night and with a wind blowing, seems extremely implausible. Morison originally dismissed the light as imaginary, conjured up by Columbus's eager anticipation of a landfall. But later he appears to have changed his mind. In his translation of the *Journal* he refers approvingly in a note to an

[18] Morison, *Admiral*, 1:300.

40

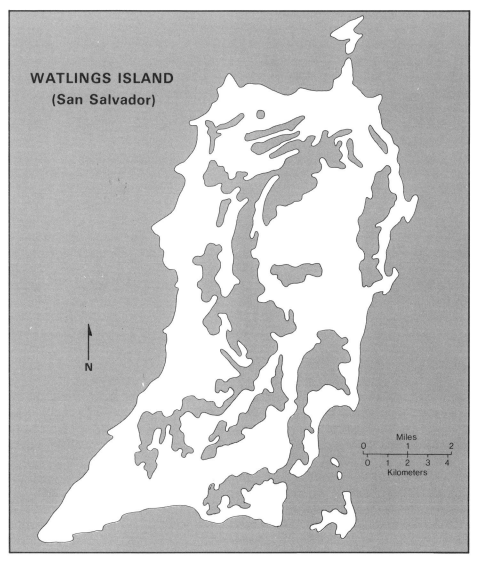

Figure 1: Outline of Watlings Island, now called San Salvador.

experiment carried out by Ruth G. Durlacher Wolper, a part-time resident of Watlings, "of having a bonfire kept lighted on top of High Cay, off the southeastern point of San Salvador [i.e., Watlings] on an October night," where she was able to see it from shipboard twenty-eight miles offshore "even to photograph it" for an article published by the Smithsonian Institution. Wolper maintains that nowadays such fires are built by black residents of the island to ward off sand flies, and that they formerly were built by Indians for the same reason.[19] Such a fire might have been the light that Columbus saw "lifting and rising."

The *Journal* description of San Salvador as "very level" ("muy llana") is somewhat puzzling, since Watlings is far from being a sandbar. High Cay is 114 feet in height, and Kerr Mount, farther north on the east coast, is 140 feet. Yet Wolper writes that "when Columbus approached the island it must have impressed him as large, level and green, and as he explored away from First Landing Bay up to the ridge where the settlements were, he could see for miles around. Trees of a wide variety grow in abundance all over the island. From this ridge he could see the great lake in the middle, surrounded by many lakes and ponds. In October, when the rains have almost ceased, the island takes on the freshness of spring in New England."[20] In my opinion, Columbus, in describing the island as level, may well have been comparing its appearance with that of such mountainous islands as those he knew in the Canaries or the Azores.

Another difficulty may lurk in the account of the exploratory voyage in ships' boats to the harbor presumably located at the north end of the island. Most probably the boats were rowed, not sailed, and if the distances from an anchorage near the break in the reef on the west coast, to Graham's Harbor, at least part way across the harbor towards the peninsula there, and a return trip to the anchorage are scaled on a map, the total distance turns out to be between twenty and twenty-five miles: a very long distance to cover between dawn and the fleet's midafternoon departure from the island. However, it should be pointed out that the *Journal* does not rule out the possibility that the fleet sailed a course parallel to that followed by the boats, standing by near the north end of the island and picking up Columbus and the boat crews there. This would reduce the total distance rowed to much less and make the schedule more plausible.

Those who think that Columbus first landed in the Caicos or Turks groups have questioned the view that Columbus's landing took place on the western side of San Salvador, since the *Journal* says nothing to this effect. Morison has the support of a practicing sea captain, Edzar Roukema, in arguing that no seaman in his right mind would have tried to anchor off San Salvador's exposed eastern shore with a sea running. Roukema forthrightly declares that "common sense alone dictated that on the morning of October 12 an anchorage be sought on the island's protected western side."[21]

None of the objections made to Watlings seems fatal to the view that it was the island on which Columbus landed, for each can be reasonably, if sometimes con-

[19] Ruth G. Durlacher Wolper, "A New Theory Identifying the Locale of Columbus's Light, Landfall, and Landing," *Miscellaneous Collections of the Smithsonian Institution* 148 (1964):21. Morison, *Journals*, p. 64, n. 5.
[20] Wolper, pp. 27–29.
[21] Edzar Roukema, "Columbus Landed on Watlings Island," *American Neptune* 19 (1959):92.

jecturally, answered. Nevertheless, it must be acknowledged that the case for Watlings is not so airtight as definitely to exclude all others. Can we be as certain as Morison that Watlings alone "fits Columbus's description"? If the description is taken in isolation, I think not and believe that much of Morison's confidence actually derives from his third line of argument, that "the position of San Salvador and of no other island fits the course laid down in the *Journal* if we work it backwards from Cuba." But first let us look at the details of Columbus's voyage through the islands in the direction in which it took place. The day before Columbus departed from San Salvador, he had understood, from signs made by Indians, that there was more land to the south, to the southwest, and to the northwest; and that by going to the south, or "around the island to the south," he would find a king who had a great deal of gold, including "large vessels of it." And he had decided then to go to the southwest. So, although, when he actually sailed from San Salvador, he failed to record his course, presumably it was to the southwest.[22]

If San Salvador is Watlings, the closest island to the southwest, presently called Rum Cay, is relatively small and is the only one in its vicinity. How, then, can this be squared with Columbus's statement in the *Journal* entry for October 14 that, after setting sail "I saw so many islands that I could not decide where to go first; and those whom I had captured made signs to me that they could not be counted, and called by their names more than a hundred. Finally, I looked for the biggest, and decided to go there, and so I did, and it is probably distant from this island of San Salvador 5 leagues, and some of them more, some less."[23]

Commenting on this passage, Morison writes: "This statement misled earlier historians into the belief that Columbus's landfall was in an archipelago like the Turks Islands."[24] But he, and Wolper also, insist, from personal experience, that from certain directions off the coast of Rum Cay, it presents the appearance of a string of islands. Morison says that, from ten miles southwest of Rum Cay, he could see six islands. Wolper goes even further and includes in her article drawings of Rum Cay from three distances, the island first seeming to be twenty-one separate islets, at a closer approach eight, and even from quite close three. The apparent multiplication of islands, she says, is due to Rum Cay's topography, "consisting of hills and bays," and the fact that, from a distance, the shoreline is below the horizon.[25]

Not only "earlier historians" have found difficulties for the Watlings Island theory in this passage and support for rival views. One point is clear, however: Columbus did not sight the "many islands" until after his departure from San Salvador, although the *Journal* gives no clue as to how far or how long he had sailed before they came into sight. Nor are we required to believe that, even if Columbus was right in thinking that his Indian captives named more than a hundred islands, he could see them. However, the "many island" problem, in my opinion, is not very convincingly settled by Morison and remains troublesome for his views. If Watlings is San Salvador and the island toward which Columbus next sailed is Rum Cay, the

[22] Arce and Gil Esteve, Oct. 13 (my translation).
[23] Morison, *Journals*, p. 68.
[24] Ibid., p. 69, n. 6.
[25] Wolper, p. 34.

approximate distance between the two is 17.5 nautical miles. Columbus first estimated this distance as five leagues, but later increased the figure to seven.[26] Seven leagues, taking the league as four "short" miles, equal about 18.5 nautical miles, a fairly close agreement with Columbus's estimate. When, after spending the night at sea lying to, he approached the island on the morning of October 15, he found that the coast that "lies over against" San Salvador ("aquella haz que es de la parte de la isla de San Salvador") ran north–south for a distance of five leagues, and "the other" which, he writes, "I followed," ran east–west for ten leagues.[27] Morison understands Columbus's route to have been south along Rum Cay's east coast, then west along its south coast to its southwestern extremity. There the fleet anchored and spent the night.

Several points in this interpretation of the *Journal* are disputed. Some think Columbus means that he did not land on and did not give a name to this second, five-by-ten–league island, but sailed past it and landed on a "bigger one to the west" which he had sighted in the morning while coasting the unnamed island and to which, later, he gave the name Santa María de la Concepción. The text of the *Journal* does not support such a view. The hypothesis ignores the fact that when on Tuesday, October 16, Columbus departed from Santa María because of a shift of wind, it was to head for "the other island, which is very big." The use of the definite article, and not the indefinite, in referring to "the other island," indicates that it was the same "bigger one to the west" that had been sighted the day before. But there may be an error in the *Journal* regarding the time at which the big island was first seen. The island west of Rum Cay is Long Island and justifies its name by its north-northwest–south-southeast stretch of almost sixty miles. But, according to Morison, it could not have been visible from the eastern part of Rum Cay's south coast early on October 15.

Another view diverging from Morison's is that Columbus sailed west along Santa María's north coast, then south along its west coast, doubling its southwest point before reaching the anchorage. It is true that the *Journal* does not say which coast, north or south, the fleet sailed along, although it is certain that the anchorage was on the south side. This is because, next day, Columbus cut short his stay on the island when the wind changed and began to blow southeast and south, "a la traviesa," which can mean only "toward shore."[28] The *Journal* says nothing about rounding the southwest cape of the island before anchoring, an omission that, to me diminishes the likelihood of a north coast route.

Another, and surprising, theory is that Santa María consisted of more than one island, not just in appearance at a distance, but in fact. Its supporters base their view on the opening line of the *Journal* entry for October 16. Three Spanish editions (Navarrete, Guillén y Tato, and Sanz) read: "Parti de las islas de Santa María"; one (Arce) reads: "Parti de la isla." Both Morison and Vigneras translate: "the islands," Morison without comment, Vigneras with a note saying that the plural "islands" probably refers to both Rum Cay and Conception Island, "which are very close together."[29] The Las Casas manuscript actually reads: "Parti de las isla": the article

[26] Morison, *Journals*, pp.68–69.
[27] Arce and Gil Esteve, Oct. 15 (my translation).
[28] Ibid.
[29] Cecil Jane, trans., *The Journal of Christopher Columbus*, rev. and annot. by L. A. Vigneras, Hakluyt Soc., extra ser. 38 (London, 1960), p. 32 and p. 205, n. 26.

and the noun do not agree in number. As there are no other references in the *Journal* to plural Santa Marías, the use of the plural article in this one instance should be regarded as a slip, probably a copying error.

From Santa María Columbus's fleet sailed west, departing from the island about noon, October 16. Columbus estimated the distance between Santa María and the large island towards which he headed as eight leagues, later revised to nine. He also wrote that the latter's coast ran north-northwest–south-southeast and was twenty-eight leagues in length. To this island Columbus gave the name Fernandina.

If, as Morison believes, Fernandina is Long Island, Columbus's estimates are off the mark. The actual distance from one island to the other approximates eighteen nautical miles, whereas the estimate converts to more than twenty-four miles. The shoreline estimate is suspect too. Columbus first wrote that "there might well be" ("bien avría") twenty-eight leagues of coast on the side he faced, and later wrote that from his landing place he could see twenty leagues of coast, but that it did not end there.[30] Using the short mile and league, Columbus's twenty-eight league estimate is the equivalent of about seventy-five nautical miles, and the twenty league estimate converts to more than fifty-three miles. But in any case it seems very unlikely that Columbus could see as far as such figures make it appear that he claimed to. Long Island is in fact somewhat less than sixty miles in length.

The difficulties in making sense of Columbus's estimates of shoreline distances have led Morison to question whether, in stating such distances, Columbus was using the sea league at all. The problem first arises in connection with his description of Santa María as an island five by ten leagues in size. In terms of sea leagues of 2.67 nautical miles each, Santa María's size turns out to be 13.3 nautical miles by almost 26.7, whereas its real dimensions are about five by ten nautical miles. The problem arises again in the estimate of Fernandina's coastline, and again in the account of his fourth island, Isabela, and in that of his voyage along the north coast of Cuba.

Although Pieter Verhoog, in his article "Columbus Landed on Caicos," pours scorn on the idea that Columbus used a standard of measurement for shoreline distances differing from the sea league,[31] Morison, when he checked actual shore distances in Cuba against Columbus's reports, found that the latter's shore leagues averaged out to about 1.6 nautical miles. Using a league of this length reduces the estimate of Santa María's size to eight by sixteen miles, still too large, but an improvement over the dimensions obtained by using sea leagues. Fernandina's twenty-eight league coastline would then convert to less than forty-five miles, and the twenty-league stretch would reduce to thirty-two miles, greatly increasing the plausibility of Columbus's account.

Roukema believes that Morison is right in thinking that Columbus estimated shore distances in very short leagues. He speculates that Columbus was deliberately confusing in giving two different units of measurement the same name: the purpose of the confusion was to make the islands he discovered seem bigger than they were. "Of course," Roukema writes, "he was painting the lily. His discoveries were important enough. But I am afraid that his thirst for glory got the better of his

[30] Arce and Gil Esteve, Oct. 15–16.
[31] *Proceedings of the U.S. Naval Institute* 80 (1954):1105.

45

honesty."[32] James Kelley, while not denying that there may have been a very short land league in use, says that he knows of no historical basis for it. To explain Columbus's shoreline estimates he prefers the view that on the north coast of Cuba Columbus's dead reckoning did not compensate for swift ocean currents, with the result that his estimates of distances traveled through the water differed from the distances actually made good along the shore. This view, however, does not account for the seeming use of a very short league before Columbus reached Cuba.

Although it appears unlikely that Columbus would invent a new league out of thin air to increase the seeming importance of the new lands he had discovered, I am inclined to believe, with Roukema, that Columbus purposely exaggerated their dimensions. But whether an initial estimate in terms of sea leagues was increased by a certain amount beyond the facts, or whether the estimate was made in terms of short shore leagues, the result would be the same: the shoreline would be taken by a reader of the *Journal* to be longer than it really was. It is much more plausible to believe that Columbus simply overstated shoreline distances than to believe that he estimated their lengths in terms of a hypothetical shore league. And if they are nothing but overstatements, then the ratio of the length of the sea league (2.67 nautical miles) to that of the shore league as calculated by Morison (1.6 nautical miles) is really a measure of Columbus's exaggeration. A reduction of the island dimensions recorded in the *Journal* by this ratio produces better (although by no means perfect) fits to the actual dimensions of Rum Cay, the east coast of Long Island, and the west coasts of Crooked-Fortune islands than does the sea league.

After sailing from Santa María for Fernandina at noon on October 16, the wind died and the fleet had to spend the night at sea. The following morning the ships anchored off a small village where the men were well received and where they replenished the fleet's supply of water. Then Columbus sailed northwest along the coast to the north end of the island, on the way stopping to explore a harbor that turned out to be disappointingly shallow. Later, after rounding the northern cape, the ships turned back because of a change of wind and a time of dark cloudy weather. They sailed east and southeast in order to stay clear of Fernandina's east shore, but there was little wind and the fleet spent the night at sea. A heavy rain continued from after midnight until near daybreak. Although the wording of the *Journal* is not entirely clear, it seems to say that Columbus expected, or at least hoped to anchor at the southwest end of the island, there to await better weather. Apparently he did not succeed in reaching that point, since, on the following day, October 18, he sailed around the island as far as he could and anchored whenever the sailing was bad ("surgi al tiempo que no era de navegar") but did not go ashore. Probably on this day the fleet reached a position from which the south cape of the island was visible, since the *Journal* later reveals that Columbus gave it a name, Cabo Verde.

When dawn came on October 19, the fleet set sail in search of an island called "Samoet" by Columbus's Indian captives. The ships fanned out, *Pinta* to the east–southeast, *Niña* to the south–southeast, and *Santa María* to the southeast. Columbus gave instructions that *Pinta* and *Niña* were to follow these courses until noon and were then to rejoin the flagship. But in less than three hours the island was sighted

---

[32] Roukema, p. 84.

and all three ships steered for it, reaching its north point before midday. At the point they found an islet ("isleo") offshore with a reef extending outward to the north and another between the islet and the larger island, which Columbus named Isabela. In Morison's view, the island is Crooked Island and the islet Bird Rock. Columbus writes that Isabela lay on an east-west line from Fernandina, which is true of Long Island's south end and Crooked Island's north end, while the distance between them, about 25.5 nautical miles, seems about right for a seven or eight-hour morning's sail.

There are some difficulties in Columbus's (or the *Journal*'s) account of Isabela. He writes that from the north point of the island the coast ran *west* twelve leagues (presumably shore leagues) and that at the west end there was a cape, "round and very deep, without shoals outside, at its extremity low and stony and farther inland composed of sandy beach." But if the fleet, on its generally eastward course from Fernandina, reached Isabela at the latter's north point, it is impossible for the coast to have run from that point west. It looks as if someone, Las Casas or a copyist, misread "sueste" as "gueste," that is, "southeast" as "west." This is Morison's view, and I believe he is right. Very probably Columbus wrote that from the islet at the north point of Isabela, to which he gave the name Cabo del Isleo, the coast ran southeast (as, on Crooked Island, indeed it does) to a cape twelve leagues distant which he name Cabo Hermoso. In terms of shore leagues, this is a quite close estimate of the actual distance to the southeast end of Fortune Island. The beeline distance scales to about 18.5 nautical miles, and Columbus's estimate is equivalent to 19 miles.

During the afternoon of October 19 the fleet sailed to Cabo Hermoso and spent the night at anchor there, Columbus noting in the *Journal* the discovery that Isabela and the island ending in Cabo Hermoso were separate, and that there was a small island in between. On a modern chart, this small island would be Rat or Goat Cay, again bearing out Morison's identification of the larger islands. From Cabo Hermoso, Columbus could see to the northeast a large, protected body of water, corresponding to the Bight of Acklins lying between Crooked, Fortune and Acklins islands. Columbus calls this water a "grande angla," and wanted to take his ships into it and to go ashore. But since he found the bottom so shallow that he would have had to anchor far from shore, he did not enter. Guillén believes that Columbus, in calling the body of water an "angla," which means "cape," really had in mind the Portuguese word *angra*, which means "cove." Morison, on the other hand, thinks that "Columbus obviously means an 'angle' in the shore; the so-called Bight of Acklin, between Crooked, Fortune and Acklin Islands." However, the Spanish word for angle is *ángulo*, not *angla*. I believe that Morison was misled by the similarity of *angla* to our word, *angle*.[33]

There is a gap in the *Journal* account of October 20, since it begins with the statement that at sunrise the ships raised anchor from a "Cabo de la Laguna." Nothing is said previously about the fleet's arrival there. Morison's translation says nothing about the omission, and in his *Admiral of the Ocean Sea* he fills the gap without comment. Apparently, very early in the morning of October 20, perhaps

[33] Morison, *Journals*, p. 76, n. 5. Cf. Guillén y Tato, *La parla marinera en el diario de primer viaje de Cristóbal Colón* (Madrid: Instituto histórico de marina, 1951), p. 29 and n. 10; and *Diccionario de la lengua española*, s.v. "angla" and "angra"—the latter is defined as "ensenada," "seno," "parte de mar que se recoge entre dos puntos o cabos de tierra."

after a brief landing at Cabo Hermoso, the fleet must have raised anchor and sailed to the south end of Isabela, named Cabo de la Laguna, "laguna" another reference to the lagoon or *angla* between Crooked, Fortune, and Acklins islands. Here again Columbus tried to find a way in, but again could not because of the shallow bottom.

Because of the difficulties encountered in reaching the parts of the islands where the Indians said there were towns and a king who had much gold, Columbus decided to sail back to the Cabo del Isleo and to go around the islands in a clockwise direction. While this summary account of the matter makes sense in relation to the shapes and locations of the three islands, the *Journal* entries for October 19 and 20 are full of puzzling references to the compass bearings of the island coastlines and to the directions in which Columbus planned to sail to accomplish his objective.

On the morning of October 20, Columbus describes Cabo de la Laguna as the "southwest" cape of Isabela, which perhaps it is, although the island (i.e., Crooked Island) has a west coast trending south-southeast. And from that cape, Columbus writes that he wanted to sail "northeast and east from the southeast and south." Since the fleet was at the southeast end of Isabela, sailing northeast and east would have taken it across the "laguna" to the island (i.e., Acklins) where the king and the towns were said to be. But when he found that he could not cross the "laguna," Columbus wrote (in Morison's translation): "I decided to turn back by the route whence I had come from the north-northeast, to the west, and go around the island along there."[34] The translation does not make sense. Columbus had not come from the north-northeast, and to the west there was no island to go around. The text of the *Journal* actually reads: "determine de me volver por el camino que yo avia traido del nornordeste de la parte del oueste y rodear esta isla para ahi."[35] The source of the trouble is in Morison's translation of the phrase "camino . . . del nornordeste" as "the route . . . from the north-northeast." The phrase means "the way to," not "the way from." With this change, Columbus's meaning can be made clear: "I decided to return by the route whence I had come [from the Cabo del Isleo] and from there [i.e., the Cabo] go *to* the north-northeast from the western part [again the Cabo] and go around the island in that direction."[36] This route would have taken him along the north and east coasts of the modern Crooked and Acklins islands to his hoped-for meeting with the king.

So on October 20 the ships set sail to retrace the course back to the Cabo del Isleo at the north end of Isabela. On the way, winds were unfavorable and *Santa María* spent the night offshore, while the other ships, misunderstanding signals, anchored somewhere en route. At ten in the morning of October 21, the fleet was at anchor again somewhere near the Cabo. From the anchorage, crews went ashore, explored the island of Isabela and replenished the ships' supplies of water. During a stay of several days Columbus decided not to try circumnavigating the islands after all. He learned that there was little gold there, and he feared that contrary winds might make the circumnavigation difficult. As he had received interesting reports about Cuba from his Indian captives, he decided to go there instead, thinking that it might

[34] Morison, *Journals*, p. 77.
[35] From the Carlos Sanz facsimile of the Las Casas manuscript, modernized. In the facsimile the last two words, "para ahí," are actually written "para y," indicating to me that the manuscript text, at least in parts, may have been written from dictation.
[36] Cf. *Diccionario de la lengua española*, s.v. "camino."

be Cipango—Japan. But calms and heavy rain prevented departure until midnight, October 23.

From Isabela, guided by his Indians, Columbus sailed west-southwest, at nightfall reaching a position he estimated to be located seven leagues southeast of Fernandina's southwest point, Cabo Verde. Later that night the wind rose and became so strong that the ships first reduced sail, then sailed under bare poles until morning, Columbus estimating that they made good a bare two leagues. On the morning of the 25th, after continuing on their west-southwest course until nine, Columbus changed course to west, and at three in the afternoon, after sailing eleven leagues, sighted a string of islands running north-south at a distance of five leagues. Columbus named these islands the Islas de Arena, identified by Morison as the presently named Ragged Cays. From there on Columbus followed the "canoe route" taken by the Indians when they traveled from islet to islet, south to and across the shallows now called Columbus Bank, and finally south-southwest across open water to Cuba, which the fleet reached October 28 at a river mouth and port that Columbus named Rio y Puerto de San Salvador.

Morison's account of Columbus's passage through the West Indies seems in general agreement, in spite of a few difficulties, with the course described in the *Journal*. Nevertheless, the uncertainty that lingers in regard to the initial landing place infects to some degree the remainder of the voyage. But in Morison's view the terminus of the voyage in Cuba is quite certain. It can be identified through a peculiar landmark, a mountain inland from Bahía Bariay, on whose peak there exists a protuberance said by Columbus to look like [the dome of?] a pretty mosque ("una montezuelo como una hermosa mezquita"), a mountain called La Teta de Bariay by subsequent settlers. This identifies the Cuban landing as having taken place at the river mouth nearby, located in 21° 5′ N, 76° 5′ W. This pinpointing of the end of the voyage makes Morison confident that by tracing Columbus's route backward through the islands, the initial landing site can be determined with precision. So let us follow this backward course.

Columbus's heading on the last leg of the passage to Cuba was south-southwest from an anchorage in shoal water somewhat south of a string of islands running north-south. If a line running north-northeast is drawn on a modern map, starting at Bahía Bariay, it does in fact cross through the shoals of Columbus Bank and clears the south end of the Ragged Cays. To reach this anchorage, the fleet must previously, that is, on October 26, have sailed south along the string of islands. Las Casas did not, even if, perhaps, Columbus did, record the courses and distances sailed, so that the position of the fleet when land was sighted must be worked out using the data provided for October 25. We know from the *Journal* that on that day, between nine in the morning and three in the afternoon, the fleet sailed eleven leagues west, and before that, between sunrise and nine o'clock, had sailed five leagues west-southwest. The night of October 24 was a stormy one, with such high winds that the ships had first to reduce sail, and later sail under bare poles until morning. Columbus recorded that no more than two leagues headway were made that night, presumably (although he did not say so) to the west-southwest. Tying these, so far, unattached courses and distances, to a map or chart is possible only through an added piece of information given for October 24, namely, that at sundown the fleet had reached a position seven leagues southeast of Cabo Verde, the southwest point of Fernandina (i.e., Long Island). Plotted on a chart, however, the position is inconsistent with the west-southwest course taken by the fleet leaving the Cabo del Isleo on Isabela (i.e., Crooked Island). Either that course was south-west rather than west-southwest, or the distance to Cabo Verde at sundown was only about half of what Columbus said it was. Morison says that Cabo Verde could not have been seen from seven leagues off, so he reduces the distance actually separating the fleet from the cape, and relies on the *Journal* statement that the fleet sailed west-southwest from the Cabo del Isleo.

If, beginning with that departure, the courses and distances sailed up to the time on the 25th when the Islas de Arena (i.e., the Ragged Cays) were sighted, are plotted on a modern map, they lead to a position satisfactorily close to those islands but perhaps not so precisely determinable as Morison makes out. He locates the fleet twelve miles east of the islands in 22° 34′ N, 75° 38′ W at the time of sighting. But, whatever the degree of uncertainty regarding this position, there can be little regarding the point of departure from Isabela, or the location of the anchorage at which the fleet spent the night of October 26, that is, the Columbus Bank. Working backwards again from Isabela, we next have Fernandina. Columbus records that the Cabo del Isleo on Isabela was due east, or lay on an east-west line, from Fernandina. This is true of Bird Rock, on Crooked Island, and of Cabo Verde, the south end of Long Island. It is also true that Long Island is long, although not as long as Columbus thought Fernandina was, and that its east coast, the one Columbus must have seen, runs north-northwest and south-southeast. And its north end is west of Rum Cay, so that the two islands have the same relative locations as Columbus's Fernandina and Santa María de la Concepción. But the nine leagues (about twenty-four nautical miles) said to separate the two islands is not a good estimate of the eighteen miles actually separating Long Island and Rum Cay. Nor was Columbus very accurate in his estimate of Santa María's dimensions even if he used his short land leagues in making it. However, in view of its location relative to that of Fernandina, it does look as if, in describing his route west along one coast running east-west and his previous sighting of a coast running north-south, he is describing Rum Cay.

There now remains only San Salvador. Although the fleet's course leaving that island is not recorded, it was Columbus's stated intention, recorded the day before, to sail to the southwest. So presumably it was in that direction that he did sail. The southwest point of Watlings Island and the northeast point of Rum Cay lie approximately northeast-southwest, so, working backwards, a line drawn northeast from Rum Cay leads to Watlings and to no other island.

Summing up, there is a generally good correspondence between Watlings, Rum Cay, Long Island, Crooked-Fortune-Acklins islands, the Ragged Cays, the Columbus Bank, and Bahía Bariay, and their relative distances and locations, with the description of the voyage through the islands given in Columbus's *Journal*. Although, as has been pointed out, there are some difficulties and discrepancies, no one else has yet proposed another set of islands that, with fewer difficulties, fits the facts of the *Journal* more closely. Working Columbus's course "backwards from Cuba" does not provide absolute certainty that Columbus first landed on Watlings Island, but it does provide a powerful line of argument tending, as Morison maintains, to establish that conclusion.

The *Diario de Colón*:
A Legacy of Poor Transcription, Translation, and Interpretation

Robert H. Fuson

From the standpoint of sheer significance, the first voyage of Christopher Columbus has very few historico-geographical parallels. It was one of those rare events that
altered the course of history, immediately and directly. It finalized the destruction
of the Middle Ages and it provided geographers with that complete planetary
laboratory they had so long envisioned. That this epic happening still holds much
for scholars who probe the past is not surprising, for mysteries still abound. Fore-
most is the one concerning the admiral's personal record of the voyage.

When Christopher Columbus returned to Spain from his first voyage to the New
World, he presented his *Diario de a bordo* (on-board log) to Queen Isabela. By
direction of the queen this log was copied and, just before Columbus departed on his
second voyage (in the autumn of 1493), the copy was given to him. Regrettably, both
the holograph original and the scribe's copy have disappeared. The exemplar has
not been seen since the death of Queen Isabela (1504) and there is no evidence that
more than one copy (the one given to Columbus) was ever made. It must be assumed
that the copy was a faithful one or, if it were not, that it was corrected by Columbus
during the time it was in his possession.

The *Diario de a bordo* was a careful, day-by-day account of the first crossing. In it
Columbus detailed navigational data, simple ethnography and geography, floral
and faunal characteristics, and even some of his inner thoughts. As the years after
1492 passed, the admiral must have treasured this document greatly. Upon his death
(1506), the copied log, various maps and charts, manuscripts, and personal papers
passed to Diego, Columbus's eldest son.[1] Diego, second admiral of the Indies, died in
1526 , and his son (Columbus's grandson), Luis, the third admiral of the Indies (and
later duke of Veragua), received the inheritance.

Luis was, at this time, a minor, under the guardianship of María Álvarez de
Toledo, his mother and Diego's widow. He was not to gain absolute control of the
Columbus papers for twenty-three years. It is highly probable that even María did
not possess all of the first admiral's documents until after the death of Ferdinand,
Columbus's second son, in 1539. Ferdinand was the family archivist and its only real

---

[1] Henry Vignaud, *Toscanelli and Columbus* (New York: E. P. Dutton, 1902), p. 144.

51

scholar.[2] He was a true bibliophile and assembled one of the finest private libraries on the European continent. Ferdinand opened his home and his library to the scholars of that day, who came to Seville to study and marvel at a collection of over fifteen thousand items. It is quite likely that Diego, before his death, gave some of the more important family papers to Ferdinand for safekeeping. If this were the case, María would not have had complete control until Ferdinand's death in 1539.

For all practical purposes, Ferdinand's library (and perhaps many of the important Columbus papers) was sealed for five years after his death. In 1544, María removed everything from Ferdinand's home and entrusted the collection to the Dominican monastery of San Pablo in Seville.[3] María then returned to Hispaniola (accompanied by Bartolomé de Las Casas) to take up her duties as viceroy and to rejoin Luis, who had been living in the Indies. Certain documents were still in the possession of María after she returned to the New World. Upon her death, in 1549, these passed to Luis, along with unrestricted access to Ferdinand's collection that was being held in trust in Seville. In essence, Luis was now free to run amok through the reassembled collection of Columbus memorabilia. This was one of the greatest tragedies that could have befallen future scholars. Luis was a ne'er-do-well who was, as Vignaud stated, "devoid of morality."[4] He placed his immediate financial interest above everything else, though women ran a close second. He was imprisoned in later years for having three wives (at the same time) and managed to acquire a fourth by bribing his jailers for frequent overnight passes. His only fondness for books or family papers was the price they might fetch in the marketplace, thereby providing the means to support his debauchery.

The *Diario de a bordo* was in Luis's possession in 1554, the year in which he was granted authorization to publish it.[5] Inasmuch as it was never published, it is reasonable to assume that he sold it, as he did Ferdinand's manuscript of the admiral's biography (the *Historie*).[6] Of course, Luis could have lost the *Diario de a bordo*, but his greed seems to preclude this. He probably sold it to some nobleman who placed the manuscript in a private library, from which it was destined eventually to disappear. It is unlikely that the *Diario de a bordo* ever passed to the cathedral chapter of Seville, which acquired Ferdinand's library from the San Pablo monastery in 1552. Even if it had, its survival would have been doubtful, for the library was mishandled and dwindled to fifteen percent of its original size within a few years. Today this collection, still housed in Seville, is known as the Biblioteca Colombiana.

Before the library was scattered and vandalized, Fray Bartolomé de Las Casas obtained access to the *Diario de a bordo*. Some students of Columbus believe this to have been the holograph original.[7] Las Casas said, however, that he used a scribe's

---

[2] Ibid.; Ferdinand Columbus, *The Life of the Admiral Christopher Columbus*, trans. Benjamin Keen (New Brunswick: Rutgers University Press, 1959), pp. viii–ix.

[3] Cecil Jane, *The Journal of Christopher Columbus*, ed. L. A. Vigneras (New York: Clarkson N. Potter, 1960), p. xvi.

[4] Vignaud, p. 165.

[5] Jane, *Journal*, p. xv.

[6] Ferdinand Columbus, p. xv.

[7] John B. Thacher, *Christopher Columbus: His Life, His Work, His Remains*, 3 vols. (New York, 1903–4), 1:512.

copy.[8] Apparently this was the copy made for Columbus by direct order of Queen Isabela and known today as the Barcelona copy. Las Casas never revealed how he came upon the copied *Diario de a bordo*. It could have come to him from any number of sources. Las Casas knew Columbus and Columbus's brothers, Diego and Bartolomé, as well as the entire Columbus family. The sons of Columbus, Diego and Ferdinand, were close personal friends, as was Diego's wife, María, and her son, Luis. It is known positively that Diego gave certain materials to Las Casas when they both resided in Hispaniola.[9] Ferdinand may have sent the *Diario de a bordo* to his brother in Hispaniola, who, in turn, loaned it to Las Casas; or Las Casas might have gotten the manuscript directly from Ferdinand during trips to Spain in 1515 or 1517. There is even the possibility that the Barcelona copy was copied, specifically for Las Casas. If so, that leaves us with a third missing version.

Some scholars still cling to the notion that Las Casas found the Barcelona copy among the remains of Ferdinand's library, thirteen years after Ferdinand's death and while Las Casas was residing in the San Pablo monastery, which at that time still housed the collection.[10] This is much too late, for internal evidence in the *Historia* clearly demonstrates that the sections derived from the *Diario de a bordo* were written in Hispaniola after 1527 and before 1539.[11] Las Casas was in Spain from 1539 to 1544, during the period when María de Toledo still had the library, and, if there were no evidence to the contrary, this would have been the logical time to gain access to the document, not eight years later.

The fact still remains that the epic *Historia de las Indias* was begun in 1527 and the *Diario de a bordo* had to be in Las Casas's hands at that time.[12] As a matter of record, Las Casas began almost immediately to collect materials relevant to the discovery after he reached Hispaniola in 1502. It is even possible, though not probable, that he obtained the *Diario de a bordo* before that year. Las Casas's father and uncle accompanied Columbus on the second voyage, a time when Columbus was carrying the Barcelona copy. Inasmuch as Las Casas had been enraptured with the admiral since the triumphant return from the first voyage, which he witnessed in Seville when only eighteen years of age, it is barely possible that his thirst for more knowledge of the exploit led eventually to the precious log. Regardless of when or how Las Casas came upon the *Diario de a bordo*, it is fortunate that he did. Other than Ferdinand's sketchy account of the first voyage (also derived from the same document), Las Casas is our only solid source. From the scribe's copy of the *Diario de a bordo*, Las Casas prepared a handwritten abstract, which he called *El libro de la primera navegación*. Today the abstract is generally known as the *Diario de Colón*, or simply the *Diario*.

One can only assume that the copy of the *Diario de a bordo* from which Las Casas worked was reasonably accurate. His firsthand knowledge of the general geographical area described, his personal acquaintance with many of the participants in

---

[8] Bartolomé de Las Casas, *Historia de las indias*, 3 vols., ed. Agustín Millares Carlo (México City: Fondo de Cultura Económica, 1951), 1:303.
[9] Ibid., p. lxii.
[10] Jane, *Journal*, p. xvii.
[11] Las Casas consistently used such terms as "these Indies" and "this Hispaniola" in the *Historia*. Positive references to dated discoveries establish the period of composition.
[12] Las Casas, 1:xix.

the venture, and his possession of other supporting evidence provided him with several means of verification. Further, few scholars question the honesty of Las Casas when relating geographical events.[13] Other than the fact that Las Casas omitted selected portions of the *Diario de a bordo* and edited others, the abstract must be accepted as a reasonably good synopsis of the copied original.

In addition to the abstract *Diario*, Las Casas may have provided further glimpses of the original log in his *Historia*.[14] Then again, the *Historia* may simply represent a polishing and elaboration of the original notes taken from the log. Since we know that Las Casas was still editing and rewriting the *Historia* as late as 1563 (three years before his death at the age of 92), there is a chance that he took editorial license or that he trusted to a failing memory.[15] The abstract *Diario* and the *Historia* generally agree, but not always. These discrepancies are discussed later, but the claim is made now that a document composed closer to the event, and with little embellishment, is probably more accurate than one dating from perhaps as much as a half century later and biased by passion, personal attachment to some of the participants, and failing health. Further, there are several versions of the manuscript *Historia* extant, various fragments of portions of it, and a possibility of undiscovered parts.[16] One of the advantages of the Thacher translation of the *Diario* is the inclusion of supplements from the *Historia*, properly identified.[17] The *Historie* of Ferdinand does not provide a means for checking on the accuracy of Las Casas.[18] There is some doubt as to whether it was even written by Ferdinand, and it may have been based entirely on the work of Las Casas.[19] The *Historie* appears to be largely plagiarism of the *Historia* and much beneath the capabilities of a scholar such as Ferdinand, who had access to all of his father's papers. Luis could have written it, or had it written, and there may never have been a Spanish original.

The Las Casas abstract of Columbus's log lay dormant until 1790, when it was found by Martín Fernández de Navarrete in the library of the duke del Infantado.

---

[13] Cecil Jane, *The Voyages of Christopher Columbus, Being the Journals of His First and Last Voyages, to Which Is Added the Account of His Second Voyage Written by Andres Bernaldez* (London: Argonaut Press, 1930), p. 63. Jane said, "It is easy to show that he [Las Casas] was upon occasion guilty of deliberate misstatement of fact, and that for his information he relied upon a memory which was either curiously defective or singularly convenient." Vignaud, pp. 139–52 and 156–68, while not accusing Las Casas of misstating geographical facts, directly charged him with complicity in the matter of the Toscanelli correspondence, which Vignaud claimed was forged. He viewed Las Casas as a master of cover-up and apology. Simon Wiesenthal, *Sails of Hope: The Secret Mission of Christopher Columbus* (New York: Christopher Columbus Publishing, 1979), agrees with Vignaud that Las Casas went to great lengths to conceal certain aspects of Columbus's personal life and that he would not hesitate to alter the facts if they furthered what he considered to be a just cause.

[14] Las Casas, 1:179–327.

[15] Ibid., p. xxxiii.

[16] Ibid., pp. xxxiii–xxxv.

[17] Thacher, 1:513–86, 604–70.

[18] Ferdinand's biography of his father is generally cited as the *Historie*. The title of the 1571 Venice edition is *Historie del S. D. Fernando Colombo; Nelle quali s'ha particolare, & vera relatione della vita, & de' fatti dell'Ammiraglio D. Cristoforo Colombo, suo padre: Et dello scoprimento, ch'egli fece dell' Indie Occidentali, dette Mondo Nuovo, hora possedute dal Sereniss. Re Catolico: Nuovamente di lingua Spagnuola tradotte nell'Italiana dal S. Alfonso Ulloa.* This is the edition translated by Keen. The original Spanish manuscript has been lost, if there ever was one.

[19] Vignaud, pp. 130–32, 153, 164–66.

This was transcribed by Navarrete and published in 1825.[20] The first three English translations of the complete *Diario* (Kettell, Markham, and Thacher) were derived from this transcription.[21] In addition, there have been several partial translations, usually beginning a day or so before landfall and continuing until the discovery of Hispaniola. Between 1892 and 1896 an Italian publication of fourteen massive volumes (the *Raccolta*) appeared, to commemorate the fourth centennial of the discovery.[22] It includes not only the *Diario* but also most of the other documents pertinent to the first voyage. Jane and Morison based their English translations of the *Diario* on the *Raccolta*.[23] A third Spanish-to-Spanish transcription of the *Diario* was published in 1962 by Carlos Sanz of Madrid.[24] To date, no English translation of the Sanz transcription has been made. In 1971, Joaquin Arce published a fourth transcription.[25] Again, there is no English translation. Like its predecessors, it is not a truly diplomatic version and there is no accompanying copy of the Las Casas manuscript. Two recent transcriptions have been made for the period October 10–27. One, by Oliver Dunn, which appears in this journal, has not been translated. The other, prepared for the National Geographic Society by Eugene Lyon, has a translation. Both transcriptions are superb, and Lyon's partial translation is the best yet to appear.

An examination of the principal English translations and Spanish transcriptions (excluding the very recent works of Dunn and Lyon), and comparisons of them with the manuscript of Las Casas, reveal a number of transcriptive, translative, and interpretative flaws. These are discussed in the pages that follow. Inasmuch as the 1963 English translation by Samuel Eliot Morison is probably the best *complete* version (despite many shortcomings), it has been chosen for most of the examples cited.

[20] There are many editions of Martín Fernández de Navarrete's transcription of *El libro de la primera navegación*. Perhaps the most readily available may be found in the edition of Navarrete's *Colección de los viajes y descubrimientos que hicieron por mar los españoles desde fines del siglo quince*, edited by Carlos Seco Serrano in his *Obras de D. Martín Fernández de Navarrete*, Biblioteca de autores españoles (Madrid: Ediciones Atlas, 1954), 75:86–166. All references to Navarrete in this paper are to this edition. Identical (other than pagination and typographical errors) are Navarrete, *Viajes de Cristóbal Colón*, 2d ed. (Madrid: Espasa-Calpe, 1934), and Navarrete, "Relaciones, cartas, y otros documentos concernientes a los cuatro viages que hizo el almirante Don Cristóbal Colón para el descubrimiento de las Indias occidentales," in J. Natalicio González, ed., *Colección de los viages y descubrimientos que hicieron por mar los españoles desde fines del siglo quince* (Buenos Aires: Editorial Guarania, 1945), 1:147–296.

[21] Samuel Kettell, *Personal Narration of the First Voyage of Columbus* (Boston: T. B. Wait, 1827), also reprinted as Van Wyck Brooks, ed., *Journal of First Voyage to America by Christopher Columbus* (New York: Albert and Charles Boni, 1924); Clements R. Markham, *The Journal of Christopher Columbus (During his First Voyage, 1492-93), and Documents Relating to the Voyages of John Cabot and Gaspar Corte Real* (London: Hakluyt Society, 1893); Thacher, vol. 1.

[22] Cesare de Lollis, ed., *Raccolta di documenti e studi pubblicati dalla Real Commissione Colombiana pel quarto centenario dalla scoperta dell'America*, 14 vols. (Rome: Ministerio Pubblica Istruzione, 1892-96). Pt. 1, vols. 1–2, is titled "Scritti di Cristoforo Colombo."

[23] Jane, *Journal*, p. xxiii; Samuel Eliot Morison, *Journals and Other Documents on the Life and Voyages of Christopher Columbus* (New York: Heritage Press, 1963), p. 43.

[24] Carlos Sanz, *Diario de Colón: Libro de la primera navegación y descubrimiento*, 2 vols. (Madrid: Gráficas Yagües, 1962). Vol. 1 is the facsimile of Las Casas's manuscript; vol. 2 contains a line-by-line pseudo-diplomatic transcription. Throughout this paper, the citation "Sanz, fol." refers to the manuscript reproduction in vol. 1. The transcription by Oliver Dunn carries the same folio designations.

[25] Joaquin Arce and M. Gil Esteve, eds., *Diario de a bordo de Cristóbal Colón: Estudio preliminario de Joaquín Arce* (Turin: A. Tallone, 1971).

A translation is no better than the material being translated, in this case one of the several transcriptions. A direct English translation of the Las Casas holograph would be possible, but it has never been accomplished. Each one so far has been made from a modern printed (and usually a modern spelling) rendition of the sixteenth-century Spanish script of Las Casas. A majority of the translations (English and foreign) have relied on the transcriptions of 1825 (Naverrete) or 1892 (*Raccolta*).

Everything considered, Navarrete's transcription is a good one that has stood the test of time. For one thing, he was perhaps the best equipped scholar in Spain for the task he set out to do at the time he did it. Navarrete was one of Spain's leading authorities on Spanish orthography, cacography and paleography.[26] He was also an eminent historian and maritime expert. There are some problems with the Navarrete transcription, however. First, it is not a diplomatic transcription. Navarrete eliminated the numerous abbreviations and generally modernized the words. Second, his footnoted comments often contain opinions that reach beyond the work at hand. Third, he or the typographer made mistakes. There are numerous errors of transcription, though some of these are unfootnoted corrections of obvious errors.[27] Only two of these errors have any real navigational substance.[28] Nevertheless, even one directional mistake early on can create a domino effect, with all subsequent parts of the voyage being affected. Another transcriptional problem associated with the several editions of Navarrete is the infamous typographical error. Sometimes those of us surrounded by old manuscripts and books, and acutely aware of their shortcomings, forget that modern printers also make mistakes. The Seco Serrano edition (utilized for this paper) appears to be the most carefully edited one, but the reader should be warned that other editions may not always agree.[29]

The *Raccolta* transcription gained wide acceptance after it appeared almost a century ago. It contains fewer errors of transcribed words than does Navarrete, but there are several significant technical errors.[30] Furthermore, it is even less diplomatic than Navarrete's work. A serious drawback is the lack of ready availability of this edition today. Its large folio size and its cost relegate the *Raccolta* to only the largest of libraries.

Sanz's two-volume transcription provides, for the first time, a facsimile of the original *Libro de la primera navegación*. The modern transcription follows the manu-

---

[26] Navarrete, 75:vii–lxv. Navarrete's classic work, *Ortografía de la lengua castellana* (Madrid: Real Academia Española, 1815) established him as an authority on the Spanish language. He also produced the definitive work on Cervantes, *Vida de Miguel de Cervantes Saavedra* (Madrid: Real Academia Española, 1819). More than fifty major works were written by Navarrete, including many on maritime discoveries and nautical history.

[27] Navarrete, 75:94. "Guesueste" ("west-southeast") in the manuscript was corrected to west-southwest. On p. 148, "sursueste" ("south-southeast") was corrected to south-southwest to fit the only possible course.

[28] The only two errors in Navarrete's transcription that would affect a reconstruction of the voyage are "norueste" ("northwest"), transcribed as "nordeste" ("northeast"), and "sursudueste" ("south-southwest"), transcribed as "sursueste" ("south-southeast"). Navarrete, 75:89, 99.

[29] In the Espasa-Calpe edition (1934), there are numerous typographical errors totally unrelated to the original transcription. These cannot be blamed on Navarrete.

[30] The *Raccolta* transcription alters the punctuation in several critical passages; these are carried over by Morison in his translation.

script, line for line, enabling the user to locate quickly any desired word or passage. Unfortunately, the transcription is not as accurate as those produced by Navarrete or the *Raccolta*. Morison stated that it is the best transcription of the three, a point open to serious question.[31] Sanz commited four errors of mistranscribed directions that are substantive (twice as many as Navarrete).[32] In all four instances the script of Las Casas is clear and distinct; there is no way the original may be misunderstood. This may be an example of poor editing, and it is a strong argument for use of primary sources by any researcher.

Arce's transcription closely follows the *Raccolta*, though some Italianisms crop up now and then (the volume was printed in Italy). All in all, it is a good transcription, though not diplomatic and carrying over several mistakes from earlier efforts.

Another transcriptional problem, affecting all four Spanish-to-Spanish transcriptions, involves the written language of Columbus. It is almost impossible to distinguish between transcription and translation in those cases where the transcriber has modernized the Spanish of Las Casas. Inasmuch as all four published transcriptions are less than diplomatic we will have to await Dunn's version before a good translation of Las Casas can be effected. Some of the words may not be Castilian, if Las Casas abstracted faithfully. Non-Castilian words may have been reformed by a well-meaning transcriber.

Columbus was a partially educated, multilingual Genoese citizen.[33] He spoke the Genoese vernacular as a native language and was reasonable adept in the then-spreading peninsular Italian. He knew Portuguese and Castilian Spanish, but not perfectly, and some Latin. Las Casas mentioned his imperfect Castilian on several occasions.[34] As Virgil Milani has pointed out, in a brilliant little book, Columbus "was outside and ahead of fifteenth century Spain."[35] In other words, he was a foreigner who used words that were not to enter Castilian until much later. In fact, Milani documents more than a hundred words (mostly from the *Diario*) that were not known in Spanish literature before the *late* sixteenth or early seventeenth centuries. These words are Genoese, not Portuguese corruptions. Milani's linguistic evidence is overwhelming: Columbus was Genoese by birth, that is, in speech. That should end the debate concerning the admiral's linguistic heritage.

[31] Morison, p. 43. Morison did not use the Sanz transcription because it appeared just before his book went to press. Had Morison had time to study the Sanz version he would not have stated that it was the best transcription.

[32] Sanz made the following substantive errors in transcribing the *Diario de Colón*: fol. 6, "sudueste" ("southwest") for "sudeste" ("southeast"); fol. 10, "norueste" ("northwest") for "nornordeste" ("north-northeast"); fol. 13, "norueste" ("northwest") for "nornorueste" ("north-northwest"); fol. 27, "norte" ("north") for "norte a sur" ("north to south"). Also, Sanz's failure to adhere to original spellings causes some difficulty in comparing the transcription with the facsimile of the holograph manuscript and vice versa. While Navarrete's transcription is not perfectly diplomatic, it is much closer than is the Sanz version.

[33] Virgil I. Milani, "The Written Language of Christopher Columbus," *Forum Italicum*, Supplement (1973), p. 11.

[34] Las Casas, 1:244. Commenting on a rather poetical passage, Las Casas said, "All of these are [his] formal words, although some of them are not in perfect Castilian Romance, since that was not the mother tongue of the admiral." This is one of five instances where Las Casas referred to the Castilian of Columbus, and it indicates an exact transcription of the holograph *Diario de a bordo* by the scribe. For the other four comments on the Spanish of Columbus, see Las Casas, 1:474 and 2:25, 44, 72.

[35] Milani, p. 11.

But more importantly, Las Casas (and others) often "corrected" the written language of Columbus when excerpting his writings. The original form is preserved in the Columbus autographs, but only some of it has survived in the Las Casas abstract of the log. Las Casas, in effect, edited the words of Columbus when he claimed to be quoting verbatim. How are we to know when he altered a Genoese word, i.e., "corrected" it to conform to Castilian usage? And what if the correction resulted in a word of another meaning? Attempted corrections by a well-wishing Las Casas may be one reason why certain portions of the *Diario* are vague, confusing, and even nonsensical. A word that is incorrectly transcribed cannot be correctly translated. We may only surmise what the original was. And, when words seem archaic or poorly spelled Castilian, we rush to *Spanish* dictionaries—old ones, if we are careful students. But, do we consult dictionaries of the Genoese vernacular of the fifteenth century?

We have, then, four less-than-perfect transcriptions of the sixteenth-century Spanish script into modern Spanish print. A direct translation into English of any one, or some combination of all, will be incorrect, unless the handwritten *Libro de la primera navegación* is used for a word-by-word comparison. Morison attempted to do this, by using a photocopy of the Las Casas document as he followed the *Raccolta* transcription.[36] His efforts produced the best version of the *Diario* that has appeared in English, but it is deficient in a number of places and falls somewhat short of what a definitive translation should be.

Alteration of the Original Text

An alteration is an error of transcription. Typically, the alteration involves shifting a punctuation mark or inserting one. Fifteenth-century manuscripts were often poorly punctuated or not punctuated at all. Capitalization was either non-existent or meaningless. Not only is there a temptation for the modern scholar to polish long, complex, unpunctuated sentences, but it is often essential to do so. Las Casas punctuated rather well for his time. Periods, semicolons, and even commas are fairly clear, although he often used symbols somewhat distinct from those of today. His hand reads as well as most modern Spanish script. While the handwriting of Columbus differs from that of Las Casas, the variation is no greater than between two modern scripts. Scribes of the time certainly had little difficulty abstracting from a Columbus holograph, though Las Casas occasionally complained of the scribe's copy of the *Diario de a bordo* that he used.[37]

There is no way to know whether Las Casas punctuated correctly when he abstracted the *Diario de a bordo*; we can only reason that he did at least as well as would someone removed by five centuries. There are, nevertheless, several instances where Morison refused to accept the authority of Las Casas and relied on the

---

[36] Morison, p. 43.
[37] Navarrete, 75:150. Next to the entry for January 13, Las Casas added a marginal note, which translates as, "Here it appears that the admiral knew something of astrology [*sic*], although these planets seem not to be well placed through the fault of the bad scribe who transcribed it." For the same date, Las Casas said in the *Historia*, 1:303, "Although I think that the letter is corrupt, through the fault of the one that transcribed the admiral's log."

incorrect *Raccolta* transcription. In two extreme cases the entire meaning of the original was altered. For October 29, the Las Casas manuscript reads, "Vna punta dla ysla le salia al norueste seys leguas de alli /. otra punta le salia al leste diez leguas /."[38] Morison translated the *Raccolta*: "A point of the island made out to the NW 6 leagues; from there another point made out to the E 10 leagues."[39] This is a correct translation of an incorrect transcription; for the period (/.) has been changed to a semicolon and moved two words closer to the beginning of the sentence. The altered sentence now means that the second point of land was viewed *after* the admiral had arrived at the first point. Las Casas clearly stated that both points of land were viewed from the starting position. In this instance, Thacher's translation is close to the original: "One point of the island projected to the north-west six leagues from there, another point projected to the east ten leagues."[40] Thacher did shift from a period (or semicolon) to a comma, but the sentence retains its original meaning. Markham botched this passage completely: "They doubled a point six leagues to the N.W., and then another point, then east ten leagues."[41] The above-mentioned passage is one of the most critical in the *Diario*, for it helps to establish the first port of call in Cuba. An incorrect reading will result in an erroneous landfall on Cuba's northeastern coast.

After Columbus departed from the harbor (October 30) he sailed westward, to a place he called Río de Mares. Las Casas continued: "salio dl rio de mares al norueste y vido cabo lleno de palmas y pusole cabo de palmas dspues de avia andado quinze leguas/. los yndios q̄ yvā en la caravela pinta dixerō q̄ detras de aq̄l cabo avia un rio."[42] The *Raccolta* once again shifted punctuation, thus leading Morison to translate the passage as, "Departed from the *Rio de Mares* to the NW, and saw a cape covered with palms, and called it *Cabo de Palmas*. After having gone 15 leagues, the Indians on board the caravel *Pinta* said that behind that cape was a river."[43] This is another point in the text that assists in establishing the route along the Cuban coast. If Columbus saw a cape after sailing fifteen leagues from Río de Mares (as the original text reads), and if that cape can be identified today, we have another piece of the puzzle. If, on the other hand, Columbus saw the palm-covered cape as he left Río de Mares and *then* sailed fifteen leagues, as the *Raccolta* interpreted it, the itinerary must be rearranged.

Another form of text alteration occurs when the transcriber selects a particular word from among several alternate spellings of the same word, and uses the one form consistently throughout the transcription. For example, beginning with the journal entry of November 12, Columbus made frequent reference to an island the Indians had told him about. This island is consistently transcribed by Navarrete as "Babeque," but the Las Casas manuscript first calls it "Baveque," then "Babeque," "Beneque," and "Baneq̄" ("Bane*que*").[44] In Morison the word is also rendered as "Babenque" and "Veneque."[45] Maps of the sixteenth century indicate that, through

[38] Sanz, fol. 18.
[39] Morison, p. 83; *Raccolta*, p. 31.
[40] Thacher, 1:552.
[41] Markham, p. 61.
[42] Sanz, fol. 19.
[43] Morison, p. 84; *Raccolta*, p. 31.
[44] Sanz, fol. 22, 23, 24.
[45] Morison, pp. 93–94.

normal Castilian reduction, the name evolved into "Jabeque," then "Yabaque."[46] It may have also been rendered as "Babueca" and, possibly, "Babuca" and "Babucca."[47] Alternate forms should not be standardized; an omitted one might be correct. According to Herrera, Ponce de León visited an island he called La Isla del Viejo ("The Island of the Old Man").[48] This was one of the Turks Islands, near the Babueca Reefs. If Babueca is associated linguistically or geographically with Babeque, then El Viejo might be San Salvador, despite the claim that Guanahaní lay farther north. It should be remembered that if Europeans mixed spellings, pronunciations, and locations, so might have the Indians. Further, the Indians may have had two names for the same island, or Bahamian Arawaks and Cuban Arawaks, though speaking the same language, may have had different names for a single place that was home to neither.

One last example of selection (or interpretation) by a transcriber may be noted. Under the entry for October 15, Las Casas said, "parti dlas ysla de Scta maria de Concepciō."[49] Every transcription renders "dlas ysla" as "from the islands." Armed with this information, various scholars have made a strong case that the island Columbus named Santa María de la Concepción must, in reality, be a cluster of several islands. Maybe this is the case; maybe not. The sentence is not written correctly, for it contains a plural article and a singular noun. It must either read "las islas" or "la isla." As it stands, it may be either singular or plural, and no clue is provided by the error. We will never know if Columbus made the original mistake, or the scribe, or Las Casas. But we may rightly charge the transcribers with exercising too much editorial license.

Errors of Translation and Interpretation

Translation from one language to another is never easy. Absolutely literal translations are not necessarily better than free translations. Literal translations may be stilted, awkward, and convey an erroneous meaning (or feeling) even if each word is rendered correctly. A Spaniard "touches a bell" while an English speaker "rings a bell," and a Spaniard "has thirst" when an English speaker "is thirsty." And words of the fifteenth century may possess different meanings today, or they may have numerous meanings.

On several occasions Columbus said that he was "in the gulf," or "mid-gulf"

[46] Henry Harrisse, *The Discovery of North America: A Critical, Documentary, and Historic Investigation* (1892; reprint, Amsterdam: N. Israel, 1961); Turin Map of 1523 is contained in the end-jacket; Alonso de Santa Cruz, "Ysla de los Lucayos," *El yslario general de todas las yslas del mundo enderesçado a la S. C. C. Magestad del emperador y rey nuestro señor por Alonso de Sancta Cruz su cosmógrafo mayor, La quatre parte* (manuscript of three pages with map, ca. 1541, in Osterreiches Nationalbibliotek, Vienna). Juan López de Velasco, *Geografía y descripción universal de las Indias*, ed. Don Marcos Jiménez de la Espada, Biblioteca de autores Españoles (Madrid: Ediciones Atlas, 1971), pp. 65–66. Antonio de Herrera y Tordesillas, *Historia general de los hechos de los Castellanos, en las islas, y tierra-firme de el mar occeano*, 5 vols., preface by J. Natalicio Gonzalez (Asunción: Editorial Guarania, 1945); this is a facsimile of the edition of 1726–30, ten volumes bound as five; see vol. 1, maps facing pp. 43 and 73.

[47] Harrisse, maps in end-jacket: Cantino (1501–2), Canerio (1504), and anonymous Portuguese (1514).

[48] Herrera, vol. 2, p. 207; Harrisse, p. 147. Harrisse claims that latitudes given by Herrera were added at least fifteen years after the voyage of Ponce de León and are in error.

[49] Sanz, fol. 12.

("golfo," "medio golfo"). "Golfo" may be translated as "gulf" in English. But it also means channel, open sea, main, faro (the game), bum, vagabond, or vagrant. Obviously, Columbus was not sailing among bums or Las Vegas games, but gulf, open sea, and channel are three totally different maritime environments. The translator must make a judgment. It must be in context. "Island" is another little word that appears dozens of times in the *Diario*. Spanish has four common words for island, while English only has three (island, isle, islet). An *isla* may be any island, large or small; an *islote* is a small, rocky, barren island; an *isleo* (rare in modern Spanish) is a small island; an *isleta* is a small or tiny island. As in English, these terms may be modified (big island, very big island, pretty big island, etc.).

Much has been made of the terminology of the *Diario* in attempting to nail down the size of San Salvador. Honestly done it may be a valid clue, but a sloppy translation (or one designed to fit a preconception) merely muddies the water. Morison, for example, translates *isleta* as "island."[50] Watlings (his San Salvador) is much too large to be an *isleta*, and the translation seems to be an intentional distortion. Molander translates the word correctly (as islet), but attributes the description to Columbus.[51] Las Casas called San Salvador an *isleta*, not Columbus.[52] Any Bahamian island would probably have been an islet to Las Casas, who regarded Hispaniola and Cuba as *islas*. The first mention of San Salvador by Columbus, when he is quoted verbatim, uses the word *ysla* (*isla*), and even Las Casas uses *isla* after his initial mention of *isleta*.

On October 14 Columbus saw a little peninsula on San Salvador and said, "y vide vn pedaço de tr̄ra q̄ se haze cōmo ysla aunq̄ no lo es" ("and I saw a piece of land that was shaped like an island although it is not").[53] Note the use of the word *island*. The peninsula was so small that he said it could be made into an *island* in two days. Then he refers to the peninsula as an *isleta*, which it was not but could have been, with some heavy digging. In other words, Columbus was not precise in his use of the word *isla*. Ferdinand Columbus mentions this same peninsula in the *Historie*.[54] But the translation from Spanish to Italian changes "two days of hard digging" (to make an island) to "three days of hard rowing to round."

On October 24 Columbus used the word *isleo*.[55] Morison needed an island smaller than that to fit his reconstruction of the voyage at that point, so he translated the word as "islet" (*isleta*).[56] It is interesting to note that Morison selected the word he wanted, not the word that was correct. The frequency with which this occurs throughout his translation can only lead to the conclusion that it was deliberate. The entry for October 18 is most interesting. It reads simply, "dspues q̄ aclarescio segui el viento y fui en derredor dla ysla quāto pude y surgi al t̄po q̄ ya no era de navegar: mas nō fui en tr̄ra y en amaneçiendo di la vela" ("After it cleared up, I followed the wind and went round about the island as much as I could and anchored at the time

[50] Morison, p. 64.
[51] Arne B. Molander, "Columbus Landed Here — or Did He?" *Américas* (1981)33:3.
[52] Sanz, fol. 8.
[53] Sanz, fol. 11.
[54] Ferdinand Columbus, p. 64.
[55] Sanz, fol. 14.
[56] Morison, pp. 75, 80.

when it was no longer possible to navigate: but I did not go ashore and at daybreak I made sail".[57] Morison renders this passage as, "After it cleared up I followed the wind and went around the island as far as I could, and anchored when the weather was no longer suitable for sailing; but I didn't go ashore, and at break of day made sail."[58] There are some significant differences between the two translations.

"En derredor" may mean "around," but Columbus used *rodear* throughout the *Diario* to mean a "circuit." "Round about" is not exactly the same as "around." "Quāto pude" (*cuanto pude*) better translates as "as much as I could," not "as far as I could." "Al t̄po" (*al tiempo*) is a time reference, not a weather report. It was getting too dark to see reefs and shoals. "Navegar" definitely means "to navigate." It may mean "to sail," but the translator should select the nearest equivalent term.

October 18 is a very important day for those interested in reconstructing the first voyage. It is, in essence, a wild card day. An entire twelve-hour sailing period is covered by a single sentence; a time span that may have permitted the fleet to cover seventy miles or more. The previous day's entry (October 17) offers good evidence that there was a strong norther followed by rapid clearing after sunrise. Columbus apparently sailed all that day, "round about," and anchored at sunset, when he could no longer see to navigate. And he sailed with the wind, which was from the north. In other words, he sailed to the south. Another vague log entry was made on October 24. It reads, "y de vn rato creçia mūcho el viento y hazia mūcho camino de q̄ dudava" ("and after awhile the wind increased a lot and I covered a great deal of a course of which I was doubtful").[59] Morison's translation yields, "And shortly after the wind increased greatly, and I was very doubtful of the way"[60] What happened to the great amount of distance covered? A goodly distance and a doubtful direction are important clues for identifying the island of Isabela.

A careful comparison of the Las Casas abstract with Morison's translation of it reveals another fascinating error. Prior to the first landing, Columbus said (on October 7), "y poner la proa guesueste con determinacion de andar dos dias por aq̄lla via" ("and to turn the prow toward the west-southeast with the determination of going two days in that direction").[61] Morison translated the phrase as, "and to turn the prow WSW, intending to proceed two days on that course."[62] This is an incorrect translation of the *Diario*, which uses the impossible direction of west-southeast ("guesueste"). It is, however, a good translation of Navarrete, who corrected the Las Casas abstract without footnoting his action.[63] Navarrete may be faulted for altering the *Diario* when he transcribed it; but by not telling us, he placed Morison in an awkward position. Morison could not have derived "WSW" from any source but Navarrete, whom he was translating at this point. Yet he claimed that he used a photocopy of Las Casas to correct the *Raccolta* transcription as he went along.[64] This

[57] Sanz, fol. 14.
[58] Morison, p. 75.
[59] Sanz, fol. 17.
[60] Morison, p. 81.
[61] Sanz, fol. 7.
[62] Morison, p. 94.
[63] Navarrete, p. 94.
[64] There is no way that the photocopy could be misread here.

causes one to wonder just how carefully Morison used the Las Casas manuscript in other instances or whether he was willing to follow the incorrect *Raccolta* and Navarrete versions.

Two glaring errors—mistakes of immense proportions—center on the little word *de*. In both instances the direction of travel is altered by 180 degrees and the entire first voyage through the islands is rerouted. On Sunday, October 14, Columbus set out to explore the coast of San Salvador, using the small rowboats carried on the ships. There was a morning of rowing, and the activity probably extended into the afternoon. Las Casas said, "fue al luēgo dla ysla en el camino del nornordeste pa ver la otra pte que era de la pte del leste q̃ avia" ("He went along the island on the route from the north-northeast in order to see the other part which was the eastern part that was there").[65] Two significant details may be noted. First, the fleet was anchored on the western side of San Salvador, a precaution that any seasoned sailor would take in the Bahamas region. Second, Columbus followed his original intent to sail southwest from his first New World anchorage.[66]

Morison agreed that the fleet was on the western side but, in order to reach the reef harbor that Columbus explored with his small boats on the morning of October 14, it was necessary to have the crew row *to* the north-northeast. Only in that direction would they have been able to fetch Graham's Harbor at the north end of Watlings. Not only did Morison mistranslate the direction, but he set up a rowing ordeal of some twenty-five miles![67] The harbor behind the reef, large enough for all the ships in Christendom, may be discovered by going southwesterly along the west coast of San Salvador. And the first landing site should be near the southern end in order to make the rowing episode feasible.

De is also a key word in explaining Columbus's actions on October 20. On that day he turned the *Santa María* about and wrote, "y por esto determine de me bolver por el camino q̃ yo avia traydo dl nornordeste dla pte del gueste" ("and therefore I determined to return by the route that I had taken from the north-northeast from the western part").[68] Morison's translation yields, "and therefore I decided to turn back

---

[65] Sanz, fol. 10.

[66] Ibid. Lyon and others translate "en el Camino del nornordeste" as "on a north-northeast course." If correct, the fleet was re-tracing its course of October 12.

[67] The routing of Columbus to any direction other than the southwest is illogical. The log states that he would sail southwest on the 15th; it states that he wanted to see some of the other (east) coast; it states that he sailed from the north-northeast; it states that the great harbor was discovered while accomplishing the first three. In the *Historia* (1:208), Las Casas contradicts the *Diario* and says the small boats rowed north-northeast. Ferdinand Columbus (p. 64) and Herrera (vol. 1, p. 232) sent the boats northwest. Despite the later confusion, the original document leaves little doubt that the direction was south-southwest. Nevertheless, all of the Watlings School have selected the direction that best suits the predetermined course. Juan Bautista Muñoz, the first Watlingsite, argued for the island (in 1791) without offering any evidence; see Navarrete, pp. 57–58, for a discussion of this. Thacher's lengthy defense of Watlings as island I (pp. 587–603) seems to be one that Morison accepted verbatim. The first important English spokesman for Watlings was Alexander B. Becher, *The Landfall of Columbus* (London: J. D. Potter, 1856). For the case against Watlings, see Pieter Verhoog, "Columbus Landed on Caicos," *Proceedings of the U.S. Naval Institute* 80 (1954): 1101–11; Edwin A. Link and Marion C. Link, "A New Theory on Columbus's Voyage though the Bahamas," *Smithsonian Miscellaneous Collection* 135 (1958): 1–32; and, Robert H. Fuson, "Caicos: Site of Columbus' Landfall," *Professional Geographer* 13 (1961): 6–9. Additional arguments against Watlings are made by H. E. Sadler, *Turks Island Landfall* (Grand Turk: 1981), vol. 1; Molander, pp. 3–7; L. Anthony Leicester, "Columbus's First Landfall," *Sea Frontiers* 26 (1980): 27–78; and lastly, Robert H. Fuson, "Grand Turk was Guanahani," *Turks & Caicos Current* (July/August 1982), pp. 21–30.

[68] Sanz, fol. 15.

by the route whence I had come from the NNE, to the west."[69] The *Diario* stated that the fleet had sailed from the north-northeast and was going to return *from* the western part. Morison sailed the fleet even farther west (*to* the west).

Presumption of Error in the Original Text

One may presume error in the Las Casas manuscript if a statement is logically impossible. For example, the direction corrected by Navarrete (west-southeast) cannot be right.[70] On the other hand, error may not be presumed merely because a thing seems unorthodox. In no case may the original be deemed incorrect simply because it does not fit a predetermined conclusion. The strangest example of error presumption occurred when Morison (following the lead of Thacher) applied the dimensions of an unnamed island to the second named one. Morison's translation is perfect, and it places a large island *between* San Salvador and Santa María de la Concepción.[71] Inasmuch as there is no island between Watlings and Rum Cay (Morison's islands I and II), the *Diario* was presumed to be incorrect. Once Morison blended two different islands, he set off a chain reaction that required a new unit of measurement in order to reconcile the discrepancies. The unnamed island is five by ten leagues, but Rum Cay is only 1.8 by 3.6 leagues. Voilá! Morison invented the "land league."[72] Such a unit of 1,800–2,700 meters is not mentioned in any Spanish, Italian, or Portuguese document of the period; it never existed. The irony is that Morison was forced to explain the dimensions of the only named island that Columbus neglected to measure, at least in part.

The unnamed second island was reached by Columbus at noon, October 15. The *Diario* states,

> y como la ysla fuese mas lexos de çinco leḡuas antes sera siete y la marea me detuvo seria medio dia quādo llegue a la dh̄a ysla y falle q̄ aq̄lla haz que es dla parte dla ysla de san salvador se corre norte sur y an ella .5. leguas: y la otra que yo segui se corria leste gueste: y an en ella mas de diez leguas /. y comō desta ysla vide otra mayor al gueste: cargue las velas por andar todo aq̄l dia fasta la noche: porq̄ avn no pudiera aver andado al cabo del gueste: a la cual puse nōbre la ysla de sancta maria dla concepçion y quasi al poner del sol sorgi acerca del dh̄o cabo.[73]

> (And since the island was further than five leagues, nearer to seven, and the current detained me, it was about midday when I arrived at the said island and I found that the side that faced San Salvador ran north-south for five leagues, and the other which I followed ran east-west, and it was more than ten leagues. And when from this island I saw another large island to the west, I hauled in

---

[69] Morison, p. 77.
[70] Navarrete, p. 94. Morison, p. 61, either translated Navarrete at this point or, as Navarrete did, corrected Las Casas without footnoting the correction. See Sanz, fol. 7. Sanz transcribed "guesueste" ("west-southeast") as "ouesu[du]este" ("west-southwest"). Since "guesueste" also appears in the *Historia* (Las Casas, 1:196), it tends to indicatae that the word was in the copy of the *Diario de a bordo* abstracted by Las Casas, and it also suggests that he copied it faithfully.
[71] Morison, p. 69.
[72] Ibid., pp. 71, 84.
[73] Sanz, fol. 11.

sails in order to sail all that day until night, because otherwise I would not have been able to reach the western cape, to which I gave the name the island of Santa María de la Concepción and almost at sunset I anchored near the said cape.)

This large (fifteen by thirty-plus nautical miles), unnamed island is mentioned in the manuscript *Diario* and in the transcriptions of it. In the *Historia*, Las Casas refers only to the named islands, as does Ferdinand in his *Historie*. An element of the unnamed island, however, remains in both of these post-*Diario* works. The *Historia* and the *Historie* state that San Salvador was fifteen leagues (sixty Columbus miles; forty-five nautical miles) in length. Nowhere in the *Diario* does Columbus give the dimensions of San Salvador; the fifteen leagues came from the unnamed island. Though the Island-without-a-Name was dropped from later histories of the first voyage, its dimensions survived and were at first assigned to San Salvador.[74]

Morison, on the other hand, did not pick up on the error of Las Casas (and repeated by Ferdinand), but he, too, had fifteen leagues (five by ten leagues) to dispose of. He merely applied them to Rum Cay, which he thought was Santa María de la Concepción. Since there was no comparison between the large unnamed island and tiny Rum Cay, Morison assumed the log entry was faulty. This may be the *single most important clue* in the *Diario* for anyone attempting to reconstruct the voyage. There must be five islands, not four, before Cuba is reached. Between San Salvador and Santa María de la Concepción there is a large island about twenty-one nautical miles west of San Salvador. It has a north-south coast facing San Salvador that extends for about fifteen nautical miles; the north coast runs east-west for more than thirty nautical miles; from the western end of this coast you can see a large island to the west (Santa María de la Concepción).

On October 16, Columbus described the coast of Fernandina (the fourth island visited and the third named) as trending north-northwest and south-southwest ("se corre nornorueste y sursudueste").[75] Morison translated this as "trends NNW and SSW [*sic*]"[76] The *sic* supplied by Morison obviously implies error. Rather than accept the statement as valid and use it to assist in determining a specific location, Morison was compelled to alter the *Diario* to force its conformance to an arbitrary scheme. Later, when Columbus wrote, "porq̃ asi se corre toda nornorueste y sursueste" ("because thusly it all trends north-northwest and south-southeast"), Morison accepted the log at face value.[77] It would be just as reasonable to accept the reference to

<hr>

[74] Columbus, p. 59; Las Casas, 1:195–241. Herrera (vol. 1, p. 233) applied the ten leagues of the unnamed island's east-west coast to Santa María de la Concepción, but stated that the north-south length was fifty leagues. Assuming that "5" was mistranscribed as "50," then Herrera also carries over the error of Las Casas. Most errors of a geographical nature can be traced to Las Casas's *Historia* or to his *Apologética Historia Sumaria*, 2 vols., ed. Edmundo O'Gorman (México: Universidad Nacional Autónoma de México, 1967). In this work (1:9), Las Casas said that island I was shaped like a bean ("haba"), a statement repeated by Ferdinand, but never mentioned in the *Diario*. Las Casas also (1:9) called island I "Triango" and did not use the name San Salvador. There is no way to prove one way or the other whether Triango was also called "Triángulo" (Santa Cruz and Velasco) or "Triangula" (Herrera). "Triango" means nothing in Spanish; if it is a misspelling of Triángulo, then it was not San Salvador, for Santa Cruz clearly describes Triángulo as "three uninhabited barren islands that form a triangle and lie east of Guanahaní."

[75] Sanz, fol. 13.

[76] Morison, p. 72.

[77] Sanz, fol. 13; Morison, p. 73.

south-southwest in the first instance and presume as incorrect the mention of south-southeast later. But would not the best course of action be to presume that *both* statements are correct and find a place that meets both conditions? Not only are both entries probably correct, but half a dozen islands can satisfy the stated directions, if viewed at different times and from different locations. Long Island, Morison's firm choice for Fernandina, has a north-northwest–south-southeast trend, if viewed from about midway along its long coast. Near the northern tip, where there is a large hook, the trend is first north-northwest and then south-southwest. The same applies to Acklins-Crooked and Mayaguana. It is perfectly reasonable to describe the trend of a coast with one set of directions and then redefine the directions later during a coastal voyage. The *Diario* entry—right or wrong—makes little difference, for several islands fit either or both sets of directions.

Other matters that cannot be taken too seriously are certain estimates of shoreline distance. Referring to Fernandina, Columbus said that he "saw" at least twenty leagues of the coast and that it did not end there.[78] For one thing, Columbus could not see twenty leagues (sixty nautical miles) and, secondly, he did not claim to sail the distance. The fleet reached Fernandina at sunset on October 16 and departed at noon on the next day. The twenty-league reference was simply a superlative, as if to say, "It was endless—I could not see it all," or, as the song goes, "On a clear day you can see forever."

Perhaps one of the best examples of presumed error on the part of Columbus—and certainly one of the most interesting—was Morison's claim that Columbus did not know how to determine latitude by Polaris.[79] On the surface this is such a ridiculous charge that it is hardly worth refuting. Columbus and the twelve other pilots and masters of the fleet were perfectly capable of this simple manipulation. Morison's belief that the admiral was unable to read the elevation of the Pole Star stemmed from the fact that the *Diario* records three instances (October 30, November 2, and November 21) when Columbus supposedly reported a position of 42° north latitude, and one instance (December 13) when 34° north latitude was given.[80] Quite obviously these are erroneous positions for a ship sailing the waters off northern Cuba and Hispaniola, where the latitude lies between 19° and 22° north. In order to understand how such values were obtained, one must have a passing acquaintance with fifteenth-century quadrants.

Fifteenth-century (and later) Mediterranean quadrants usually had trigonometric scales (tangent, cotangent, sine, cosine) as well as (or in addition to) the equal-interval scale.[81] Concerning the quadrant, Navarrete said, "The quadrants of that time measured a double altitude; and, consequently, the 42° north latitude reading should be reduced to 21° north latitude, which is approximately the parallel where Columbus navigated."[82] This is an oversimplification, that the readings were exactly double, but it explains readings that differ from standard measurements

[78] Sanz, fol. 13.
[79] Morison, pp. 85, 87, 99, 120. Also see Morison, "Columbus and Polaris," *American Neptune* 1 (1940): 1–35.
[80] Navarrete, pp. 107–8, 116, 129.
[81] See the article by James E. Kelley, Jr., "In the Wake of Columbus on a Portolan Chart," also published in this issue.
[82] Navarrete, p. 107.

above the horizon. Columbus undoubtedly had a quadrant that carried a tangent/cotangent scale, such as the one pictured in Jane.[83] All four "latitude designations" appear to be tangent readings; the arc tangent is the correct latitude and the fleet was exactly where it should have been. A number of similar quadrants have been recovered from Spanish ships that sank in Florida waters as late as the seventeenth century. It is highly probable that Columbus did not designate these readings as latitude in the *Diario de a bordo*, but Las Casas assumed as much when he made the abstract. This may well be an instance where Las Casas presumed the *Diario de a bordo* to be in error (or, by the omission of standard latitude reference, to be incomplete) and took it upon himself to amend the text.

Morison, seemingly unfamiliar with early quadrants, stated emphatically that, "Columbus simply mistook another star for Polaris."[84] He went on to say, "I figure that he 'shot' β Cephei (*Alfirk*) instead of Polaris."[85] To prove how easy it was for Columbus to have done this, Morison admitted, "Made the same 'blooper' myself in November 1939."[86] Alfirk is a fourth magnitude star that is barely visible in the circumpolar constellation of Cepheus (between Cassiopeia and Draco). Although it is almost impossible to see with the naked eye (and Columbus had no optics), we are expected to believe that Columbus made *repeated* sightings on it. Morison's inability to find a brighter star does not confirm that Columbus was as inept. By not understanding the type of quadrant used by Columbus and its calibration, Morison searched the sky for a star at 42° elevation. As dim as Alfirk is, it is the only star that meets this requirement—sometimes. Inasmuch as Alfirk revolves about the pole, it will only be at 42° once each night. It is an amazing coincidence that three of the sightings by Columbus and the one by Morison all occurred at precisely the same time, for any variation in time would produce an angle other than 42°. Columbus was not only fully capable of shooting Polaris but he knew that he was in the approximate latitude of the Canary Islands (though a little south, since he did not follow a due westerly course across the Atlantic).[87] His ability to hit the Azores dead on during the return trip suggests rather dramatically that he was a master navigator. Morison's claim that Columbus was obtaining a quadrant reading near Cuba that equated with the northern limit of Portugal (a position well known to Iberian sailors) was weak indeed.

Other presumptions of error in the *Diario* included numerous restatements of distances, directions, sizes of islands, and descriptions. The island called Isabela by Columbus serves to illustrate one of these presumptions. Morison was unequivocal in his identification of Crooked Island as the island of Isabela.[88] Its northern tip lies twenty-seven nautical miles east of the southern end of Long Island, which Morison

[83] Jane, *Journal*, p. 73. Also see Peter Bienewitz (Petrus Apianus), *Quadrans astronomicus* (Ingolstadt, 1532).
[84] Morison, p. 87.
[85] Morison, p. 99.
[86] Ibid.
[87] Navarrete, p. 96. Before 1475, Regiomontanus published almanacs and true astronomical ephemerides at Nürnberg. From these tables it was possible to determine the coordinates of a ship at sea anytime the moon was visible (the so-called method of lunar distances). Columbus used these tables, as did every other important navigator of the period. See Giorgio Abetti, *The History of Astronomy* (New York: Henry Schuman, 1952), p. 54.
[88] Morison, pp. 75–76.

identified as Fernandina. After reaching Isabela, Columbus said that he sailed westward along the coast for twelve leagues.[89] Since such a course would have put the fleet back at Fernandina, Morison said the *Diario* was corrupt, and that the word "west" must be changed to read "southeast" for the first few leagues of this cruise, then should be read "south-southwest" for the latter part of it.[90] Also, this course (as proposed by Morison) included the coasting of two islands (Crooked Island and Long Cay), though Columbus only referred to one. Nothing in the admiral's description of Isabela, or in his sailing directions along its shore, fits the condition of modern Crooked Island and Long Cay. Therefore, Morison presumed an error in the log.

Presumption of Correctness in the Original Text

For some reason Morison was willing to alter a series of events in order to explain a single event. In other words, by assuming one statement to be correct he had to bend several others to fit his procrustean frame. The *Diario* does not state unequivocally that Columbus sailed from Fernandina to Isabela. As mentioned earlier, October 18 was a wild card day. There is nothing to suggest that the fleet did not depart Fernandina and anchor at an unspecified spot on the night of October 18.

To illustrate the confusion that arises when facts are selected to support a prior conclusion (and others are discarded when they do not), we may consider the location of two capes on Fernandina. On October 17, Columbus said, "y nos al cabo dla ysla dla pte dl sueste" ("and we are at the southeast cape of the island").[91] A week later (October 24) Columbus had a bearing on *another* cape on the same island and said, "el cual es dla pte de sur a pte de gueste" ("which is in the southern part at the western part").[92] Morison assumed that both references were to the same cape.[93] He then proceeded to place the first cape on the southwest tip of Fernandina (the *Diario* said "southeast") and the second cape on the southeast tip of Fernandina (the *Diario* said "southwest"). In reaching the first (southeast) cape, Columbus had a difficult night at sea, with high winds, heavy rain, and a rough sea. He variously sailed east-southeast, east, and southeast.[94] He also had to keep well offshore for fear of reefs. Early on the morning of October 18 the ships anchored at the unnamed southeastern cape on Fernandina. After the weather cleared, the fleet moved on.

Cabo Verde, mentioned on October 24, was located at the western end of the southern part of Fernandina. If the *Diario* is faithful, this is not the same cape visited on October 18. Morison was certain that they were one and the same, but he became so tangled up that he located his single cape in two different places! Furthermore, to reach the first (southeast) cape, Morison insisted that the fleet reversed its direction and sailed for a number of hours against the wind.[95] Not only is such an action not

---

[89] Sanz, fol. 14.
[90] Morison, p. 76.
[91] Sanz, fol. 14.
[92] Ibid., fol. 17.
[93] Morison, pp. 74–75, 80–81.
[94] Sanz, fol. 14.
[95] Morison, pp. 71, 75.

recorded in the log, but the carefully cited positions allow no time for such an erratic maneuver, even if it had been possible. There is simply no way that Columbus could have been where Morison placed him on October 19. While willing to accept as absolute the sailing directions for a stormy night at sea, Morison was unwilling to accept events that occurred in good weather during broad daylight.

After departing Isabela (October 25), Columbus said that he sailed west-south-west.[96] Had he actually done so he would have been retracing the route taken on October 19.[97] The *Diario* is probably incorrect here, for all evidence points to the fact that the Indians on board were guiding the fleet: "y me amostro q̃ al guesudueste yria a ella" and "creo q̃ si es asi como por señas q̃ me hizierō todos los yndios" ("and they showed me that I could get to it [i.e., Cuba] to the west-southwest," and "I believe that it is thus as all of the Indians have indicated to me by signs").[98] The intent may have been to sail west-southwest, or it may have been to go to the west-southwest by the safest possible course, that is, first sail west to the edge of the Great Bahama Bank and then follow a southerly course to Cuba. In any event, Columbus became somewhat confused that evening and reported that, for all practical purposes, he was lost.[99]

Verhoog raised the interesting possibility that compass variation may have played a role in this and other aspects of the voyage.[100] In fact, the problem of compass variation raises a question concerning the entire course from the Canary Islands to America. Morison, along with most other researchers, assumed that the course was one of dead reckoning, and the evidence for this seems abundant. Compass directions were carefully recorded in the *Diario* and some special notations were made about deviation of magnetic north from true north. But could Columbus have sailed due west for most of the first voyage crossing by means of a compass? Other than for a brief period when the agonic line was crossed (September 13), the compass declined from true north, first easterly and then westerly. Further, there is no way of knowing whether or not another agonic line was crossed later in the voyage. An additional complication (fully known to Columbus) arises when we consider the fact that the several compasses carried by the three ships did not agree with one another.

European compasses in the late fifteenth century were corrected for true north in the city of manufacture; a Flemish compass did not correspond with one made in Lisbon. There was probably as much as five degrees difference between two such instruments. This variation could have been corrected on a daily basis by observing Polaris or the sun, assuming that the admiral knew which compass to correct and further assuming that his celestial readings were precise. If, however, Columbus had so much trouble shooting Polaris from the calm waters of a sheltered harbor, as Morison claimed, how could he have been exact on a rolling ship in the open ocean? There was a much easier, and more accurate, method to navigate the Atlantic in 1492: by means of the sun. Peter Martyr, a principal source for our knowledge about Columbus, said, "From these Ilandes [i.e., the Canaries] *Colonus* directynge his viage towarde the weste, folowinge the fallinge of the sonne, but declining somwhat

[96] Sanz, fol. 17.
[97] Ibid., fol. 14.
[98] Ibid., fol. 17.
[99] Ibid.
[100] Verhoog, p. 1110.

towarde the left hande, sayled on forwarde xxxiii. dayes continually, hauynge onely the fruition of the heauen and the water."[101] Inasmuch as Columbus was cognizant of winds, currents, and compass variation, as well as the difficulty of shooting Polaris with his crude quadrant, it is reasonable for him to have chosen the most reliable navigational aid of them all—the sun. At sunrise, noon, and sunset he would have had an absolutely precise celestial guide. Pedro de Medina, a senior member of the scientific office of the pilot major in Seville, when asked how to navigate the ocean without a chart or compass, answered, "The sun will serve as compass and his knowledge of winds [i.e., directions] as a course."[102]

This is the fundamental principle underlying solar navigation. It was well known to Mediterranean pilots before 1492 and is explained in detail in Pedro de Medina's classic work. There is every reason to believe that Columbus followed the "falling of the sonne," as Martyr declared, and declined "somwhat towarde the left hande" as the sun moved south after the autumnal equinox. The *Diario* may be technically incorrect in its record of compass headings during the Atlantic crossing, for west most probably was toward the setting sun, not a true compass course of 270°.[103] There is also the tantalizing thought that the trip was planned to coincide with the autumnal equinox, in order to provide a window that would ensure a reliable westerly course for at least the first week out. Columbus departed the Canaries on September 8 (Julian calendar), which was September 17 by our present Gregorian reckoning. With the autumnal equinox occurring on September 11 (Gregorian September 20), no better date of departure could have been chosen if solar navigation were to be employed. The next window would have been in March, 1493. Although a navigator of Columbus's ability could have employed solar techniques at any time during the year, it is a simpler procedure near either equinox and, if a coincidence, the departure was fortuitous.

Claimed Corrections of the Original Text

These are rare occurrences that almost defy explanation. The entry for October 27 reads, in part,

> levāto las anclas 'salido el sol' de aq̃llas yslas q̃ llamo las yslas de arena por el poco fondo q̃ tenian dla ̲p̲t̲e̲ dl sur hasta seys leguas / anduvo ocho millas por ora hasta la vna del dia al sursudueste.[104]

> (He raised anchors (the sun having risen) from those islands he called the Sand Islands because of the shallowness that they had from the southern part up to six leagues [northward]. He made eight miles per hour until 1:00 in the day to the south-southwest.

[101] Peter Martyr, "The Firste Booke of the Decades of the Ocean," in Richard Eden, trans., *The First Three Books on America (? 1511)–1555 A.D.*, ed. Edward Arber (Birmingham: Turnbull and Spears, 1885), p. 66.
[102] Pedro de Medina, "The Libro de Cosmographía of 1538," in Ursula Lamb, ed. and trans., *A Navigator's Universe: The Libro de Cosmographía of 1538* (Chicago: University of Chicago Press, 1972), p. 200.
[103] Robert H. Fuson and Walter H. Treftz, "A Theoretical Reconstruction of the First Atlantic Crossing of Christopher Columbus," *Proceedings of the Association of American Geographers* 8 (1976): 155–59.
[104] Sanz, fol. 17.

First, Morison mistranslated this:

> They weighed anchors at sunrise from those islands which he called *las islas de Arena*, owing to the slight depth which they had in the southerly direction, for a distance of 6 leagues. He made 8 Roman miles an hour until 1 P.M. to the SSW.[105]

Columbus was looking at the shallow Great Bahama Bank, with the Islas de Arena (Sand Islands, Ragged Islands) stretching northward for six leagues. Morison believed that Columbus recorded that he sailed south for six leagues, and then changed course for the south-southwest. Morison "corrected" this in a footnote and blamed Las Casas for "a bad job of editing." The footnoted comment is a non sequitur, for the passage reads well in the original Spanish and only Morison's poor translation needs correcting.

In another footnote for October 30, Morison said, "I do not think that this records an observation for 30 October, but that it is an interpolated remark of Las Casas based upon the observation on 1 November, which see."[106] The reference is to the 42° angle obtained by Columbus on a sighting of Polaris. There is no mention in the *Diario* of Polaris on November 1, hence, the footnote is meaningless. Yet another claimed correction appears in a footnote of Morison. Referring to November 14, the note reads, "*sueste* in the Spanish text, an obvious scribe's error for *oueste*."[107] The original text reads *gueste* (= oueste). This makes for a scholarly looking comment, but only to the reader who does not check it against the original.

Errors of Omission

An error of omission occurs when the translator fails to take into account a relevant fact that has a direct bearing on the document under consideration but which, for any number of reasons, was omitted by the original author. In the case of the *Diario* the items omitted were (1) also omitted from the *Diario de a bordo* because they were so well known to Columbus and his fellow pilots that he saw no reason to mention them, (2) those passages that Las Casas believed to be too technical for the layman and, therefore, not essential to the abstract, or (3) events or situations that were unknown to either Columbus or Las Casas.[108]

Columbus (or Las Casas) told us virtually nothing about the ships and navigational techniques. We do not know, for example, how Columbus determined his speed or even the unit of measurement he used. We are able to extrapolate from other contemporary sources about these things, but there is still room for error. The Columbian mile measured somewhere between 4,060 feet (1,237 meters) and 4,850

---

[105] Morison, pp. 81–82.
[106] Ibid., p. 85.
[107] Ibid., p. 96.
[108] Sanz, fol. 24 ("y por otros inconvenientes q̃ alli refiere."), and Las Casas, 1:237 ("y por inconvenientes que vía"). These may have been navigation matters. It is unfortunate that Las Casas omitted them from his abstract.

feet (1,478 meters).[109] The lower value tends to equate better with the Atlantic crossing and the larger one with the sail through the islands. It is difficult to believe that Columbus reached the speeds he often claimed unless he used the shorter value. Six knots would have been an exceptionally good speed for the *Santa María*. No specific dimensions of the three ships have come down to us, and we must assume that they were similar to known craft of the period. Apparently, a man on the sterncastle of the *Santa María* had an eye level about thirty to thirty-five feet above the water, and the height of eye from the crow's nest was probably seventy to seventy-five feet above water. These heights were, of course, substantially lower on the two smaller vessels. Such values are relevant; they determine how far an object (such as an island) can be seen at sea.

The horizon, as viewed from the *Santa María*'s crow's nest, was about 11.5 statute miles (10 nautical miles) distant; from the sterncastle it was about 7 or 8 statute miles (6 or 7 nautical miles).[110] High, forested islands would have been observed beyond these limits. And there are other ways that experienced navigators "see" islands: clouds, birds, water color, deflected currents, and depth are some of the things that provide positive reference. Additionally, landfall does not mean landing; it is the first sighting, and may occur several hours before the actual act of anchoring and going ashore.

Columbus passed many islands that he did not name, visit, or describe.[111] These he deemed unimportant to his mission or claims, and he felt that he did not have sufficient time to visit them all. Had these unmentioned islands been recorded (or, if they were, had Las Casas only included them in his abstract) the problem of reconstructing the first voyage would have been greatly simplified. The fact that Las Casas dropped the second island Columbus visited from all of his later works suggests that he deemed the tiny islands north of Cuba and Hispaniola to be relatively unimportant. Those named for God, Mary, and the royal family, however, could not be omitted.

Certain navigational techniques have already been discussed, but the question of compass variation needs elaboration. The plotted course through the Bahamas indicates that variation may have approximated fifteen degrees easterly, not a few degrees westerly as Morison indicated.[112] Though Columbus probably did not rely very much on his undependable compasses on the open Atlantic, he may have used

---

[109] We are not sure of the precise value of the Roman (Italian) mile, as there were several. Morison uses 4,842 feet (p. 44) and 4,855 feet (p. 116). George E. Nunn, *Geographical Conceptions of Columbus* (New York: American Geographical Society, 1924), pp. 17–18, gives a value of 4,855.584 feet. Kelley offers a good argument for 4,060 feet, basing it on his exhaustive study of Portolan charts. A Columbian league of four Roman miles would, therefore, have a value that lies between 2.5 and 3.2 international nautical miles (1 INM = 6076.11549 feet).

[110] A rule of thumb for determining the distance of an object at sea is this: take the square root of the height of the observer (above sea level) and add it to the square root of the above-sea-level height of the viewed object; multiply the added square roots by 1.5 for statute miles or by 1.3 for INMs.

[111] Sanz, fol. 11.

[112] Verhoog, p. 1105. Morison mapped the supposed magnetic variation for 1492 in *Admiral of the Ocean Sea*, facing p. 222. This was pure conjecture. The U.S. Coast and Geodetic Survey can supply information on geomagnetism, but states that there is no known way to derive agonic lines for 1492 (personal communication from K. L. Svendsen, chief, Analysis Branch, Geomagnetism Division, U.S. Coast and Geodetic Survey, Washington, D.C., May 19, 1967).

them most of the time while zigzagging through the Bahamas for two months. Unfortunately, there is no way to predict secular (i.e., long-term magnetic) change; no known method for working backward through time to establish what it used to be; no law that will even describe the phenomenon.[113] Secular change can be determined only by empirical observations, such as are made today in the United States at thirteen magnetic observatories and one hundred repeat stations.[114] The few observations made by Columbus shed very little light on magnetic declination for the year 1492.

Declinations differs from place to place, and often there are large differences within a small area. Sometimes there is a variation of several degrees within a hundred feet or less.[115] It is now known that there is no magnetic pole and that compass needles are not attracted to anything. A needle merely points in the direction of the horizontal projection of the magnetic field at the point of observation. The earth's magnetic field results from some cause or causes distributed throughout a large volume of the earth; a magnetic polar region is one of its manifestations, and the magnetic declination at any particular place is another. There is no possible way to construct a map of magnetic declination across the Atlantic Ocean for the year 1492, such as Morison attempted to do.

A number of omissions from the *Diario* occurred because they were unknown to the participants. For example, we can plot the speed of the ocean current between the Canaries and the Bahamas, but Columbus had no independent means for establishing this speed. He probably assumed a current but could not have proven its existence in the open sea. Longitude was another thing that could not be determined with any degree of precision. Not until the eighteenth century did time reckoning become precise enough for this measurement. Until we identify with absolute certainty where Columbus landed, we cannot derive exact coordinates or come up with the precise number of miles by which he overran or underran his target. Open-ocean estimates of elapsed distance cannot be verified until the length of the Columbian mile is established beyond question.

Since the first voyage, the Western world has changed from the Julian to the Gregorian calendar; nine days must be added to all Columbian references to bring them into line with our modern system of date keeping. Columbus and Las Casas had no idea that the calendar would be revised, but this fact must be taken into account if one is interested in celestial navigation and the several lunar references. Further, even the celebration of Columbus Day on October 12 is incorrect; October 21 is the true discovery day.

Lastly, Columbus had no way of knowing that the lands he discovered would undergo so much change between then and now. The discovery unleashed an unforeseen force that was to alter greatly the natural and cultural environments. This force was, by and large, a human one. From the moment a nameless Arawak saw the little fleet approach Guanahaní that October morning long ago, change began.

---

[113] H. H. Howe and L. Hurwitz, *Magnetic Surveys*, USDC, Coast and Geodetic Survey, Serial 718 (Washington, 1964), p. 6.
[114] Ibid., p. 8.
[115] Ibid., p. 13.

At first it was cultural—a new god, perhaps. Then came technology and, quickly, disease. The old world of the Indian was rushing to become the New World of the European and African.

During the last 500 years the islands between Florida and Cuba–Hispaniola have suffered severe deforestation. Plantation agriculture (especially cotton and sisal), salt production, and the gathering of firewood have been largely responsible. Erosion following the removal of vegetation has caused some alteration of the topography, and siltation has affected water depths. Destruction by hurricanes has intensified as the islands have been exposed by human activity. Particularly devastated have been those islands chosen for salt production. Even the Arawak seems to have played a role in this, for archaeological evidence indicates that Indians were producing salt in the southernmost islands before Columbus arrived, and transporting it in large canoes to Cuba and Hispaniola.[116] Europeans merely expanded the operation at a later date. And, in doing so, they flooded the interiors of several islands with seawater and cut every tree in sight in hopes that rainfall would decline and solar evaporation in the salinas would increase. Could Columbus have anticipated this when he recorded in his journal that the groves of trees were more beautiful than those of Andalucia in spring? Could he have guessed that virtually every Arawak would be banished to the mines of Hispaniola or dead within thirty-five years of his fortnight in the islands? Could he have known that the Indians he described as handsome, well proportioned, and gentle would be replaced by African slaves?

The *Diario* is a good account of what was, not what is. Nature and culture went through an upheaval after 1492. Omitting these changes is, obviously, not anyone's fault. After all, Columbus was not a fortune-teller. But one must always bear in mind that Columbus described a New World that no longer exists; in other words, America is no longer New.

Conclusion

The discovery voyage of Christopher Columbus was the greatest voyage in recorded history, and it is still a subject for scholarly debate. This is, in large part, due to the transcriptive, translative, and interpretative flaws derived from the *Diario* and briefly discussed in the preceding pages. Although some errors were in the holograph original, and others appeared in the Las Casas abstract, the greatest source of error is to be found in the collective works of those who have transcribed and translated the Las Casas narrative. It is the closest thing we have to a primary source, and should take precedence over *any* later commentary, even one by Las Casas himself. A faithful, diplomatic transcription is close to completion. Hopefully, the long-overdue rendering of the *Diario* will become the standard for future research and will lead to a near-perfect English translation.

Columbian scholars have too long worked in isolation. Perhaps this is because they are so few and, being from different academic disciplines and backgrounds, they rarely communicate. This mold was broken in 1981, when the Society for the

---

[116] Shaun Sullivan, "Pre-Historic Caicos," *Turks & Caicos Current* (July/August, 1982), p. 34.

History of Discoveries sponsored a well-attended Columbus session at its annual meeting. Mountains of correspondence among Columbus students followed that meeting, and this paper is largely a result of that event. By Columbus Day 1982, twenty-five scholars from America, Europe, and Africa assembled in Miami, Florida, for the First International Columbus Symposium. Plans call for nine additional symposia, one each year until the five hundredth anniversary of the discovery.

From these recent gatherings of Columbus-philes, several important matters have surfaced. First, most of the previous Columbus research has been carried out by historians, linguists, and maritime-related persons, with a scattering of geographers and cartographic historians involved. Almost conspicuous by their absence were geologists, anthropologists, oceanographers, biologists, meteorologists, and remote-sensing specialists. The Miami symposium made a start at correcting this. Especially valuable is the archaeological fieldwork that has already been done; it simply had not been connected with the ongoing Columbus research. Another matter concerns fieldwork—not enough has been done. Some of the leading theories about the first landing have been proposed by people who have never set foot in the islands. And, some of the theories smacked of religion more than they did science. Science is tentative; it is always subject to reevaluation and change. Since Navarrete, only two people have ever changed their original positions on the question of the first landing site. Additionally, perception, in the psychological sense, should be investigated. Language, for instance, is conditioned by culture, and a Mediterranean sailor might regard an island as green and flat while his Danish counterpart would disagree. We should never forget that the *Diario* is an expression of Columbus's cultural heritage.

Lastly, most scholars agree that the Las Casas abstract is a fairly reliable document, but it is imperfect and certainly incomplete. The pieces of the puzzle will never fit exactly; some are forever lost. But there are enough to satisfy the laws of statistical probability. We know certain inarguable facts, many probabilities, and some possibilities. With a rekindled desire to solve the landfall riddle by 1992, and with the assistance of newfound allies from other disciplines, there is every reason to believe that a precise map of the 1492 October sojourn may be finally executed.

In the Wake of Columbus on a Portolan Chart

James E. Kelley, Jr.

The question of just where Columbus first landed in the New World on October 12, 1492, is taking on renewed interest as we approach the five hundredth anniversary of the discovery of America. As John Parker shows elsewhere in this volume, the identification of Columbus's first landfall has been debated for some considerable time, with many solutions proposed.[1] In more recent years, Watlings Island in the Bahamas has become the generally accepted landing site. It has been renamed San Salvador, Columbus's name for his first landfall, and it is almost universally identified in school texts, encyclopedias, and maps as the landing site. But can this identification be verified with certainty?

The prime source of information on the first landfall is the summary or paraphrase of Columbus's *Journal* done by the Dominican historian Bartolomé de Las Casas. This document is of great intrinsic interest and of considerable value to scholars in a variety of disciplines. Among other things, it contains a unique record of late medieval European navigational practice—virtually a complete daily accounting of the course made good, plus many associated navigational details. The great wealth of information in the Las Casas redaction is what makes it possible to have a meaningful debate over the first landfall issue. The quantity of information allows a number of plausible hypotheses to be developed and tested. The researcher soon discovers that a plethora of possible assumptions can be supported by the data Las Casas provided. The possibilities of missing essentials and false information compounds problems of interpretation. Finally, it is most difficult to use consistently all of the information Las Casas presents.

To most students of the debate, identifying the first landfall means tracing a route forward or backward from a known position to San Salvador, using clues in the *Journal* and other contemporary background information. Reconstructing Columbus's route across the Atlantic in terms of geographic latitudes and longitudes is most difficult to do accurately. Several attempts of varying sophistication and underlying assumptions have been made.[2]

[1] See John Parker's introductory essay to this volume.

[2] See, for example, J. W. McElroy, "The Ocean Navigation of Columbus on His First Voyage," *American Neptune* 1 (1941): 1–20, 123–27; Robert H. Fuson and Walter H. Treftz, "A Theoretical Reconstruction of

The mathematical difficulties of modeling Columbus's voyage are both theoretical and computational. Considerations of winds, currents, leeway, course made good, estimation errors, and the like, must be quantified in relation to the voyage. Use of a modern computer is a must to do the overwhelming amount of arithmetic involved. One criterion of acceptability for such a mathematical/statistical model is that it correctly reconstruct the homeward voyage from Hispaniola to the Azores—two known points on the course. If this can be done with reasonable accuracy from the *Journal* data, then applying the model to estimating the endpoint of the outward course from the Canaries would seem to be credible. If anything, this requirement may be too restrictive since the homeward voyage presents technical complications regarding drift and leeway that are not so significant for the outward voyage. A number of background studies, founded on current knowledge and methods, are needed for building such a model. At the head of the list is a study of the course data given in the *Journal*. How is it to be interpreted? What insights emerge to strengthen the modeling efforts?

This paper analyzes the *Journal* course data from the point of view of the fifteenth-century south European mariner. By reconstructing the whole voyage on the equivalent of a contemporary portolan chart, a few long-held opinions about Columbus and his navigational techniques can be corrected, or recast. The importance of allowing for ocean currents when interpreting the *Journal's* sailing directions is underscored. This factor is illustrated with a simple computer simulation of part of the voyage which identifies Acklins-Crooked Island as Isabela, Columbus's third island after his landfall. If these results hold up to scrutiny, perhaps from a more finely tuned analysis, they will tend to confirm Watlings Island as Columbus's first landfall.

The reason this analysis provides a new perspective is that the marine maps available to Columbus, the so-called portolan charts, were constructed on an implied assumption that the earth is practically flat over the region depicted. This assumption served well enough for the normal navigational practice of his day since the limited north-south and east-west strips of the Atlantic coasts of Europe and Africa and the coasts of the Mediterranean which they covered were sufficiently flat. Using a portolan chart to map Columbus's whole transatlantic voyage, however, reveals distortions which probably misled Columbus and his pilots. From such a reconstruction of the voyage, statements in the *Journal* that are puzzling or easily overlooked can be explained or revealed. This is not possible when a chart based on a more modern projection such as Mercator's is used.

The Journal Data

The Las Casas *Journal* of Columbus's voyage is a compilation of some quotes, abstracts, and Las Casas's personal interpretations and opinions, arranged in chron-

the First Atlantic Crossing of Christoper Columbus," *Proceedings of the Association of American Geographers* 8 (1976): 155–59; G. E. Nunn, *The Geographical Conceptions of Columbus* (New York: American Geographical Society, 1924), esp. p. 36, n. 5, for earlier serious analyses; P. Verhoog, "Columbus Landed on Caicos," *Proceedings of the U.S. Naval Institute* (1954), pp. 1101–11; and Arne B. Molander, "Columbus Landed Here—Or Did He?" *Americas* 33 (1981): 3–7.

ological order.[3] It naturally divides into three parts: the outward voyage, the voyage through the islands, and the homeward voyage.

The open ocean legs are quite similar in style and extent of information. Essentially the text recites sunrise and sunset course summaries—the number of leagues made good on a bearing with a given wind. But other information is interpolated which provides insights into life aboard ship, managing and recording the ship's pilotage, and the like. The voyage through the islands is of considerably different character. The rather dry repetitiveness of ocean navigation is replaced by a series of adventures. Given an abundance of interesting material to select from, Las Casas was not consistent in giving complete navigational data on this leg of the voyage. Then again, Columbus may have omitted this data himself, though this does not seem likely.

Tables 1, 2, and 3 summarize the salient navigational data as abstracted from the *Journal*. The computer simulations are based on these data. Interpretations of the *Journal* are documented in the notes to these tables at the end of this paper.

Columbus's Method of Navigation

To fully appreciate the results of this computer reconstruction of Columbus's first voyage, it is necessary to understand how the *Journal* data derive from Columbus's probable method of dead reckoning. In reconstructing this method from fourteenth- and fifteenth-century materials, three steps appear to have been involved. These are developed as follows:

(1) Data Collection. Every half hour—measured by a sandglass—or with a change in course, the speed of the ship was estimated using a "Dutchman's Log." That is, the pilot threw a wood chip or spit in the water and timed its passing with counting rhyme. By ratio and proportion, the distance traveled during the past half hour was calculated. This calculated distance and the helmsman's magnetic compass bearing were entered on a plotting board called a *toleta del marteloio*—the "table of the bell" that was rung or struck when the sandglass was turned.[4] The *toleta* is a type of analog computer for solving trigonometric problems graphically. Before radar and digital computers took over, tactical problems at sea were solved on a maneuvering board almost identical to the *toleta,* a mariner's device which must date from at latest the

[3] Articles 240 and 241 of *Il Consolato del Mare*, the maritime law of the time, required the patron of a vessel to make a full accounting of all transactions and activities to the shareholders after a voyage. Apparently a diary or journal, supplemented by other documents of detail, was the usual method of satisfying this requirement. It is instructive to compare Columbus's *Journal* with other survivors of the time (e.g., the Albizzi Diary in Michael E. Mallett, *The Florentine Galleys in the Fifteenth Century* (Oxford, 1967).

[4] More precisely, *toleta del marteloio* means "the hammer grate," possibly because an iron grate and hammer may have been used as a gong, and the *toleta*, with all its crisscross lines, looks like a grate. A few contemporary examples survive (e.g., in Andrea Bianco's atlas of 1436, Bib. Marciana, Venice, and in Egerton MS 73, British Library fol. 47v). The use of a rhyme for measuring time is conjectural. We do know that the Miserere and the Pater Noster, repeated a certain number of times, were used for short-interval timing (e.g., for cooking, preparing medicines, etc.). For background on the sandglass, see R. T. Balmer, "The Operation of Sand Clocks and Their Medieval Development," *Technology and Culture* 19 (1978): 615–32. For the magnetic compass and its impact, see Barbara M. Kreutz, "Mediterranean Contributions to the Medieval Mariner's Compass," *Technology and Culture* 14 (1973): 367–83, and Fredrick C. Lane, "The Economic Meaning of the Invention of the Compass," *American Historical Review* 67 (1963): 605–17.

TABLE 1
Data for the Outbound Course: September 6–October 11, 1492

Date	Hours	Course	Degrees	Leagues	Reckoned	Wind	Discourse
Sept. 6	24	W	270.00	0.0	0.0	Calm	Left Gomera in a.m.; becalmed
Sept. 7	24	W	270.00	0.0	0.0	Calm	Becalmed
Sept. 8	3	W	270.00	0.0	0.0	Calm	Becalmed
Sept. 8	9	W	270.00	9.0	9.0	NE	Started 3 a.m. between Gomera and Tenerife
Sept. 9	12	W?	270.00	15.0	0.0		Las Casas notes C. to reckon less than he makes; bad steering
Sept. 9	12	W by N	281.25	30.0	0.0		Speed 10 mph; notes *legua* = 4 *millas*; Morison interpolates "Roman" miles
Sept. 10	24	W?	270.00	60.0	48.0		
Sept. 11	12	W	270.00	20.0+[a]	0.0		
Sept. 11	12	W	270.00	20.0	16.0		
Sept. 12	24	W	270.00	33.0	0.0		
Sept. 13	24	W	270.00	33.0	29.5		Reckoned 29–30 miles; compass turned NW, but declined NE a little in a.m.
Sept. 14	24	W	270.00	20.0	0.0		Saw tern and tropic bird that never go 25 leagues from land
Sept. 15	24	W	270.00	27.0+	0.0		Saw a meteor
Sept. 16	24	W	270.00	39.0	36.0	Mild	Some clouds and a little rain; start of temperate breezes; began seeing many tufts of seaweed
Sept 17	24	W	270.00	50.0+	47.0	Soft	Currents assisted them; compass declined 1 point NW, but pointed true in a.m.
Sept. 18	24	W	270.00	55.0+	48.0		Sea smooth
Sept. 19	24	W?	270.00	25.0	22.0	Calm	Voyage estimates: 440, 420, and 400 leagues (C.'s log =436); supposed islands to N and S
Sept. 20	24	W by N, WNW	286.88	7.5	0.0	Var./Calm	7–8 miles made good; more birds land on ship
Sept. 21	24	W and W by N?	275.63	13.0	0.0	Calm	Sea choked with weed; saw a whale; some wind
Sept. 22	24	WNW	292.50	30.0	0.0		Hardly any vegetation at first but did see some later in day; experienced head wind
Sept. 23	24	NW/W/NWbyN	315.00	22.0	0.0		Sea calm; men begin to complain they will never get home
Sept. 24	24	W	270.00	14.5	12.0		
Sept. 25	12	W	270.00	4.5	0.0	Calm	Islands thought to be nearby; C. plotted position on

Date		Wind					Remarks
Sept. 25	12	SW	225.00	17.0	13.0		Veered to investigate supposed land sighting; more on C.'s keeping two distance figures
Sept. 26	6	W	270.00	7.8	0.0	Mild	W till noon; thence SW till loom of land seen as cloud (say 3 hrs); McElroy takes WSW for the day
Sept. 26	3	SW	225.00	3.9	0.0		
Sept. 26	15	W	270.00	19.3	24.0		Compare day's total of 31 to 24
Sept. 27	24	W	270.00	24.0	20.0		
Sept. 28	24	W	270.00	14.0	13.0	Calms	Saw birds and vegetation
Sept. 29	24	W	270.00	24.0	21.0	Calms	C. remarks on the position of the Guards and compass variations
Sept. 30	24	W	270.00	14.0	11.0	Calms	
Oct. 1	24	W	270.00	25.0	20.0	Calm	Heavy rain; C.'s Pilot's est. = 578 leagues west of Hierro; C.'s (map?) est. = 707, but reckoned 584; log total = 676.5
Oct. 2	24	W	270.00	39.0	30.0		Smooth sea; weed floating E to W (backward)
Oct. 3	24	W?	270.00	47.0	40.0	Freshened	Many birds
Oct. 4	24	W	270.00	63.0	46.0		Made 11 mph; sea calm and smooth; Many flying fish
Oct. 5	24	W	270.00	57.0	45.0		Considered changing course SW by W for Cipangu
Oct. 6	24	W	270.00	40.0	33.0		Made 12 mph for 2 hrs., 8 mph thereafter; 23 leagues in total implies 10.5-hr period
Oct. 7	11	W	270.00	23.0	18.0		Bird migration from N to SW; C. notes Portuguese discoveries from observing birds
Oct. 7	13	WSW	247.50	5.0	0.0		
Oct. 8	24	WSW	247.50	11.5	0.0	Soft breeze	At times made 15 mph if text not corrupt (Morison has "if the log is to be trusted")
Oct. 9	6	SW	225.00	5.0	0.0		Wind changed during the day, forcing them to tack a bit; text may be read that they went 20.5 leagues at night instead of during 24-hr. period; 17 leagues is C.'s published figure for 20.5
Oct. 9	4	W by N	281.25	4.0	0.0		
Oct. 9	2	WSW	247.50	2.0	0.0		
Oct. 9	12	WSW	247.50	9.5	17.0		Made at times 7, 10, 12 mph; men complained of long voyage
Oct. 10	24	WSW	247.50	59.0	44.0		Roughest sea of outward voyage
Oct. 11	12	WSW	247.50	27.0	0.0		Made 12 mph; land apparent at 10 p.m.; land appeared 2 leagues ahead at 2 a.m.
Oct. 11	7	W	270.00	22.5	0.0		
Oct. 11	0	W	270.00	2.0	0.0		Landed on Guanahani (San Salvador?) in the Lucayos on the morning of the 12th

[a] Plus signs indicate that the *Journal* figure was greater.

TABLE 2

Data for the Islands: October 14, 1492–January 13, 1493

Date	Hours	Course	Degrees	Leagues	Reckoned	Wind	Discourse
Oct. 14, 1492	0	—	0.00	0.0	0.0		Sailed about Guanahani exploring; stood off all night
Oct. 15	6	SW?	225.00	7.0	0.0		At daybreak sailed to S. Maria; experienced strong E tidal current
Oct. 15	2	S	180.00	5.0	0.0		S. Maria's E shore 5 leagues long; S shore 10 leagues
Oct. 15	4	W	270.00	10.0	0.0		Anchored off W point of S. Maria for the night
Oct. 16	21	W	270.00	8.5	0.0	SE and S, Calm	Went ashore at daylight; departed 10 a.m. for Fernandina; stood off all night
Oct. 17	4	NNW	337.50	4.0*[a]	0.0	SW and S	Set out about noon to round island at N; C est. island runs NNW-SSE, 20–28 leagues
Oct. 17	12	ESE, E, SE	157.50	20.0*	0.0	WNW	Sailed length of Fernandina, anchoring off SE end
Oct. 18	0	NW?	315.00	2.0*	0.0	SSE?	Continued circuit of island, anchoring when weather foul
Oct. 19	3	SE	135.00	7.0*	0.0		Saw island of Samoet to east
Oct. 19	3	E	90.00	7.0*	0.0	N	Made N point at noon; called island Isabela; due E of Fernandina
Oct. 19	0	SSW?	202.50	12.0	0.0		Anchored at Cabo Hermosa
Oct. 20	0	NNE?	22.50	12.0	0.0	Light	Stood off N point all night
Oct. 21	0	—	0.00	0.0	0.0		Anchored at Cabo del Isleo on Isabela at 10 a.m.; learned of Colba and Bofio
Oct. 22	0	—	0.00	0.0	0.0		Explored Isabela
Oct. 23	0	—	0.00	0.0	0.0	Calm	C. observed variability of winds in Bahamas
Oct. 24	0	WSW	247.50	9.5*	0.0		Set sail at midnight bound for Cuba; period extends to dawn Oct. 25
Oct. 25	0	WSW	247.50	5.0	0.0		Sailed from sunrise to 9 a.m.
Oct. 25	0	W	270.00	11.0	0.0		9 a.m. to 3 p.m.; saw 7–8 islands 5 leagues distant
Oct. 26	0	S?	180.00	10.0*	0.0		Along Islas de Arena and across Columbus Bank(?) to an anchorage
Oct. 27	12	SSW	202.50	17.0	0.0		Weighed anchor at sunrise and sighted land before nightfall; stood off all night
Oct. 28	0	SSW	202.50	5.0*	0.0		Est. distance to land; landed at river and harbor called San Salvador

Date							Remarks
Oct. 29	0	NW	295.50	6.0*	0.0		Weighed anchor and proceeded to Rio de Mares
Oct. 30	0	NW	315.00	15.0	0.0		Continued to Cabo de Palmas and beyond; est. latitude, 42 deg N
Oct. 31	0	SE	135.00	15.0*	0.0		Returned to Rio de Mares
Nov. 1	0	—	0.00	0.0	0.0		Concourse with natives
Nov. 2	0	—	0.00	0.0	0.0		Est. latitude, 42 deg N; C. est. 1,142 leagues from Hierro (map distance?)
Nov. 3	0	—	0.00	0.0	0.0		From Nov. 3–11, they careened ships and explored
Nov. 12	12	E by S	101.25	18.0	0.0		Set out for Babeque; made Cabo de Cuba by night and stood off
Nov. 13	4	SSW?	202.50	5.0	0.0		At dawn made sail for land
Nov. 13	8	E	90.00	14.0	0.0	N	10 a.m. to sunset; coast runs ESE and WNW
Nov. 13	12	E by S	101.25	6.0	0.0	NE	Wind failed; went E by S to maintain E movement; beat about all night
Nov. 14	4	S	180.00	10.0*	0.0	Strong	Est. distance to shore
Nov. 14	6	NW by W	303.75	16.0	0.0		Coasted looking for harbor C. called Puerto del Principe
Nov. 15	0	—	0.00	0.0	0.0		From Nov. 15–18, explored harbor area; low tide estab. = SW by S
Nov. 19	0	NNE	22.50	7.0	0.0	Calm, E	Weighed anchor at dawn; Babeque 15 leagues E at sunset position
Nov. 19	14	NE	45.00	15.0	0.0		Sailed all night to 10 a.m. on 20th
Nov. 20	1	NE by N	33.75	3.0	0.0	ESE	Isabela 12 leagues away; Babeque lay to ESE
Nov. 20	7	SSW?	202.50	25.0*	0.0		Returned to Puerto del Principe; NW currents prevented making it
Nov. 20	6	NE	45.00	7.0*	0.0	High	At sunrise, Puerto del Principe lay SW by W, 12 leagues
Nov. 20	6	E by N	78.75	7.0*	0.0	SSE, S, SE	Sailed dawn to vespers; sea against fleet
Nov. 21	10	E	90.00	6.0	0.0	S	Sailed dawn to vespers; sea against fleet
Nov. 21	2	S by E	168.75	3.0	0.0	E	Vespers to sunset; notes quadrant reading of 42 N is error
Nov. 22	6	S by E	168.75	4.0*	0.0	Calm, NNE	10 leagues from land at dawn owing to contrary currents; same position as on the 21st
Nov. 22	0	—	0.00	0.0	0.0	Light	Sailed within sight of land all night
Nov. 23	0	S	180.00	0.0*	0.0	ENE	Contrary current kept fleet in same relative location

[Table 2 continued on next page.]

TABLE 2 (*continued*)

Date	Hours	Course	Degrees	Leagues	Reckoned	Wind	Discourse
Nov. 24	15	S	180.00	10.*	0.0		Made land at a point passed on the 14th
Nov. 25	0	–	0.00	0.0	0.0		Explored in and around Cabo Moa Grande (?); a little confusing here
Nov. 26	12	SE	135.00	8.0	0.0	SW	Departed at dawn for Cabo el Pico; approached Cabo Campana and stood off for night
Nov. 26	0	SE	135.00	6.0	0.0		Current carried fleet 5–6 leagues during night
Nov. 27	0	NW	315.00	7.0*	0.0	SW	Backtracked to observe large bay
Nov. 27	0	SE	135.00	7.0*	0.0	N	Anchored in harbor of Puerto Santo
Nov. 28	0	–	0.00	0.0	0.0		Stayed ashore through Dec. 3 because of weather and contrary winds
Dec. 4	6	ESE	112.50	5.0	0.0	Light	Made Cabo Lindo and stood off for the night
Dec. 5	4	SE	135.00	7.0	0.0	NE	Saw land to SE (Bohio); had gone 120 leagues along Cuban coast
Dec. 5	8	SE	135.00	15.0	0.0	N-SE	Went 22 (7 + 15) leagues SE on 5th; beat off Hispaniola all night
Dec. 6	0	S by W	191.25	4.0	0.0		Entered Puerto de San Nicolas after daybreak
Dec. 7	0	NE	45.00	2.0	0.0	SW	Left harbor at the dawn watch
Dec. 7	0	E by N	78.75	5.0	0.0		
Dec. 7	0	E	90.00	7.0	0.0		Reached Cabo Cinquin; Tortuga lay 8 leagues NE
Dec. 7	0	E	90.00	6.0	0.0		Anchored in Puerto de la Concepción; stayed through Dec. 13
Dec. 13	0	–	0.00	0.0	0.0		C. measured daylight as 20 half-hour glasses; quadrant read 34 degrees N
Dec. 14	0	NNE	22.50	2.5*	0.0	E	Sailed to Tortuga
Dec. 14	0	SSW	202.50	2.5*	0.0		Returned to Puerto de la Concepción
Dec. 15	0	ENE?	67.50	5.0*	0.0	E	Dec. 15–18 C. explored and beat about channel between Hispaniola and Tortuga
Dec. 18	0	ESE?	112.50	5.0*	0.0		Here we est. course to Cabo Torres
Dec. 19	0	–	0.00	0.0	0.0	E	Left Cabo Torres but made no headway; 60 *millia* to Monte Caribata
Dec. 20	0	ESE?	112.50	7.0*	0.0		Made Puerto Mar de S. Tomas at sunset

Date							
Dec. 21	0	—	0.00	0.0	0.0		Explored harbor area
Dec. 22	0	—	0.00	0.0	0.0		Set sail, but weather unfavorable so anchored again
Dec. 23	0	—	0.00	0.0	0.0		Stayed in port for lack of wind
Dec. 24	0	ENE?	67.50	2.5*	0.0	Calm	Weighed anchor before daybreak; Made Puerto Santa at 11 p.m.
Dec. 25	0	E by S?	101.25	2.9*	0.0		Santa Maria wrecked; established La Navidad on Dec. 26–Jan. 4
Jan. 4, 1493	0	E	90.00	10.5*	0.0	Light	Coast trends NW and SE; C. est. Monte Cristi due E of Puerto Santo 18 leagues
Jan. 5	0	SE	135.00	6.0	0.0	E	Anchored below Monte Cristi
Jan. 6	0	—	0.00	0.0	0.0		Made 10 leagues E but returned to Monte Cristi
Jan. 7	0	—	0.00	0.0	0.0		Stayed in port until Jan. 9
Jan. 9	0	ENE	67.50	15.0	0.0	SE	Sailed at midnight and reached Puerto Roja (Puerto Rucia), 60 miles due E of Monte Cristi
Jan. 10	0	SE	135.00	3.0	0.0		Made Rio Gracia
Jan. 11	0	E	90.00	4.0	0.0		Made Bel Prado (Puerto Patilla)
Jan. 11	0	E by S	101.25	32.0	0.0	Land	Passed Cabo del Angel (Puerto Sosua), Cabo del Hierro, Puerto Seca, Redondo (Cabo de la Roca)
Jan. 11	0	E	90.00	2.0*	0.0		Passed Cabo Frances
Jan. 11	0	E	90.00	1.0	0.0		Passed Cabo del Buen Tiempo
Jan. 11	0	S by E	168.75	1.0	0.0		Made Cabo Tajado; wind and currents with fleet all day
Jan. 11	0	NNE	33.75	7.0	0.0	Fresh	Jogged off all night
Jan. 12	0	E	90.00	5.0	0.0		Dawn watch until day
Jan. 12	2	E	90.00	6.0	0.0		For two hours after dawn
Jan. 12	0	S	180.00	12.0	0.0		Sailed toward Cabo de Padre y Hijo (Cabo Cabron)
Jan. 12	0	E	90.00	2.0	0.0		Passed Puerto Sacro
Jan. 12	0	E	90.00	8.0	0.0		Passed Cabo del Enamorado (Cabo Samana)
Jan. 12	0	S?	180.00	2.0*	0.0		Anchored in Gulfo de las Flechas (Samana Bay)
Jan. 13	0	—	0.00	0.0	0.0		Stayed in port exploring through Jan. 15

a Asterisks indicate guesses.

TABLE 3

Data for the Homebound Course: January 16–February 10, 1493

Date	Hours	Course	Degrees	Leagues	Reckoned	Wind	Discourse
Jan. 16	1	E by S?	101.25	2.0*ᵃ	0.0	Land (N?)	Departed 3 hrs. before day for Carib Island
Jan. 16	8	E by N	78.75	16.0	0.0	W	Indians indicated Carib lay to SE
Jan. 16	1	SE	135.00	2.0	0.0		
Jan. 16	6	NE by E	56.25	12.0	0.0	Strong	Changed course until sunset, bound for Spain; Indians said this is course to Matinino
Jan. 17	15	NE by E	56.25	21.0	0.0		
Jan. 17	9	E	90.00	11.0	0.0		
Jan. 18	8	E by S	101.25	10.0	0.0	Little	
Jan. 18	4	SE by E	123.75	7.5	0.0		Course until sunset
Jan. 18	12	N by E*	11.25	15.0	0.0		Course average
Jan. 19	7	N by E	11.25	14.0	0.0		
Jan. 19	7	NE by N	33.75	16.0	0.0		
Jan. 19	5	NE	45.00	10.0	0.0	ESE	
Jan. 19	5	NE by N	33.75	11.0	0.0		
Jan. 20	7	NE	45.00	5.0	0.0		
Jan. 20	4	SE	135.00	2.8	0.0	Soft	
Jan. 20	13	NNE	22.50	9.0	0.0		
Jan. 21	7	NE by N	33.75	26.0	0.0	E?	
Jan. 21	11	NNE	16.88	21.0	0.0	E	Wind getting colder
Jan. 22	4	NNE	22.50	8.0	0.0	E	Wind veered SE; *Journal* gives insights into dead reckoning accounting, but is very corrupt
Jan. 22	3	N by E	11.25	4.5	0.0		
Jan. 22	2	NE	45.00	3.0	0.0		
Jan. 22	9	ENE	67.50	15.0	0.0		
Jan. 22	6		0.00	0.0	0.0	Calm	Wind fell off; Indians went swimming
Jan. 23	13	NE by N	33.75	21.0	0.0	Variable	
Jan. 23	6	NE	45.00	7.5	0.0		

Date		Wind					Notes
Jan. 23	5	ENE	67.50	7.5	0.0		
Jan. 24	13	NE	45.00	11.0	0.0		
Jan. 24	11	ENE	67.50	14.0	0.0		
Jan. 25	7	ENE	67.50	9.5	0.0		
Jan. 25	4	NNE	22.50	1.5	0.0	Variable	
Jan. 25	13	ENE	67.50	7.0	0.0		Wind fell; running low on provisions
Jan. 26	13	E by S	101.25	14.0	0.0		
Jan. 26	4	ESE, SE	123.75	10.0	0.0		Average bearing
Jan. 26	7	N	0.00	6.0	0.0		Ran close hauled
Jan. 27	13	NE, N by E	28.13	16.5	0.0		Average bearing
Jan. 27	6	NE	45.00	6.0	0.0		
Jan. 27	5	ENE	67.50	3.0	0.0		
Jan. 28	24	ENE	67.50	14.0	0.0		
Jan. 29	24	ENE	67.50	17.5	0.0	S, SW	Temperate breezes; smooth sea
Jan. 30	13	ENE	67.50	7.0	0.0		McElroy thinks bearing may be error in *Journal* for N by E
Jan. 30	11	S by E	168.75	13.5	0.0		
Jan. 31	6	N by E	11.25	7.5	0.0		
Jan. 31	7	NE	45.00	8.8	0.0		
Jan. 31	11	ENE	67.50	13.5	0.0		
Feb. 1	13	ENE	67.50	16.5	0.0		
Feb. 1	11	ENE	67.50	29.3	0.0		
Feb. 2	13	ENE	67.50	10.0	0.0	WSW	Sea choked with weed; breezes soft
Feb. 2	11	ENE	67.50	19.3	0.0		
Feb. 3	13	ENE?	67.50	29.0	0.0	WSW	Polaris as high as Cape St. Vincent; too much roll to use quadrant
Feb. 3	11	ENE	67.50	27.0	0.0		
Feb. 4	13	E by N	78.75	32.5	0.0		Overcast, rainy and cold, so not near Azores
Feb. 4	11	E	90.00	19.3	0.0		
Feb. 5	13	E	90.00	13.5	0.0		
Feb. 5	11	E	90.00	27.5	0.0		Saw petrels and small sticks, signs of land
Feb. 6	13	E	90.00	35.3	0.0		Much weed
Feb. 6	11	E	90.00	38.5	0.0		Yanez: Flores to N, Madeira to E; Roldan: Fayel to NNE, Puerto Santo to E

[*Table 3 continued on next page.*]

TABLE 3 (*continued*)

Date	Hours	Course	Degrees	Leagues	Reckoned	Wind	Discourse
Feb. 7	13	E	90.00	32.5	0.0		
Feb. 7	11	E	90.00	22.0	0.0		C.: 75 leagues S of Flores; Alonso: Terceira and St. Mary to N, 12 leagues N of Madeira to E
Feb. 8	13	E, E by S	98.65	12.0	0.0		
Feb. 8	11	SSE	157.50	13.0	0.0		
Feb. 9	3	SSE	157.50	3.0	0.0		
Feb. 9	3	S by E	78.75	3.0*	0.0		*Journal* only indicates going S by E for a while
Feb. 9	11	NE	45.00	5.0	0.0		
Feb. 9	7	E	90.00	9.0	0.0		
Feb. 10	13	E	90.00	32.5	0.0		Pilots: 5 leagues E of St. Mary on parallel of Puerto Santo and Madeira
Feb. 10	11	E	90.00	24.8	0.0		C.: S of Flores on parallel of Casablanca
Feb. 11	13	E?	90.00	39.0	0.0		
Feb. 11	11	E?	90.00	16.5	0.0		
Feb. 12	13	E?	90.00	18.3	0.0		Heavy seas and stormy weather begin
Feb. 12	11	E?	90.00	11.5	0.0		
Feb. 13	13	E?	90.00	13.0	0.0		Went with "bare poles" most of the night
Feb. 13	11	E?	90.00	13.5	0.0		
Feb. 14	13	NE by E	56.25	13.0	0.0		Waves terrible
Feb. 14	6	ENE, E by N	67.50	7.5	0.0		Wonderful description of terror at sea
Feb. 14	5	NE	45.00	2.5	0.0		
Feb. 15	13	ENE	67.50	13.0	0.0		Land sighted to ENE; C. declared it to be the Azores; others declared Castile

[a] Asterisks indicate guesses.

thirteenth century, and probably much earlier as a surveyor's aid.[5] Maintaining the *toleta* was pilot's work. Each pilot in the fleet may have maintained his own during the watch he stood. Columbus himself could have done only about half of this type of detail work on the voyage. Otherwise, he would never have slept or accomplished his other administrative tasks as fleet commander.

(2) Twelve-Hour Summaries. At dawn and sunset a line was drawn on the plotting board, between the start and end points of the traverse, to give the resultant course made good for the half-day period. This bearing and distance data is what Columbus put in his *Journal*, and it is used here for the computer plot. The pilots also plotted this summary data on a map by a process later called "pricking the chart" to provide a visual record of daily progress relative to land. This formal observational data was meticulously compiled and *never* tampered with.

(3) Interpretation and Decision. Now other observational evidence of position—so-called sea marks—were taken into account, but in a more informal and subjective way. Included here were winds, currents, color of the water, birds, fish, bottom depths and sediments, and weather, as well as star and sun positions. The navigator would have to interpret all this information to estimate his actual position and decide what course to make from that point. The *Journal* includes many examples of these kinds of interpretations and decisions, some seeming rather silly to modern minds.

It is important to appreciate that some of the inconsistencies in Columbus's statements may be recordings of results at two different stages of the dead reckoning process, one being the raw observational data as plotted, the other being the interpretation of it. For instance, on February 7, 1493, Columbus placed the fleet to the south of Flores in the Azores. Only the day before, Roldan and Yanez, two of the pilots, had placed them at about the same spot. Thus, the admiral's dead reckoning was just about thirty leagues behind the pilots. But a few days later, on Feburay 10, having gone another eighty leagues or more, Columbus found himself "much out of his course" and fixed his position back where he had plotted it on the 7th. This was clearly a case of his reinterpreting the log or chart data.

Plotting Columbus's Course

The calculations involved in plotting Columbus's half-day course data are quite simple since the portolan charts he used assume the the regions represented are flat. Thus, the more complicated trigonometry utilized by McElroy, Fuson, Treftz, and others to plot Columbus's data on a Mercator chart is avoided. The portolan grid is a simple square one. One simply picks a starting point and lays off successive *Journal* distances in the associated directions as shown on the computer-generated plot (figure 1). For the outward and homeward voyages these successive points are marked. Through the islands, the points were often too close together to be distinguished at this scale. To give meaning to this analysis it is essential to view the course

[5] The *raxon de marteloio* is the digital version of the *toleta*—a table of trigonometric ratios for resolving courses by ratio and proportion. It was to be memorized. Andrea Bianco writes of it, "Whoever uses this rule . . . must know how to multiply and divide well." This "mental" method cannot begin to compare with the *toleta* as a practical alternative.

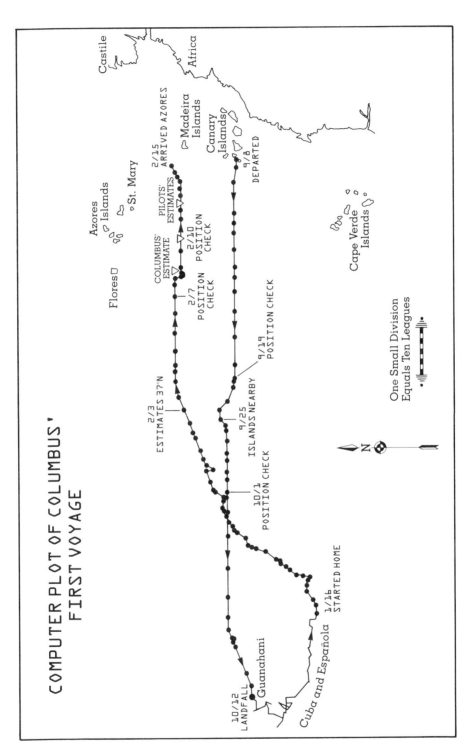

Figure 1: Plot of the first voyage of Columbus to the New World, 1492–93. (Adapted from a computer-generated version produced by the author.)

progress relative to various landmarks along the western coast of Africa and the Azores. Thus, it is relevant to ask what sort of map Columbus used for his adventure. For our purposes, the fairly well-known "Ginea Portogalexe" in the British Library is used. The basis for this choice and how it was employed are described in appendix A.

An essential step is to associate Columbus's *Journal* data quantitatively with the chart, so that daily course positions are properly located. The question is: how long is Columbus's league? It is widely believed that Columbus used the Roman mile of about 4,856 English feet. Morison is so strong in this belief that he substitutes "Roman mile" explicitly for "mille" throughout his translation of the *Journal* and other Columbian documents.[6] There is, however, no explicit statement by Columbus, either in the *Journal* or elsewhere, that he navigated using it. Yet, to model Columbus's first transatlantic voyage requires knowing the length of his mile unit with high credibility. Morison reports that D'Albertis thought Columbus's mile was 4,028 English feet (i.e., 2.665 nautical miles per Columbus league).[7] In appendix B, evidence is given showing that Columbus used a 5,000-palm mile of 4,060 English feet, and a league of four of these miles. In figure 1, the course data and chart outlines are normalized to this league at 100 leagues per inch, as indicated by the scale in the bottom border.

The Outward Voyage and the Columbus Conspiracy

Columbus's fleet got underway on September 8, 1492, from a point between Gomera and Tenerife in the Canaries. A week and a half later, on September 19, Columbus recorded a position check verified by polling his fellow pilots (see appendix C). Their individual estimates of position were within six percent of the average, namely, 420 leagues west of the Canaries. Figure 1 notes this position for reference. It is easily seen, from the league scale on the map, that this position is 420 leagues from Hierro, the westernmost of the Canaries. The close agreement among the estimates indicates a certain high degree of consistency in the pilots' dead reckoning. It also raises questions about the two estimates Columbus gave each day for the outward voyage.

Starting with Las Casas, it has often been believed that Columbus intentionally falsified his daily progress by giving smaller figures to the crew to ease their fears should the voyage become a long one. How could Columbus hide the truth from the crew unless he conspired to do so with all who could function as pilots, or unless he had a crew who were ignorant of ocean sailing — and unobservant as well? In view of the facts, these assumptions are unwarranted. Considerations of safety at sea, the stiff maritime laws of the time, the openness of life aboard small ships, and the general experience of the crew would seem to preclude the possibility of conspiracy. Furthermore, on at least one occasion (September 25), Columbus fixed his estimate of current position on Martín Alonso Pinzón's chart in the presence of his pilot and sailors.

The explanation of the two distance figures given in the *Journal* lies in Columbus's

---

[6] S. E. Morison, *Journals and Other Documents on the Life and Voyages of Christopher Columbus* (New York: Heritage Press, 1963).

[7] Morison, *Admiral of the Ocean Sea* (Boston: Little, Brown, 1942), p. 261.

desire to make the truth known in terms the crew could better understand. It appears that Columbus made his personal estimates in terms of a 5,000-palm mile, while his Spanish crew worked with the Portuguese maritime league of four neo-Roman miles (see appendix C for an analysis). Columbus had to convert his mile estimates to a league unit by dividing by four. To obtain the equivalent Portuguese maritime leagues he then had to multiply this result by five-sixths. Additional verification of this explanation occurs on October 1, when Columbus checked his position with his pilot. The pilot estimated 578 leagues west of the Canaries; Columbus told the crew that the distance was 584 leagues or approximately five-sixths of his estimate of 707 leagues. Appendix C discusses this assumption at length.

Was Columbus a Latitude Sailor?

On October 12 Columbus's fleet made landfall at the island called Guanahaní. The next day, the admiral wrote that this island was on an east-west line with the island of Hierro, the southwesterly island in the Canaries. This statement is true to within twelve or fifteen leagues on the plotted reconstruction of his landfall, figure 1, suggesting that Columbus was basing his observation on a map reading and not on an independent estimate of latitude.

It has been argued that Columbus was a latitude sailor who, by shooting Polaris, was able to maintain a constant westerly course along about the same parallel of latitude. Therefore, since the plotted landfall is in the latitude of Hierro, he must have landed a good bit north of the generally accepted landfall on Watlings Island — perhaps near Eleuthera. Another argument holds that Columbus maintained his constant westerly course by shooting the sun, not for latitude, but to define west as the position of sunset. Since the fleet sailed about the time of the autumn equinox, this horizon position was nearly constant throughout the voyage, though enough south of west to bring them to a southern landfall near Caicos Island.[8]

It is important to resolve this technical issue since it is fundamental to bracketing San Salvador between a landfall based on a reconstruction of the outward voyage and a retracing of the fleet's progress backward from Cuba. The hypothesis followed in the computer simulation divides the relevant contemporary sailing methods as follows. The traditions of northern sailors suggest they sailed squared courses more or less along meridian and latitude lines. But the traditions of the south European navigation in which Columbus was steeped seem to be based on the formal geometrical method of dead reckoning described earlier, which depended on the magnetic compass and the estimation of ship's speed underway. The fifteenth-century Portuguese who charted Africa seemed to have used a combination of the Italian dead reckoning process and sun shots.[9]

It seems inconceivable that Columbus and his contemporaries avoided considerations of latitude totally. In fact, lists of latitude positions of various European places

[8] Molander opts for Eleuthera; Fuson and Treftz follow the sun to Caicos.
[9] For "square" courses see J. E. Kelley, Jr., "Non-Mediterranean Influences That Shaped the Atlantic in the Early Portolan Charts," *Imago Mundi* 31 (1979): 19–35. The way the chart scale along the west coast of Africa varies with distance from the Canaries suggests that the Portuguese did not correct for the sun's changing declination until Zacuto's tables became available generally.

were available to fifteenth-century mariners.[10] Further, Columbus was probably familiar with the Portuguese methods of taking sun shots, having sailed down the coast of Africa with them. In spite of this, latitude observation does not appear to have been formally incorporated into Columbus's dead reckoning process on the voyage. Given the available evidence, it is difficult to justify assumptions that identify him as a latitude sailor in the usual sense of that term. Appendix D is devoted to an analysis of Columbus's latitude measurements.

Although the study is old, Van Bemmelen's estimate of a western magnetic declination in the Atlantic at the time would tend to put the landfall much to the south of the due west position from Hierro seen in the computer plot.[11] It took some years for Columbus's "error" in the relative positioning of the islands to be "corrected" on the charts. The early charts of the north Atlantic—La Cosa, Cantino, and others—locate Cuba well to the north of the tropic of Cancer, whereas the tropic actually only cuts through the northwest portion of the island. It appears that this error was due to charting positions from the dead reckoning data in ships' logs. Apparently the latitude error could not be "corrected" until enough mariners made sufficiently accurate star and sun shots with a quadrant or astrolabe to make it necessary to shift the charted positions of the islands farther south. In fact, some sixteenth-century maps have two latitude scales—one for western Europe and one for America. In this way, both latitude information and magnetic bearing information were made available in the same document.

For the magnetic-bearing–distance navigator of Columbus's time, placing Guanahaní due west of Hierro provided a more practical direction for getting there than if it were placed some four degrees farther south to satisfy latitude conceptions. In the latter event, the sailor of Columbus's time would likely have arrived in the Virgin Islands, his course being bent there by the westerly declination of the time.

Threading the Islands

Figure 2 gives an expanded view of Columbus's course through the islands, from first landfall on October 12 until he started home on January 16, 1493. The dashed lines represent distances not explicitly given in the *Journal*. There are also a few missing bearings denoted in table 2 by question marks. The course trends southward to Cuba, then eastward along the north coasts of Cuba and Hispaniola. The islands are omitted on the map to avoid making a commitment on the location of the first landfall and to avoid misleading distortions in fitting landforms to the data at this stage of the analysis.

It is quite evident that the course data for the island threading is very incomplete as compared with data for the outbound and homebound courses. The fact that the island data are incomplete does not imply that they are any less accurate than the ocean voyage data.[12]

---

[10] See Mallett, p. 200.

[11] W. Van Bemmelen, "Die Abweichung der Magnetnadel," in *Observations of the Royal Magnetical and Meteorological Observatory at Batavia* 21 (1899). This obscure reference is often cited, but little seen.

[12] There is a temptation born out of frustration to discount these data, or only to accept as correct what is consistent with the particular landfall theory under consideration at the moment. There is, however, no

There is another problem in interpreting this *Journal* data: the distances along Cuba and Hispaniola are far larger than they ought to be. This can be seen from the true crow-fly distances in figure 2, shown by the heavy bars. It has been proposed that Columbus used two leagues: one for ocean navigation and one for land distances. If he used two different leagues, the one used for Cuba and Hispaniola would have to lie in the range 10,450 to 10,900 English feet. There is no historical basis for believing that Columbus employed two different leagues of these lengths. It is preferable to assume that Columbus's dead reckoning did *not* compensate directly for swift westerly currents which occur in winter along the coasts of Cuba and Hispaniola. They move at 4.5 to 7 leagues in twenty-four hours.[13] There are a number of instances of the influence of currents in the *Journal*.

On January 9, for example, the fleet sailed from Monte Cristi eastward along the north coast of Hispaniola to Punta Roja in about fourteen hours. The *Journal* distance is fifteen leagues. The actual distance is twelve Columbus leagues. But for fourteen hours the fleet was pushed westward some three leagues by the current, making up a good part of the difference in estimate. The formal data collection step of the dead reckoning process would not compensate for this current. When sailing with the current, the dead reckoning process would underestimate actual distances made good; when sailing against the current, the distance recorded would be overestimated. Another example brings out the point more clearly. The left side of figure 3 enlarges a section of the computer-plotted course, south from Isabela and along the Cuban coast.[14] Note that Puerto del Principe was passed sometime during the 13th of November. Columbus backtracked and anchored there on the 14th, where he stayed exploring through the 18th. Before dawn on the 19th he set sail in a north-northeast direction. Over the next thirty-five hours he sailed out and back toward Puerto del Principe, but not quite making it to anchorage. In that period his ship was subject to the strong currents, and must have been swept seven to ten leagues northwestward. It was nightfall and Columbus observed that the currents were carrying them northwest, so he steered northeast out to sea. But notice the distance between the two computed positions of Puerto del Principe. It is about seven leagues—the estimated drift distance. Notice also that on the 24th he made land at a point he passed on the 14th. From the computed plots, the effect of the swift currents on the dead reckoning is readily seen. The easterly and southerly headway he made in this period was totally offset by the currents. To test these observations further, Columbus's course from Columbus Bank to Cabo Lindo was recalculated on the assumption that he was subject to a half knot northwesterly current. The result is plotted in the right-hand side of figure 3.

---

reason to believe that Las Casas was any less accurate in reporting the island course data than the ocean course data. Too much should not be read into the map of figure 2. It must be studied with the *Journal* in hand.

[13] See "Pilot Chart of the North Atlantic Ocean," published monthly by the Defense Mapping Agency Hydrologic Center, Washington, D. C. The westerly currents (in knots) along Hispaniola and Cuba were estimated for 1975 as follows: October, 0.5; November, not marked; December, 0.7–0.8; January, 0.5–0.6; February, 0.7–0.8. (The November chart was for 1974.) Because of the change in calendar, these dates are shifted a fortnight ahead of the comparable dates in Columbus's time.

[14] Some of the distance estimates are missing in the *Journal*, and I had to supply them based on rationale presented in the notes to tables 1–3. However, almost all the bearings *do* appear in the *Journal*.

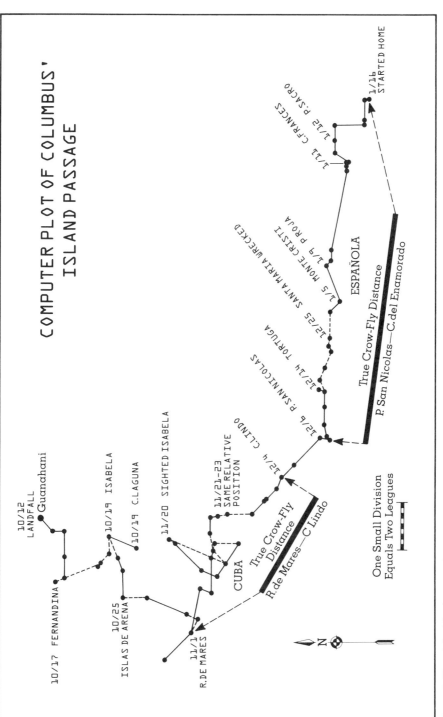

Figure 2: Plot of the island passage followed by Columbus. (Adapted from a computer-generated version produced by the author.)

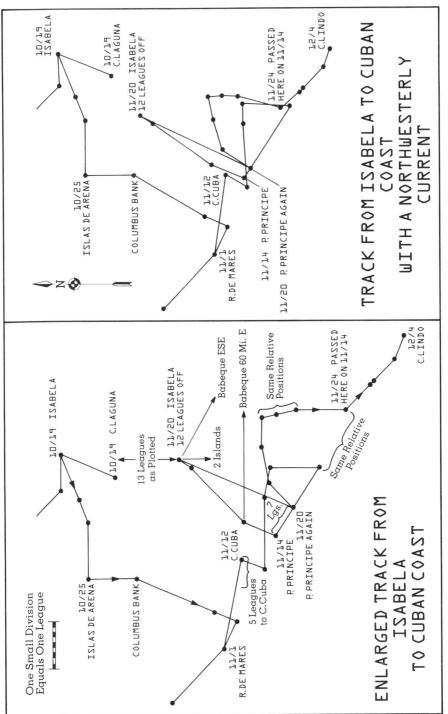

Figure 3: *Left*, an enlarged plot of the track from Isabela to the Cuban coast. *Right*, the same plot allowing for a northwesterly current.

By this the importance of the effects of currents on the interpretation of the *Journal* dead reckoning data is demonstrated. The impact may be quite startling. Note how the distance for Rio de Mares to Cabo Lindo is compressed from an unbelievable seventy-two leagues to a more realistic forty-seven leagues.[15]

The Homeward Voyage

On January 16, the fleet left Hispaniola in search of the island of Carib. They had not gone far when the wind grew stonger, "very good for going to Spain." Because his people wanted to go home without more side trips, and the caravel was leaking, Columbus turned to take "the direct course for Spain, northeast by east." This bearing, taken literally, brings Columbus's credibility into question. Instead of being a direct course for Spain, even on a portolan chart it would put the fleet on a course for England or farther north. But notice that the computer plot, figure 1, shows that the homebound trend for the first day or so is about east-northeast. This trend course gives a straight line for Spain. Certainly, attempting to average a direct course for Spain was one thing Columbus could easily try in order to control any mutinous feelings of the crew. But it is clear from the *Journal* and the computer plot that he had to change headings often in those first few days because of contrary winds. To proceed by this direct route they would have had to claw their way back to Spain. In short order everyone realized this was not the way to go and the course trend had to be changed to north-northeast.

On the trip home, Columbus recorded some interesting position checks with which the computer plot can be compared. The morning of February 7 he plotted his position as seventy-five leagues south of Flores. Just the day before, Vincente Yanez put them on the same meridian, but some fifty leagues farther south. But now on the 7th another of the pilots, Pero Alonso, placed them on a parallel twelve leagues north of Madeira and on a meridian passing between Terceira and Santa Maria in the Azores. These positions are shown on figure 1. First consider the latitudes of these estimates. Except for Columbus's estimate of February 7, placing them seventy-five leagues south of Flores, all the latitude estimates are consistent. It seems reasonable to conclude that the seventy-five leagues was an erroneous map reading for 125 leagues, the same type of error he committed on October 1, 1492. The context of the estimate is a casual remark whose statement and recording were nonessential since the correct information was recorded on his chart. Now consider the relative longitudes of the various position estimates. For both February 7 and February 10, the computer plot is shifted to the west of all the estimates except the admiral's for February 10. This shortfall is probably the result of substituting actual distances along the coast of Hispaniola for those missing in the *Journal*. The pilots' distance estimates would be larger because they fought a westerly current along that coast.

Columbus's position estimate for February 10 is another matter. It seems to be based on an interpretation of his chart and notes, not the charted positions themselves. He found himself "much out of his course," that is, out of his dead reckoning

---

[15] The crow-fly distance from Gibara (=Cabo de Mares?) to Cabo Lindo on my Mercator navigation chart is about 120 nautical miles, which translates to about 45 Columbus leagues.

estimate. He said he was due south of Flores and due west of Casablanca—back where his own estimate placed him on February 7. This example vividly illustrates the difference between the formal dead reckoning process, which produced half-day summaries of "course made good," and the interpretive step that followed it. Columbus probably analyzed his *Journal*, maps, and ship's log on the trip home. He noted that his dead reckoning distances for Cuba and Hispaniola did not jibe with his visual estimates. It is reasonable to assume that he compensated for the strong westerly currents which run along the north coasts of these islands in winter. He put his position back some 65 leagues from the position implied by the *Journal* data to just south of Flores. In the computer plot of figure 2 the excess of the crow-fly coastal distances implied by the *Journal* over the actual is 70 leagues, just about his setback distance of February 10, but about 130 leagues behind the other pilots.

On February 10, Columbus had not yielded to the suspicion that he was some eighty leagues farther north, in the vicinity of the Azores. Remember, by February 3, he was beginning to think he was at the latitiude of Cape Saint Vincent, where Prince Henry's base of operation had been. It seems that not until landfall was actually made on February 15, at Saint Mary Island—on the parallel of Cape Saint Vincent—that he felt assured in this suspicion.

Of course, the computer plot of the *Journal* puts their arrival at Saint Mary some 120 leagues out of position to the southeast. Further, considering that the pilots placed themselves some 60 leagues ahead of the computer-plotted estimate for February 10th, it is not surprising that they thought they were off Castile on the 15th. But even on the trip outward they were running ahead of Columbus.[16]

In the storm of February 15 the *Pinta* under Martín Alonzo Pinzón got separated, to make its way home alone. Guided by his dead reckoning, which put him on the parallel of Morocco instead of the Azores, and helped by the storm, Pinzón finally ended up in Bayona in Galicia, far to the north of home base. This fact, Columbus's handling of the various position checks in the *Journal*, and the quadrant episodes certainly seem to inply that his fleet did not employ latitude measurements, if they made them, in any regular way.

Identifying Isabela

A quantitative basis for interpreting Columbus's *Journal* having been established, how can this information be used to answer the question of principal interest: where is Columbus's first landfall? To successfully identify San Salvador one must also clearly identify three other islands: Santa Maria, Fernandina, and Isabela. Virtually all students of the problem agree on this requirement.

Figure 3 and the data on which it is based provide an interesting challenge for those who deny that Isabela may be indentifed with Acklins-Crooked Island. Comparing the right-hand side of figure 3 with a modern Mercator navigation chart shows that the identifications given in table 4 are consistent within a reasonable level

---

[16] Overestimating distance may have been a safety practice among some groups of mariners, especially in the Atlantic. Thinking you are there, though a little early, would tend to sharpen the sensibilities when approaching a coast.

TABLE 4
Identifying Isabela As Acklins-Crooked Island

		Crow-fly Distances[a]			Bearings[b]		
From	To	Fig.3	True	Error (%)	Fig. 3	True	Error (%)
Rio de Mares (Gibara)	Isabela (Crooked I.- Bird Rock)	137	144	−5	51	43	8
Rio de Mares	Cabo Lindo (Puente Fraile)	125	119	5	120	115	5
Puerto del Principe (Bahia de Tanamo)	Cabo Lindo	80	67	19	124	112	12
Puerto del Principe	Rio de Mares	46	51	−10	293	298	−5
Puerto del Principe	Isabela (Bird Rock)	122	139	−12	32	23	9
Cabo Lindo	Isabela	148	153	−3	359	358	1
Average error				−1			5

[a]Leagues are converted to nautical miles using the 4,060 English-foot Columbus mile.
[b]Bearings are given in degrees proceeding clockwise from north.

of accuracy. These quantitative results are also consistent with other data in the *Journal*. At sunset on November 19, when Columbus was seven leagues north-northeast of Puerto del Principe, Las Casas has him spotting Babeque some fifteen leagues to the east, as indicated on the left side of figure 3. At 10:00 A.M. the next morning, having gone some eighteen leagues farther to the northeast, Isabela is noted as lying twelve leagues off, Babeque is located to the east-southeast, and two islands lie to the south. These data require interpretation. It is quite unlikely that Columbus saw anything but clouds fifteen leagues to eastward. To see land this far away from his probable position it would have to rise nine hundred feet or more. Great Inagua, which does lie to the east of that position, has ninety-foot mounts on its western end, which could not be seen farther away then eighteen nautical miles (about seven Columbus leagues). If the sunset and next morning bearings of Babeque are used to triangulate its position, it is found to be some forty-four leagues east from the fleet's sunset position. This is very close to the distance to Great Inagua from Columbus's probable position seven leagues north-northeast of Bahia de Tanamo (Puerto del Principe).

Here is what probably happened to make the *Journal* data inconsistent. The evening of November 19, Columbus revised his estimate of November 13 that Babeque was three days by canoe from Rio de Mares, or twenty-one leagues (at seven leagues per day, see *Journal* entry for November 14). By sunset, November 14, he had sailed some thirty-six leagues east of Rio de Mares, without sighting Babeque. At sunset, November 19, he was some ten leagues west of the most easterly position attained thus far, and likely added five leagues to reflect his optimism that Babeque had been just out of sight over the horizon that day. The Indians seemed to know just where Babeque was, and probably gave Columbus the easterly bearing of November 19 and the east-southeast bearing the morning of November 20. Columbus's estimate that the Indians could make only seven leagues per day needs discussion in this context. Seven leagues is only a day's march (about twenty-one statute miles). At this rate of progress very little headway could be made against the half knot currents common to the area, which can carry a small vessel 4.5 leagues in twenty-four hours. A trader or war canoe, operated in shifts by tens of men, might possibly make the 135 nautical miles (50 leagues) from Rio de Mares (Gibara) to Great Inagua in three days. Columbus's idea that Guanahaní was eight leagues from Isabela (November 20) probably derives form his estimate of a day's travel by canoe. In fact, Crooked Island to Watlings Island is about sixty-five nautical miles, or twenty-four leagues. Certainly the canoe that could make Gibara to Great Inagua in three days of forced paddling might well make this twenty-four leagues in twenty-four hours. It is surprising that Columbus would make such an apparent error in distance after sailing those water.

Columbus's comment that Isabela lay twelve leagues from his position at 10:00 A.M., November 2, was probably based on his mapping of the area, possibly suggested by the loom of clouds in the island's direction. To actually sight land from twelve leagues off (about thirty-two nautical miles) it would have to rise at least five hundred feet above sea level, which is much higher than any of these smaller islands. As a map reading, uncorrected for the effects of currents, Cabo de la Laguna would lie to north-northwest as indicated on the left side of figure 3. In all likelihood the cape really lay to the northeast by east as shown on the right side of the figure 3.

Finally, what were the two islands Columbus noted lying to his south the morning of November 20, which he wished to investigate? In fact, he must have investigated them on his course back south to Puerto del Principe on November 20 and found them to be like those he investigated on the outward voyage—cloud shadows, mirages, or imaginings. No other mention is made of them in the *Journal*.

Concluding Remarks

The conclusion that Isabela is Acklins-Crooked Island is certainly not immune to criticism. But if the identification holds under scrutiny then there is a strong presumption that San Salvador is Watlings Island. The chain of reasoning used here is rather long, but not too complicated. It established that the *Journal* data are internally consistent and highly credible in a quantitative sense, that the units of measurement employed have an historical basis in fact, that the navigational details are consistent with what is known of fifteenth-century, south-European methods, and that known physical conditions are reflected in them.

However, a significant error along the path of argument may vitiate the conclusions. More particularly, individual legs of the course around Cuba, shown on figure 3, might be interpreted differently. And currents in the area may not behave in exactly the simple way that was assumed for the calculation. But the real question is this: can the *Journal* data and local currents be interpreted so differently as to put Isabela in a significantly different position from Acklins-Crooked Island?

Appendix A:
Employing "Ginea Portogalexe" in the Computer Simulation

What Map Did Columbus Use?

We will probably never answer this question. Much is made of Columbus's dependence on the Toscanelli Map of 1474, the only known quantitative characteristics of which are that it had a 250-*miglia* grid overlay; Quinsay was 26 grid squares (6,500 *miglia*) from Lisbon; Cipangu was 10 grid squares (=250 *miglia*)from Antilia. Parallels with Martin Behaim's globe of 1492 have led to reconstructions of Toscanelli's map based on this production of Nürnberg cosmographers.[17]

Though Columbus's intentions might be colored by the thinking of contemporary cosmographers, he would have been hard-pressed to trust his day-by-day navigation to their idealized productions, based as they were on Ptolemy and conjecture. His probable first choice would have been charts of the Atlantic coast of Europe and North Africa, specially prepared by professional marine cartographers, showing as much as was known or conjectured of the Atlantic and its islands. Charts including blank parchment for many leagues to westward on which he could pilot his course and chart newly discovered lands were doubtlessly prepared for Columbus and his pilots.

The question is what cartographic model would he have used for this purpose? Actually very little survives that would have recommended itself to Columbus in 1492. Among the surviving charts that depict the Azores in recongnizable form are J. Bertran's chart of 1482 (Arch. Stato, Florence) and related ones like the pseudo-Roselli of c.1466 at Paris,[18] the Soligo chart of c.1475 (MS Egerton 73, British Library), the Ginea Portogalexe of c.1485 (also Egerton 73), and the anonymous planisphere c.1490 at Paris.[19]

The Ginea Portogalexe is the best of these candidates, and it is the basis for this computer voyage simulation of Columbus.[20]

Restoration and Scaling

To put Ginea Portogalexe into the computer for scaling and other manipulations, I had first to trace a copy of it from a microfilm reader. Except for the portion in the binding of MS Egerton 73, the chart appears fairly flat and undistorted. The crack of the binding runs through the Canaries. Thus, in removing the distortion of the crack by separating the north and south sections a measured amount, I had to reconstruct

---

[17] See the Toscanelli letter in Morison, *Journals and Other Documents*, and elsewhere. For a good summary of current thinking about the cartographic influences on Columbus, see R. A. Skelton, "The Cartography of Columbus' First Voyage," appendix to Vigneras's edition of Jane's translation of *The Journal of Christopher Columbus* (London, 1968).

[18] M. Foncin, et. al., *Catalogue des cartes nautiques sur velin*, (Paris: Bibliotèque national, 1963), n. 13.

[19] Foncin, n. 17. Ronciere thought Columbus personally made this planisphere, a conjecture which seems unlikely.

[20] The Azores in Ginea Portogalexe are only six percent (about 20 Columbus leagues) too close to Portugal. Their general clockwise displacement from true orientation suggests a westerly magnetic compass variation in the mid-Atlantic at the time the chart source was recorded (c.1450–90?).

the Canaries almost totally. The corrected tracing (based on fixed relationships within the rhumb net) was then copied directly into the computer on a digitizer.

Since we are dealing with quantitative matters, it is essential to have a reasonable basis for relating Columbus's units of measurement at sea with the scale of the chart. Sufficient evidence exists to presume that Columbus used a mile unit of 4,060 English feet (see appendix B). This unit is built up from 5,000 palms (=¾ foot or ⅛ cane) of a foot unit of 33 cm (Machabey's R4 foot). This palm was the most widely used in southern Europe at the time. Further, McElroy's estimate of Columbus's mile is consistent with this unit, and it is the common "short" mile of the portolan charts.[21]

To scale the chart to the presumed Columbus mile unit of 4,060 English feet required some interpretive judgment. Charts of his day were compilations from various sources that displayed different scale units among their parts. Thus, the choice of which measurements to compare with a modern map very much influences the value of the scale unit one derives. In the case of Ginea Portogalexe I have based the scale on these measurements:

	Tracing	*Statute Miles*	*Stat Mile/Inch*
C. St. Vincent to Madeira	6.475''	523.3	80.82
C. St. Vincent to Fuerteventura	7.00''	586.1	83.73
C. Razo to St. Michael	10.05''	850.0	84.58
C. Blanco to C. Verde	4.93''	400.2	81.17
		Average	82.58

These chart distances are in about the same ratio to the true distances. In addition, three are open water distances, which are not so subject to the distortions introduced by cartographers in piecing sections of coastline together from various sources. Other point pairs I tried were inconsistent with these results, or could be discounted for various reasons. Consequently, I have presumed that on the tracing of Ginea Portogalexe the scale is 107.4 (=82.58x5,280/4,060) of Columbus's 5,000-palm miles per inch. The result is shown at the right edge of figure 1.[22]

Appendix B: The Five-Thousand Palm Mile

In his analysis of Columbus's *Journal* data, McElroy calculated that Columbus used a mile of 4.393 English feet (=2.89x6,080/4) on his outward voyage and 4,104 English feet (=2.7x6,080/4) on the homeward voyage. McElroy attributed the lower figure to Columbus's unfamilarity with the sailing characteristics of *Niña*, his flagship on the return voyage. Possibly *Niña* seemed to sail faster than she really did. Morison's explanation that drift probably accounts for the inconsistency seems to be the real reason.[23]

---

[21] McElroy, p. 216.

[22] There is a scale on Ginea Portogalexe for which 450 *miglia* measure 5.08'', or 88.58 *miglia*/inch. The *miglia* in this case is equivalent to a 5,000 neo-Roman-foot mile (i.e., 88.58 is approx. 82.58x5,280/4,888 = 89.2 neo-Roman *miglia*/inch). Because of the errors inherent in the chart, one might alternatively believe that the scale is based on the Roman foot.

[23] Morison, *Admiral*, pp. 414–15; McElroy, p. 216.

According to modern pilot charts, Columbus was helped along by a 0.4 knot current, giving him a free ride for some 326 nautical miles of the 3,155 (McElroy's estimate) from the Canaries to San Salvador. Thus, Columbus's estimate of 1,090 leagues is equivalent to 2,829 nautical miles. At four leagues to the mile, this equivalence makes Columbus's mile equal to 3,945 English feet on the outward voyage, a little closer to McElroy's estimate of his mile unit on the homeward trip.

A rough analysis indicates that the cumulative effect of currents on the return trip distance that McElroy calculated was probably minimal. For the first six days there was probably a 0.5-knot set to the west. For the next twelve days, there was a 0.4-knot current opposite to Columbus's course. During the final thirteen days to the Azores, Columbus was helped along by a 0.5 knot current. This last current seems to have canceled out the effects of the others. Thus, McElroy's estimate of the length of the homeward voyage is probably directly equivalent to Columbus's total leagues traveled.[24]

The average of McElroy's outward and homeward voyage mile estimates, adjusted for currents, is 4,025 English feet. This figure is probably close to what is implied by Columbus's method of dead reckoning. His mile is about five-sixths the length of the Roman mile. Most writers seem to assume that Columbus's intended unit was the Roman mile.[25] Because his course data imply a short mile, it is generally concluded that Columbus consistently overestimated his distance sailed—by some nine percent, according to McElroy. Whether or not Columbus really thought he was using the Roman mile, this short mile is consistent with the average mile of about 4,100 English feet that Wagner and Steger found implied by the mile scales for portolan charts of the Mediterranean.[26] The unit is also found in the contemporary pilot books. Consequently, Columbus's short mile is probably real and not just the result of poor estimating at sea. The problem here is to find a reasonable basis for defining this short mile.

From Machabey's work (summarized in table 5), it is known that the most common basis of south-European units of length was the Bourgogne foot of 33.0 cm. It was the basis of the *aune* of Provins which conditioned many southern *canas*. In particular, some Genoese units of measure are based on this foot. However, among southern Europeans it is not the foot unit that was commonly used, but the palm. In fact, Columbus writes of the length of a snake (*sierpe*) as seven palms (October 21 and 22, 1492) and that of a canoe as ninety-five palms (November 30, 1492); nowhere, to my knowledge, does he mention a foot unit. The palm of the Bourgogne foot is about five-sixths the so-called neo-Roman foot (see table 5). Thus, 5,000 of these palms are

[24] This rough analysis is no substitute for a detailed analysis of the outward and homeward voyages, a task yet to be done in credible detail. Here it just makes the argument for the 5,000-palm mile appear more reasonable.

[25] This Roman mile is generally considered to be about 4,856 English feet. In Machabey's notation this mile figure lies between 5,000 R1 and 5,000 R'1, where the foot unit R1 = 29.4 cm and R'1 = 29.8 cm. (see table 5).

[26] H. Wagner, "The Origin of the Medieval Italian Nautical Charts," *Report of the Sixth International Geographical Congress* (London, 1895), pp. 695–702; "Der Ursprung der 'kleinen Seemeile' auf den mittelalterlichen Seekarten der Italiener," *Kgl. Ges. d. Wiss. Nachrichten Philolog.-histor.*, klasse 1900, heft 3, pp. 271–85; E. Steger, "Untersuchen uber italienische Seekarten des Mittelalters auf Grund der kartometrischen Methode," dissertation, Göttingen, 1896.

4,060 English feet. This is essentially the mile implied by both Columbus's (the Genoese) *Journal* data, and many portolan chart mile scales.

TABLE 5

Western European Measures of Length

Measure	Length in Centimeters	Where Used
Roman foot (R1)	29.4	Brussels, Florence
Neo-Roman foot (R'1)	29.8	Albi, Cahors, Carcassonne, Geneva, Milan, Paris, Rouen, Sens, Toulouse, Valenciennes
Foot (R2)	27.5	Antwerp, Autun, Bruges, Brussels, Flanders, Malines, Nantes, Rouen
Pied de Lorraine (R'2)	28.6	Amsterdam, Antwerp, Avignon, Geneva, Lorraine, Louvain, Montbeliard, Rouen
Rhinelandic foot (R3)	31.4	Ancona, Besançon, Dijon, Milan, Toulouse
Spanish foot (R'3)	27.9	Cantal, Castile, Corrèze, Valenciennes
Bourgogne foot (R4)	33.0	Arles, Avignon, Barcelona, Bourgogne, Cahors, Carpentras, Dôle, Genoa, Majorca, Marseilles, Montpellier, Nantes, Nîmes, Paris, Provins, Rome, Tournai, Troyes, Valenciennes, Venice
Pied manuel (R'4)	34.3	Agen (pied de terre), Bordeaux (pied de ville), Bruges, Grenoble, Lyon, Milan
Pied manuel (R5)	35.3	Chartres, Messina, Naples
Pied manuel (R'5)	35.7	Bordeaux (pied de terre), Bourgogne (pied de Comte), Dôle, Messina

Source: Abstracted from Armand Machabey, *La Metrologie dans les musées de province et sa contribution a l'histoire des poid et mesures en France depuis le treizieme siecle* (Paris, 1962).

Appendix C:
Columbus and the Portuguese Maritime League

According to Las Casas's paraphrase of Columbus's *Journal* (September 9 and 25, 1942), Columbus resolved to tell his men they traveled less than he estimated so that if the voyage were long, they would not be troubled by their great distance from home in the latter stages of the voyage. Columbus wrote down this smaller figure, perhaps on a tally conveniently placed for the men to see (see *Journal* entry for September 19). Columbus's action certainly appears to be a deliberate fabrication of the truth.[27] But this long-held belief may not be the correct interpretation. Rather, Columbus may have reduced the numeric value of the distance traveled for just the opposite reason—so as not to mislead the men. They, being Spaniards, were accustomed to a longer league than Columbus, the Genoese, was in the habit of using for his dead reckoning.[28] The numerical value of distance would be smaller in this case. The effect on the men would be the same, however. They would not be so unduly alarmed as the distance from home increased.[29]

The following analysis supports the conjecture that Columbus was simply making voyage progress available to his men in terms they could readily understand. First of all, the other pilots in the fleet were not necessarily inferior to Columbus at dead reckoning. On September 19, the four estimates of distance traveled west of the Canaries were recorded by Columbus as follows:

440 leagues—*Nina's* pilot
420 leagues—*Pinta's* pilot
400 leagues—*Santa Maria's* pilot
436 leagues—Columbus's cumulative estimate in the *Journal* and the estimate
               on the computer plot (figure 1).
424 ± 18 leagues average

All these figures are within six percent of the average.[30]

Columbus would have had difficulty hiding the truth from the pilots even if he had tried. To keep actual progress a secret from the fleet, all parties who could estimate voyage distance (at least four people and probably double that number) must have conspired to do so. But where is the *positive* evidence for such a conspiracy? Furthermore, on September 25, Martín Alonzo Pinzón sent his chart aboard *Santa Mariá* so that Columbus might record his estimate of current position theron. Columbus did so with the help of his pilot and sailors "con su piloto y marineros." At that time, his men had to see their position on the chart. But perhaps Columbus plotted a false position! What a dreadful breach of safety! If something were to happen to Columbus, the others would not have his best thinking on their current position, an important ingredient for plotting the course home. Further, at the time they were on the lookout for some charted islands, a task that is certainly not carried out well when everyone has a significantly different idea of current position.

---

[27] Morison, *Admiral*, 1:266, thought it ethically justified in the circumstances to hide the truth. He thought that it would be an easy practice since no one would bother to check the commander's calculations.

[28] Of eighty-seven men identified as members of the fleet, only four are believed to have been non-Spanish (J. M. Martinez-Hidalgo, *Columbus' Ships*, ed. Howard I. Chapelle [Barre, Mass., 1966], p. 85).

[29] Columbus's statement of intent may have been ambiguously phrased so that Las Casas, not being aware of the metrological technicalities involved, missed the true meaning and thought the smaller number to be false. In fact, Las Casas has Columbus still pretending at a time when he and everyone else thought they were in sight of land (see *Journal* entry for September 25).

[30] Morison, *Admiral*, 1:279, makes a case for estimating Columbus's position at a more comparable 418 leagues west of the Canaries, still an equivalent figure.

On October 1, 1492, Columbus calculated that they had come 707 leagues from the Canaries, but he told his men 584 leagues. Columbus's own pilot estimated 578 leagues that same day, a figure comparable to Columbus's published distance. It does not seem likely that the pilots could differ from Columbus at this point by as much as 129 leagues when they agreed with his estimate on September 19, and were running somewhat ahead of him in their estimates of September 25. Clearly there is an inconsistency here.[31]

The answer to the dilemma seems to be this: since the estimates for September 19 are comparable, it seems reasonable to conclude they are in the same units used by Columbus. Except for *Santa Mariá*'s pilot, whose estimate is noted in the *Journal* to be "exact," the figures are clearly rounded down to the nearest ten leagues, a common method of eliminating unwanted fractions. This was probably done while Columbus was converting from units used by the pilots to his own units to compare estimates, where the arithmetic was cut short at the level of significance he needed. It certainly was not for the purpose of simplifying the writing of the numbers. Otherwise why would Columbus convert so precisely from 707 to 584 leagues, which he might have written as 700 and 580, respectively?

The two sets of distances recorded in Columbus's *Journal* provide an estimate of $(82.0 \pm 7.2)\%$ as the conversion factor he used (based on twenty-three daily entries—see table 1). If he used a mile of 4,060 English feet, then his men would be thinking in terms of a league of around 19,805 English feet($=4 \times 4,060/0.82$).

A case can be made for believing Columbus converted his estimates to the published figures by multiplying by five-sixths a factor that arises naturally in conversions among various foot units (see table 5). In fact, seven of the twenty-three cases in the *Journal* are converted exactly, using this factor, except for the fractional part which Columbus dropped. Nine other cases are within two leagues of the correct integer value, likely due to arithmetic blunders. At least three more cases can be explained as being misreadings by Las Casas, as can the conversion of the cumulative 707 leagues to 584 (instead of 589) on September 25.[32] It is understandable that Columbus's men could eventually become upset if he quoted his calculated distances in Genoese units, which were numerically larger, unless they had a feel for the difference. To one who has *not* grown up with the metric system, distances in kilometers always seem so much farther than the equivalents in statute miles. And in this case the ambiguity of calling two different units (miles and kilometers) by the same name does not apply as it did in Columbus's time, when explicit distinctions among similar units were not consistently made.

It seems likely that Columbus's pilots were using the Portuguese maritime league, stated as 19,422.5 English feet ($=5,920$ m) by some authorities.[33] Six-fifths of Colum-

---

[31] Actually, Columbus probably made a common error in reading the scale on his chart, one which shows up in the contemporary pilot books and suggests that *pieleghi* (long-distance courses) given there were complied from map readings. Experiment with some dividers and figure 1 to read the distance from the point of departure to the position check of October 1. You may read 707 leagues if you made Columbus's error. You should read about 660 leagues, one major scale division less. With this last figure Columbus would probably have published his progress as 550 leagues, still comparable to the pilot's estimate.

[32] In Columbus's writing of Arabic numerals, a *9* and *4* may be confused with one another; a *1* may be read as *7* if a slight hook is formed just before the down stroke; and a poorly formed *5* may appear to be an *8*. There may be other cases.

[33] For example, Fontoura DaCosta, *A Marinharia dos descobrimentos*, (Lisbon, 1939), p. 216.

bus's league is 19,488 English feet. Note also that the league of 20,000 neo-Roman feet (Machabey R'1) is 19,554 English feet, also close to the league of Columbus's pilots.[34] There is a very good reason why these pilots did their dead reckoning in different units. When each individual first learned the art of navigation he had to learn a method of estimating ship's speed using a prayer or counting verse to be said with a certain rhythm as bubbles, weed, a wood chip, spittle, or some other thing passed a measured distance along the ship's side. With this method it is natural to tie the calibration to a specific mile or league unit. The words correspond to speed, the speed decreasing as more words are said before the wood chip runs its course along the ship's side. Once one learns such a method, one risks confusion and errors that affect safety at sea, by switching to another scheme. The internal feel for the rhythm is the key to correct speed estimating. It is better to do an arithmetical conversion of the results into other units when needed. And this appears to be precisely what Columbus did so that he could compare results with his pilots who had learned a different estimating scheme, and thought in a different set of units.[35]

Appendix D: Columbus and the Quadrant

It has bothered me that Columbus had such apparent difficulty in measuring latitude using a quadrant. On November 2, 1492, while in the harbor of Mares (21.1° N) his quadrant reading was 42° N. He got the same reading at sea on November 21. Later, on December 13, while in the harbor of Conception (19.1°N) his quadrant reading was 34°. How could Columbus make such gross errors of some twenty degrees? He knew the readings were wrong and thought the quadrant was broken. A quadrant is so easy to use that even Morison does not suggest Columbus mishandled the instrument. Rather he suggests Columbus shot the wrong star.[36] Morison's explanation does not seem valid to me. Columbus had been looking at Polaris and the "guards" all during the trip in order to tell time at night. Polaris's general position in the rigging and relative position on the horizon would be well known by the time he used the quadrant on November 2. To misselect Polaris at the latitude of Cuba would be like selecting a twenty-five-story building to survey instead of a twelve-story building while standing three hundred feet away.

---

[34] The longer league unit may be what Columbus refers to as a "great" league in his letter of Feburary 15, 1493 (Jane, p. 192; Morison, *Journals and Documents*, p. 185). In the Latin version of the letter, distances are converted to *milliaria* at 3 per league. (See Major's 1847 Latin edition published by the Hakluyt Society.) The only way I can make sense of this conversion of units is that the translator took the league as 4 of Columbus's 5,000-palm miles and converted to a 5,000-foot mile, the foot being Machabey's foot of Bourgogne (R4). Taking the "great" league as 4 Roman miles implies a mile unit four-thirds of a Roman mile. To my knowledge no such unit was in use at the time, nor was one of 5,000 R4 feet either. But there is much confusion in this area of research, which is in great need of clarification.

[35] To relate the above discussion to perhaps more familiar ground, there are a shade under 22.5 of Columbus's leagues per degree and 18.8 Portuguese maritime leagues to the degree. In the sixteenth century, Spain, under her Germanic rulers, apparently adopted a maritime league of 20,000 Rhinelandic feet (Machabey's R3 foot of 31.4 cm). There are 17.7 of these Spanish leagues to the degree, usually rounded to 17.5 in the literature.

[36] Morison, "Columbus and Polaris," *American Neptune* 1 (1941): 209–40.

I remember reading the suggestion that Columbus may have used a quadrant which, for some reason, had twice the number of degree graduations it should have had. The idea that the scales on Columbus's quadrant may have been out of the ordinary could have merit. The standard quadrant often had other scales besides the equal interval degree scale along the circumference. The large variety of scales in surviving instruments, even long before Columbus's time, must be seen to be believed.[37] Included were standard scales for the elementary trigonometric ratios: tangent (*umbra recta*), cotangent (*umbra versa*), sine (*corda recta*), cosine (*corda veras*). There were many ways to represent these functions, which found their way into everyday use by builders, military men, surveyors, pilots, and the like. It is not unlikely that Columbus's quadrant had a tangent/cotangent scale running parallel, and just inside, the degree scale, and along the circumference. Such a scale is shown in Apian's quadrant.[38] This scale gives one hundred times the trigonometric tangent of angles under forty-five degrees, and one hundred times the cotangent of angles over forty-five degrees.

Suppose that when Columbus took his quadrant readings — in the dark, of course — his thumb, which held in place the weighted thread which measures the angle, covered the numbers on the degree scale. In the light of a lantern or at the binnacle he might mistakenly read the nearby numbers on the tangent scale. If this was the case the inverse tangent (arc tangent) of his reading should approximate his true position. Let's do the arithmetic.

Date	Columbus's Latitude Reading	Arc Tangent of 1/100 Reading	Columbus's True Position
Nov. 2	42	22.8° N	21.1° N
Dec. 13	34	18.8° N	19.9° N

These are pretty good results and conform to the reasonable assumption that one could easily measure angles to within a couple of degrees with a quadrant.

On February 3, 1493, Columbus records observing Polaris to be very high, as at Cape Saint Vincent (37° N.). This observation sans quadrant or astrolabe is pretty close to the latitude calculated by McElroy to be the fleet's position that day, namely, 35° N.

I suspect that Columbus never resolved his difficulty with the quadrant during the course of the voyage. For in his letter of February 15, 1493, he notes that the new lands are twenty-six degrees from the equinoctial line.[39] This position corresponds closely with the plotted location on a portolan chart of his landfall relative to the Canaries. Hierro is in 27.7° N.

[37] R. T. Gunther, *Early Science in Oxford*, vol 2: *Astronomy* (reprint, London: Dawsons, 1967).
[38] This quadrant is pictured in *Quadrans astronomicus*, 1532, and is reprinted in Cecil Jane, trans., *The Journal of Christopher Columbus*, ed. L. A. Vigneras (New York, 1960), p. 73. The scales are labeled "umbra recta" and "umbra versa," but in the reverse of their proper positions.
[39] Jane, p. 200.

Notes to the *Journal* Sailing Directions, Tables 1, 2, and 3

In tables 1, 2, and 3, unmarked single course bearings are directly from the *Journal* and are translated into degrees. Bearings marked with a ? are educated guesses. Where multiple bearings are given, an average is taken. Leagues are the course distances, sometimes converted from mile figures in the *Journal*. Those marked with an "*" are guesses; those with a "+" were indicated in excess of the figure shown. The reckoned leagues are what Columbus told the crew on the outward voyage (a "0.0" means no entry available). Specific assumptions or interpretations are given in the discourse and below. Only the figures for degrees and leagues entered into the voyage calculations. The figures for hours were used for the calculations of drift in figure 3. In cases where drift is assumed not to be a factor (for example, around Isabela), or where the fleet position is based on an observed distance and bearing from land (for example, November 19), the hours figure is set to zero.

The notes that follow document the assumptions made to compile the sailing directions presented in table 1, 2, and 3. There are numerous instances where the *Journal* is imprecise, suspect, or silent on matters of bearings and distances, making it necessary to guess at an answer. In most cases a wrong guess is not crucial to the conclusions sought. However, providing a rationale for each guess makes the conclusions more credible to the reader and gives a basis for drawing independent conclusions, especially in crucial cases. The data for tables 1, 2, and 3 derive from the works of Jane and Sanz.[40] I have been guided by the efforts of McElroy, Morison, Fuson, and Fuson and Treftz, and cite their interpretations where they differ from my own.[41]

9/9	The implied course for the day is W. During the night the sailors steered badly, falling off W by N and WNW. I take the average W by N; McElroy and Fuson and Treftz take W for the whole day.
9/10	Implied course = W.
9/19	Implied course = W.
9/20	I average the bearings and distances of the *Journal*; McElroy has seven leagues WNW; Fuson and Treftz have twenty-five nautical miles WNW.
9/21	The fleet's tendency in these few days is to sail N of W when not on the western course. Thus I take the average of W and W by N; McElroy and Fuson and Treftz take W.
9/23	All agree on a NW average.
9/26	McElroy averages the day, 31 leagues SW; Fuson and Treftz have 10 leagues W plus 21 leagues SW. I interpret the text that the course was W except for about 3 hours in the afternoon, when they went SW to investigate the possibility of land under a cloud. I assumed a constant rate of speed for the day in allocating the 31 leagues to legs.
10/3	Implied course = W.

[40] Jane; Carlos Sanz, ed., *Diario de Colon*, (Madrid, 1962).
[41] McElroy; Morison, *Journals*; Robert Fuson, "The *Diario de Colón*: A Legacy of Poor Transcription, Translation, and Interpretation," this volume; Fuson and Treftz.

10/9	McElroy breaks the day into two legs: 5 leagues SW, 15 leagues W by N. Fuson and Treftz interpret three legs: 5 leagues SW, 4 leagues W by N and 11.5 leagues SW. The bearing of this last leg is omitted in the text. I interpret WSW because this is the course the morning of the 10th.
10/15	On the 13th Columbus resolved to go toward the SW and presumably followed through on the 15th. Fuson has them leaving on an approximately W by N course. It is not clear if Columbus sailed along the eastern shore of Santa Maria unless "y la otra que yo segui" means the "opposite," or south side of the island, and the fleet is coming from the NE.
10/16	Average of two distance estimates given in the *Journal*.
10/17	Columbus started at noon, following the coast of Fernandina NNW to about 2 leagues of the north end; they explored for 2 hours; continued to north end till sunset (?), when they turned back, sailing the length of the island during the night. I estimate they went 2 leagues in the first part of the afternoon for a total of 4 leagues NNW during a 4-hour period. On October 16, Columbus says he saw 20 leagues of Fernandina. Thus, I have taken the course resultant for the night of the 17th as 20 leagues SSE.
10/18	Purely a guess to cover the fact that Columbus rounded Fernandina into the NW quadrant.
10/19	These courses are based on the averages of an algebraic analysis of sailing times and bearings in the *Journal*, and the distance that one can see at sea from various heights. The result is that Isabela probably lies 13.7 to 18.7 leagues ESE of Columbus's starting point at Fernandina.
10/19–20	The *Journal* says that Isabela extends to the W from Cabo del Isleo 12 leagues to Cabo Hermosa where Columbus anchored the night of the 19th. The morning of the 20th he weighed anchor to steer NNE back to Cabo del Isleo, though his actual course was not direct due to light winds. Though he seems to rechristen Cabo Hermosa, as Cabo de la Laguna, Fuson interprets the latter as a cape beyond Cabo Hermosa. Since Columbus eventually gets back to Cabo del Isleo, a resultant course 12 leagues SSW and NNE is taken for the calculations.
10/24	The *Journal* is explicit only about the fleet's WSW course for some 30 hours. To be consistent with his course of 10/19 and to be 7 leagues SW of Fernandina at sunset 10/24, I calculate he made 7.5 leagues. Add 2 more for the stated headway during the night.
10/25–26	Apparently the ships made their way S along the islands for some 4 leagues and spent the 26th inching their way south the 6 leagues across Columbus Bank, reaching its southwestern margin at nightfall, where they anchored.
10/27–28	Sometime before sunset of the 27th, they sighted land but could not make shore before nightfall. I assume they jogged "a la corde" about 5 leagues offshore during the night and made this distance to the river San Salvador after dawn the 28th.
10/29	No indication is given of the fleet's activities at the river San Salvador for some 24 hours or more until they weighed anchor to sail W along the coast. They reached Rio de Mares at vespers. The text is in contention

here (see Fuson). On November 12 they sailed 18 leagues E by S to Cabo de Cuba. Cabo de Cuba may be read as being 10 leagues E of the river San Salvador. Allowing for a retarding current during the leg, I estimate Cabo de Mares is 6 leagues NW of the river San Salvador.

10/31   Reverse of course to Cabo de Palmas.

11/13   The fleet stood off Cabo de Cuba all night, adjusting the tacks to retain about the same position relative to land, a pass between two lofty mountains. They went 5 leagues SSW into a gulf.

11/14   The distance of the fleet offshore at dawn is omitted in the *Journal*. I estimate 5 leagues.

11/20   I assume Columbus was aware of the westerly current on the trip back to Puerto del Principe so that he would aim for a bearing somewhat east of the desired landfall, say SSW. He did not make it with sufficient time to anchor. During the night they went NE and N by E an unspecified distance. With a 0.5-knot current north of west they probably logged 7 leagues on each leg to come out 12 leagues NE to NE by E of Puerto de Principe.

11/21   I assume the calm cut relative progress about in half so that Columbus would only log about 4 leagues or less in 6 hours.

12/14   Missing distances are converted from map readings. Because of
1/15   westerly currents they are probably smaller than what Columbus logged, but which Las Casas omitted.

1/21   McElroy interpreted bearing as N by E; The *Journal* explicitly resolves course to NE by N.

1/26   I averaged the course leg as 10 leagues SE by E; McElroy has ESE.

1/27   I averaged the N by E and NE bearings of the *Journal*; McElroy has 16.6 leagues NE.

1/30   McElroy substitutes N by E, assuming the *Journal* is in error because the admiral gives no rationale for such an extreme change of course. However, this change puts the fleet too far north of its estimates on February 6 and February 10. Thus, I have retained the *Journal* bearing of S by E.

2/3   Bearing missing in *Journal*. But ENE is the general course these few days.

2/8   I averaged the E and E by S bearings of the *Journal*; McElroy takes 12 leagues SSE, translating "a la quarta del suests" as SSE.

2/9   McElroy omits the S by E leg.

2/10–13   The bearing E is not explicit in the *Journal*; McElroy has very slightly different distance estimates.

A New Approach to the Columbus Landfall

Arne B. Molander

Despite the recognition of Watlings Island as the San Salvador of Columbus by the Bahamas Parliament in 1926, and the imprimatur of S. E. Morison in 1942, there still remains considerable doubt as to the authenticity of this identification.[1] The continuing controversy was demonstrated by several papers presented at the 1981 meeting of the Society for the History of Discoveries, all of which postulated a landfall to the southeast of Watlings.[2] This paper argues for a northern route, with its landfall at the entrance to Northeast Providence Channel, two hundred miles northwest of Watlings Island. A comparison of my northern route with the generally accepted central route is shown in figure 1.

Any reconstruction of Columbus's route through the Bahamas must be detailed enough to address all of the available clues, not just those that are in congruence with the particular reconstruction. My methodology has been to compare all the clues in the *Journal* with the earliest available descriptions of the northern and central routes, aware that changing conditions since 1492 might have altered some of the congruences, for better or for worse. Because of its widespread availability, I have selected the Cecil Jane translation of the *Journal* as the primary data source upon which to base a comparative evaluation of the northern and central routes.[3] Nevertheless, in several instances I have referred back to the Las Casas holograph in pointing out examples of how the Cecil Jane translation was apparently adjusted to better accommodate the central route.[4] Using only these data sources, I have synthesized an alternative reconstruction which, in my opinion, fits the *Journal* clues much better than does the central route.

My arguments are presented in three parts: an analysis of Columbus's method of transatlantic navigation; an evaluation of both reconstructions against that portion of the *Journal* covering his journey through the Bahamas; and a brief discussion of the few independent contemporary data sources.

[1] Samuel Eliot Morison, *Admiral of the Ocean Sea*, 1-vol. ed. (Boston: Little, Brown, 1942).
[2] Robert Fuson, "The Search for Columbus' Guanahani — Navigation"; James E. Kelly, Jr., "In the Wake of Columbus on a Portolan Chart"; Robert Power, "The Search for Columbus' Guanahani — Cartographic and Pictorial Evidence."
[3] Cecil Jane, trans., *The Journal of Christopher Columbus*, ed. L. A. Vigneras, appendix by R. A. Skelton (New York: Bramhall House, 1960).

Columbus departed from Gomera in the Canary Islands on September 6, sailing due west along his departure latitude until October 7, or so he recorded in his *Journal*. On that date he acceded to the urging of Martín Alonzo Pinzón, captain of the *Pinta*, altering his course to west-southwest to follow the route of the migrating birds until the afternoon of October 11, when he resumed his course to the west for the final eight hours of his transatlantic voyage.

Although he never revealed his method of navigation, it was clearly his intent to sail due west from Gomera to his Oriental objective, Cipangu (Japan). For, when the daily distances and bearings recorded in his *Journal* are summed from September 6 to October 7, they describe his perceived location as about nine hundred leagues west of Gomera, while only six leagues north, an apparent bearing deviation of less than one-half degree from true west. His fixation with the Gomera latitude was revealed again on October 13, when, in trying to account for the skin coloration of the San Salvador natives, he meticulously described the island as lying "in one line from east to west with the island of Hierro in the Canaries," apparently overlooking the four-day jog to follow the birds.

Columbus's perceived location of the landfall can be obtained explicitly from the *Journal* by summation of his daily entries of distances and bearings for the entire ocean crossing. This procedure places his landfall along the south shore of North-east Providence Channel, halfway between its mouth and Nassau, if the length of his league is arbitrarily assumed to be three nautical miles. While other values of league length—such as the 3.18 nautical miles assumed by Morison—would change the distance between Gomera and his landfall, they could only slightly alter his north-south coordinate, as his perceived bearing from Gomera was only three degrees south of west. It is also true that Columbus was aided in his voyage by a pervasive half-knot current which would have been difficult for him to detect while out of sight of land.[5] This undetected western current would, of course, have made his actual bearing from Gomera even closer to true west, further reducing the likelihood of a Watlings Island landfall.

The actual location of his landfall is strongly dependent on whether Columbus navigated by latitude sailing or dead reckoning. The method of latitude sailing is more reliable than dead reckoning, since one of the ship's coordinates is always known, independent of errors in ship's speed and compass heading. In this technique, the navigator sails a fixed latitude by maintaining a constant elevation angle to the solar and stellar meridians. In this way, he knows he will eventually reach the far shore at the desired latitude, although speed errors may alter his time of arrival. The major limitation of latitude sailing is that it can only be utilized efficiently when

[4] Carlos Sanz, *Diario de Colón: Libro de la primera navegacion y descubrimiento de las Indias*, 2 vols. (Madrid: Graficas Yagües, 1962). Volume 1 is a holographic copy of the Las Casas manuscript. Volume 2 is a line-by-line transcription of the manuscript.

[5] When out of sight of land, a dipsey line could have detected the relative motion of surface currents, but unmeasurable underwater currents would have affected his perception of absolute current velocity. For example, the September 13 *Journal* entry records that the westerly north Equatorial Current was "against them."

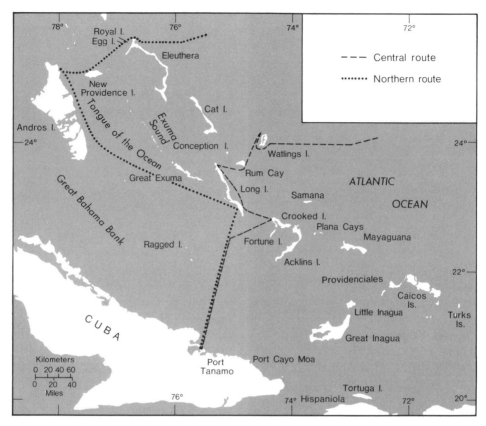

Figure 1: The central and northern routes which Columbus might have followed on his first voyage to the New World. The author advocates the northern route. Morison advocates the central route.

the objective lies at the same latitude as the point of departure, as was apparently the case with Columbus.[6]

In dead reckoning, compass headings are combined with average speed estimates to obtain the increments of ship's position. The advantage of this form of navigation is that it is applicable to any direction of sail, not just those along a fixed latitude, an attribute of no apparent use to Columbus in his quest for Cipangu. The disadvantage of dead reckoning is that it can be dangerously inaccurate, being subject to both speed estimate errors and compass variation. It was this inaccuracy which apparently led Columbus's contemporaries to rely on latitude sailing when venturing out on their first Atlantic crossings. Morison himself cites the 1497 performance of John Cabot, who employed latitude sailing to reach Newfoundland from Ireland with only four miles of error.[7] Again, in 1534, Jacques Cartier used the same method of navigation to reach Newfoundland from Saint-Malo, France, with only three miles of error.[8] Morison rightly marvels at these navigation exploits, but doesn't give any indication of what performance would normally be expected in latitude sailing.[9]

Thus, it is not surprising that G. J. Marcus gives detailed arguments on why Columbus used latitude sailing and summarizes his chapter on navigation with the unqualified declaration that "it cannot be too strongly emphasized that latitude sailing was the underlying principle of all ocean navigation down to the invention of the chronometer."[10] Morison, on the other hand, publicly argued that dead reckoning was the navigation method of Columbus, in order to explain how compass errors might have caused him to drift ninety miles south of the course described in his *Journal*. But, in 1972, Morison answered my query, responding, "Of course Columbus was attempting latitude sailing, but his Journal shows very clearly that he changed course towards the end, to follow the birds."[11] Taking this statement at face value, Morison is clearly supporting my thesis that Columbus used latitude sailing to enter the Bahamas through Northeast Providence Channel. I believe that he employed this method of navigation because it would be, according to the contemporary examples cited by Morison, from twenty to thirty times as accurate as dead reckoning for reaching an objective due west of Gomera.

During his month-long stay on Hierro, Columbus would have had ample opportunity to observe that the bright star Duhbe traced its diurnal circle around the

---

[6] Morison, *The European Discovery of America: The Southern Voyages* (New York: Oxford University Press, 1974). The Martin Behaim globe, reproduced on pp. 32–33, shows the twenty-eighth parallel slicing through the Canary Islands and northern Cipangu.

[7] Morison, *The European Discovery of America: The Northern Voyages* (New York: Oxford University Press, 1971), p. 174.

[8] Ibid., p. 346.

[9] Latitude sailing requires no knowledge of absolute latitude, only detection of latitude differences. Thus, the large refraction errors on the horizon reported by Bowditch, *The American Practical Navigator* (Washington D.C.: U.S. Government Printing Office, 1977), are of no concern in latitude sailing. However, navigation errors are introduced by random fluctuations in this refraction angle. Bowditch estimates the magnitude of these random variations at from two to three minutes of arc, tantalizingly close to the navigation accuracies achieved by Cabot and Cartier.

[10] G. J. Marcus, *The Conquest of the North Atlantic* (New York: Oxford University Press, 1981), p. 118. On this same page, Marcus claims that latitude sailing was "practised by Christopher Columbus on his voyage of 1492–3." This claim is buttressed by detailed reading of sailing directions in the sagas both before and after the introduction of the compass to the Northmen in the thirteenth century.

[11] Letter from S. E. Morison to A. B. Molander, 17 November 1972.

north celestial pole, tangent to a line 3 degrees above the northern horizon when 0.5 degrees refraction are added. Thus, the heavens provided him with an accurate and simple reference for maintaining 28 degrees of latitude by watching the Big Dipper take its nightly scoop from the North Atlantic. For the apparent elevation angle of its corner star, Duhbe, would have been reduced by half at Morison's inferred latitude of 26.5 degrees.[12] Even if Columbus had navigated by dead reckoning, rather than availing himself of this magnificent stellar navigation system, is it conceivable that he would have failed to notice on October 7 that Duhbe's diurnal circle was now brushing the horizon? According to Marcus, the Viking unit of elevation angle was the "half-wheel," or half the solar diameter.[13] It is hard to believe that Columbus would have failed to detect stellar angle changes at the northern and southern horizons which were equivalent to *five* of these Viking units.

Two additional *Journal* clues with possible potential for determining Columbus's method of navigation are his frequent references to "much weed" through October 3, and the sighting of great flocks of birds beginning on October 7. According to Morison's reconstruction, the admiral was about five hundred miles south-southwest of Bermuda on October 7, while my reconstruction places him about the same distance from that island, but in a southwest direction.[14] As the flock "passed from the direction of the north to the southwest," my northern route location is in better accord with a possible migratory flyover of Bermuda. Also, Morison's map shows Columbus in much weed while outward bound on October 3, but places the first sighting of weed on the return voyage 150 miles north of this supposed October 3 location.

Finally, there is the admiral's unexplained decision to return to his primary course (west) at sunset, about eight hours prior to the landfall sighting. If his decision was based on a specific latitude objective in Cipangu, then neither navigation candidate has an advantage. And, if his decision was based on observations of sea birds returning from their daytime feeding areas, then neither candidate has a currently measurable advantage, despite the much larger nesting area and more substantial vegetation of Eleuthera. However, if his decision was based on the identification of land by the afternoon buildup of stationary cumulus clouds over warm surface areas, a technique expertly exercised by Polynesian navigators, then Eleuthera is a much more likely landfall candidate than is Watlings Island. This is because the thousands of square miles of land and shallow water at Eleuthera do build up substantial afternoon cumulus, as does all of the Grand Bahama Bank. The average cloud tops of 5,000 to 8,000 feet systematically measured over the tropical

[12] My hypothetical explanation for the latitude-sailing precision achieved by Cabot and Cartier requires, first, a bright (first or second magnitude) star easily related to a prominent nearby constellation; second, a declination angle from the north celestial pole that will cause its diurnal circle to be nearly tangent to, but above, the horizon; and, third, an azimuth angle that would cause the tangency to occur between 10:00 P.M. and 2:00 P.M., that is, at the hours of maximum visibility. The first magnitude star, Capella, is well placed for the early summer crossings of Cabot, Cartier, and the Vikings. There are only two suitable constellations for crossings between the equator and forty degrees north latitude. It is interesting that Columbus made the best possible use of the Big Dipper (both in choices of latitude and sailing season), and that Verrazano's February crossing at thirty-four degrees was a perfect utilization of Cassiopeia.
[13] Marcus, p. 110.
[14] Morison, *Admiral of the Ocean Sea*, map facing p. 222.

Pacific are probably representative of cumulus clouds in the Bahamas.[15] At that height, the clouds would have been well above his horizon late that afternoon at a distance of seventy miles from Eleuthera. On the other hand, Watlings Island is a solitary outpost lying at least fifty miles east of the large cloud-producing areas of the bank, whose cloud tops would have had to exceed ten thousand feet to be clearly visible at 120 miles. On the northern route, Columbus probably would have seen a broad cumulus buildup extending from horizon to horizon, indicative of the mainland or a long island. On the central route, he would have only seen the buildup from Watlings extending over an azimuth angle of about ten degrees, possibly difficult to distinguish from scattered ocean cloud cover.

In summary, the first and primary leg of his crossing is better explained by the assumption of latitude sailing than by dead reckoning, if we are to believe the accuracies that Morison claims for Cabot and Cartier, his personal acknowledgment to me on Columbus's method of navigation, the detailed research of Marcus, and the oblique reference to the latitude of San Salvador made by Columbus on October 13. The northern route also has a slightly better explanation for his second leg to follow the birds, and the final return to a western course, although more study is needed in both areas.

I will now proceed to an evaluation of the alternative routes through the Bahamas on a day-by-day basis from their separate landfalls to their conjunction at the Columbus Bank. Each day's discussion begins with a paragraph condensing all *Journal* entries that could influence evaluation of the candidates. In addition to these excerpts from the Cecil Jane translation, I have included a few Spanish phrases from the holograph whenever I have felt that Jane's rendering is suspect.

Friday, October 12

The landfall was first sighted by Rodrigo de Triana, a sailor on the Pinta, "two hours after midnight . . . at a distance of about two leagues." The fleet jogged until daylight, at which time "they reached a small island [*isleta*] of the Lucayos, which is called in the language of the Indians 'Guanahaní.' Immediately they saw naked people . . . [and] when they had landed, they saw very green trees and much water and fruit of various kinds." The admiral "took possession of the island . . . [and] soon many people of the island gathered there." At this point begins an apparently verbatim transcript of the remaining twelve days in the Bahamas. Inquiring as to the cause of the Indians' wounds, he is told "that people came from other islands, which are near, and wished to capture them." But Columbus contradicted them by writing: "I believed and still believe that they come here from the mainland to take them for slaves." He then closed his first entry in the New World with the surprising observation that "I saw no beast of any kind in this island, except parrots."

A major problem with the central route is the use of the term *isleta* in Columbus's very first reference to his discovery. His exact usage of this term can be gauged by examining his applications of it to fifteen identifiable islets along the north coasts of

---

[15] Joanne S. Malkus and Herbert Riehl, *Cloud Structure and Distributions over the Tropical Pacific Ocean* (Berkeley and Los Angeles: University of California Press, 1964).

Cuba and Hispaniola, none of which is more than two miles in area. The one island along the Hispaniola route that comes closest to matching the sixty square miles of Watlings in size is Tortuga, which has an area of seventy-two square miles. Columbus always referred to this island as an *isla*, twice reinforcing the definition with the adjective *grande*.[16] Cecil Jane must have rebelled at calling Watlings an islet, so he improperly translated the term as small island. That he knew better is shown by his seventeen precise translations out of the twenty times that the term appears in the *Journal*.

For evaluation of the reference to parrots, we can turn to *The Bahama Islands*, a comprehensive survey of the natural history of the Bahama Islands published early in this century. Unfortunately, Shattuck's work is of little help as it places the Bahama parrot on Abaco, Acklin, Fortune and Inagua.[17] Only a slight advantage for the northern route results from the recent decision to establish a haven for this threatened species within its natural habitat in the forests of Abaco. But it is clear which candidate better fits the description of "no land animals," for the Smithsonian Institution attributes eight reptile species to Watlings Island, including the giant iguana.[18] In marked contrast, it reports *none* for either Egg or Royal Islands, the adjoining islets on the northwest coast of Eleuthera, which taken together are my candidate for the San Salvador of Columbus. Considering the eagerness with which the Indians demonstrated their meager possessions to Columbus and his men, it is difficult to imagine how the *Journal* could have failed to record the impressive presence of the giant iguana, if Watlings Island had indeed been his landfall.

Of less certainty is the answer to the question of why the landfall was detected at a mere six miles range, when the moon was only five days past full and positioned over the shoulder of Rodrigo so as to reflect its light off the limestone rocks of Watlings.[19] Even without the tree cover that the central route advocates attribute to fifteenth-century Watlings, these 140-foot hills would have been a prominent target for a sharp-eyed sailor who had been promised a lifetime sinecure for their discovery. The horizons can be calculated as thirteen miles for the barren hills, and at least eight miles for Rodrigo in the rigging of the *Pinta*, giving a total detection range of about twenty miles in daylight. This estimate is confirmed by *The Yachtsman's Guide to the Bahamas*, the bible of modern-day mariners, which notes the exceptional clarity of the local atmosphere.[20] This question may not be worth much further study since, even if the longer detection range of Watlings's hills can be shown for similar lighting conditions, the central route could be rescued by sliding Morison's suggested approach course about ten miles south.

Turning to the northern route, the six-mile detection range is certainly consistent with the low elevations of Bridge Point and Man Island at the north end of Eleuthera. And, the two hundred acres of Egg Island closely match the size of the Hispaniola "isletas." Also, Egg Island is the first land that would have been

---

[16] Sanz, entries for December 11 and 15.

[17] George Burbank Shattuck, *The Bahama Islands* (New York: Macmillan, 1905), p. 363.

[18] William P. Mclean, Richard Kellner, and Howard Dennis, *Island Lists of West Indian Amphibians and Reptiles*, Smithsonian Herpetological Information Service, No. 40 (1977).

[19] Morison, *Admiral of the Ocean Sea*, p. 225.

[20] Harry Kline, ed., *The Yachtsman's Guide to the Bahamas*, 22d ed. (Tropic Isle Publishers, 1972), p. 10.

accessible to the fleet at the entrance to Northeast Providence Channel that Friday morning, because of the reefs that front the north shore of Eleuthera (see figure 2). Finally, it may be significant that Las Casas refrains from identifying the first sighting as Guanahaní, which was not reached for at least four hours of jogging in a strong east wind with the mainsail up.

Three other points also favor the northern route. One is the flora and water, which exist on Egg and Royal islands in greater abundance than they do on Watlings. In fact, Didiez Burgos, in his study of the landfall issue, claims that there is no sweet water on Watlings and that the island would not have been capable of supporting an Indian population.[21] The second point is that the reported slaving attacks from nearby islands would have been a lot more feasible for narrow canoes operating on the Bahama Bank near Egg Island. The third point can be inferred from the absence of any quantitative dimensional estimates of San Salvador. This is the only one of Columbus's four Bahama discoveries that doesn't have at least one length measurement, and usually more. The explanation for this omission on the northern route is that either Egg Island was too small to warrant an estimate, or that Columbus found it difficult to characterize the relationship of Egg and Royal islands with the mélange of islets and sandbars on the bank. No such problem exists with Watlings, which is simply four leagues in length and two leagues in width.

On the basis of the meager clues in the *Journal*, I have given a significant advantage to the northern route, primarily because Watlings is not an *isleta* and because its awesome giant iguanas were not reported by Columbus.

Saturday, October 13

At daybreak, the Indians "came to the ship in boats, which are made of a tree trunk . . . and large, so that in some forty or forty-five men came, . . . and they travel wonderfully fast." Columbus reasoned that they were the color of Canarians, "since this is in one line from east to west with the island of Hierro." The Indians communicated the idea that "going to the south or going round the island to the south, there is a king who . . . possessed much gold . . . [and] that there was land to the south and to the south-west and to the north-west." Columbus "resolved to wait until the afternoon of the following day, and after that to leave for the south-west . . . to seek the gold and precious stones." Then turning his attention to San Salvador, Columbus described it as follows: "This island is fairly large and very flat; the trees are very green and there is much water. In the center of it, there is a very large lake [*laguna*]; there is no mountain, and all is so green." He added that "cotton . . . grows here in this island; . . . here also is produced that gold. . . . But . . . I wish to go and see if I can make the island of Cipangu."

Looking first at the major clues, Watlings Island lies 4 degrees south of Columbus's emphatic description of the latitude that San Salvador supposedly shared with Hierro, while Egg and Royal islands are only 2.5 degrees south of Hierro, all of this difference imposed by the four-day jog to the west-southwest suggested by Pinzón.

---

[21] Ramon J. Didiez Burgos, *Guanahani y Mayaguain* (Santo Domingo: Editora Cultural Dominicana, 1974), p. 413.

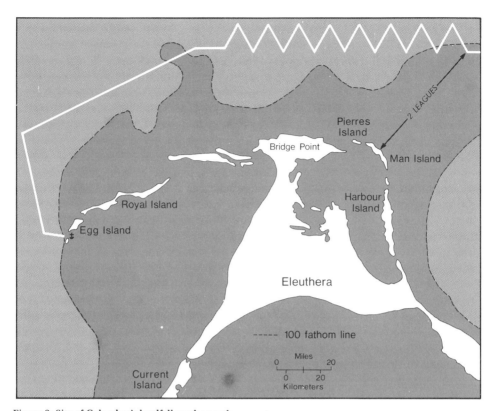

Figure 2: Site of Columbus's landfall on the northern route.

While this discrepancy may tell us something about the mind-set of the admiral, objective scoring leads to only a marginal advantage for the northern route.

The second major clue, the Indians' alternative sailing directions to the land of gold, is nonsensical from his supposed Watlings Island anchorage at Fernandez Bay, which has a direct deep-water route to Cuba. On the other hand, these alternative directions fit perfectly for an anchorage off the south beach of Egg Island because, while the Indian canoes could easily traverse the direct shallow-water route across the Bahama Bank, some of the more perceptive Tainos could well have suggested an indirect route around Eleuthera or New Providence Island in water deep enough to handle his imposing fleet. The third major clue, defining the directions of nearby lands, fits both candidates (and almost every other island in the eastern Bahamas). Watlings does have a clear-cut advantage on the fourth major clue, which describes San Salvador as "fairly large" in apparent contradiction to the previous use of *isleta*. But, even here it is at least possible to understand how Columbus might have used these contradictory terms on the northern route, yesterday applying *isleta* to his Egg Island landfall, and today using *isla* to describe the Egg and Royal combination or possibly Eleuthera itself.

The final important clue, and the only one that has attracted much attention from earlier analysts, is the description of the *laguna* in the center of the island. It is interesting to observe that of the eight times that this term is used in the *Journal*, this is the only time that Cecil Jane incorrectly translated it as "lake." Columbus demonstrated a distinction between *lago* and *laguna*, once using the former term while on the island of Cuba.[22] Thus, it appears that Jane may have been influenced by the prevailing acceptance of the central route and an awareness that the multiple lakes on Watlings do not fit the classic definition of lagoons.[23] Watlings Island fails to match the *Journal* description in quantity as well as in kind, for U.S. Hydrographic Chart 26281 shows not one, but dozens of independent lakes on Watlings, several of which are now interconnected by man-made canals. In contrast, the center of Egg Island is, in fact, covered by a single large lagoon, fed from Northeast Providence Channel at high tide and occupying about twenty-five percent of the islet's total area. Only in the important factor of absolute size does the water on Watlings better fit the "laguna" clue.

The other clues tend to favor the northern route because of its greater rainfall, more abundant vegetation, and its proximity to the forests of Andros and the little Bahama Bank, the most likely sources for their dugout canoes.[24] The *Yachtsman's Guide* tells us that the English named nearby Spanish Wells for the sweetest water in the Bahamas, and even today Eleuthera has plenty of good water.[25] In summary, each route has a distinct advantage on about one and a half of the major clues. As the northern route is favored by the minor clues, I am inclined to give it a slight edge on Columbus's first full day in the New World.

---

[22] Sanz, entry for November 3.

[23] *Webster's Third New International Dictionary* defines *lagoon* as "a shallow sound, channel, pond, or lake near or communicating with the sea."

[24] Meteorological Office, Nassau, *Rainfall Distribution over the Bahamas* (1971); these data show that the rainfall in the northwestern Bahamas averages more than twice the rainfall in the southeastern Bahamas. Shattuck, pp. 185–270, p. 223.

[25] *Yachtsman's Guide*, p. 183.

Sunday, October 14

On Sunday morning, Columbus "ordered the ship's boat and the boats of the caravels to be made ready, and I went along the island in a north-northeasterly direction, to see the other part, which lay to the east" to explore the landfall firsthand. Beckoned ashore by the natives, who "brought us water, . . . I feared to do so, seeing a great reef of rocks which encircled the whole of that island, while within there is deep water and a harbour large enough for all the ships of Christendom, the entrance to which is very narrow. It is true that inside the reef there are some shoals, but the sea is no more disturbed than the water in a well." Looking for a suitable fortress site, Columbus "saw a piece of land, which is formed like an island although it is not one, on which there were six houses; it could be converted into an island in two days." Before returning to his ships, he noted "the loveliest group of trees that I have ever seen . . . near the said islet." Leaving the anchorage, "I saw so many islands that I could not decide to which I would go first. . . . Finally I sought for the largest and resolved to steer for it, which I am doing. It is five leagues away from the island of San Salvador, and of the others, some are more and some less distant."

Watlings Island fits these detailed descriptions no better than dozens of other randomly selected islands of the Bahamas, and in several important particulars is a total mismatch with the *Journal*. First, there is the matter of the grueling twenty-four-mile rowing circuit imposed by the selection of Fernandez Bay as his anchorage and Graham's Harbor as his objective.[26] Not only is this distance impossible for small boats fending off the surf and the friendly Arawaks, but also the precise NNE direction can't be achieved from Fernandez Bay. This raises the question of why Columbus did not use the speed of his fleet or the convenience of a land party to explore the "other part of the island" which the Indians certainly must have described to him during the Saturday parleys. Most of his subsequent explorations were accomplished by sail, and he surely demonstrated in Cuba that he was not afraid to send out a land party among these docile inhabitants.

But the most damning limitation of Watlings lies in the character of the "puerto" that was the objective of the rowing expedition. While this was the only body of water seen in the Bahamas that rated this recognition by Columbus, he used this term over fifty times each on Cuba and Hispaniola, invariably to describe the flask-shaped harbors that are characteristic of these shores. Although he sailed by many shoal areas similar to Graham's Harbor, he never dignified them with the term *puerto*. For example, when forced to anchor on January 4 between Santo Tomas and Monte Cristi, he carefully refrained from describing this somewhat protected shoal area as a *puerto*. Morison's selection of the exposed shoal area on the northeast corner of Watlings as the marvelous "puerto" with a narrow entrance is unjustified, both by casual inspection of charts and by careful study of the admiral's restrictive application of this term.

As for being as quiet as water in a well, this deficiency of Graham's Harbor is revealed by the *Yachtsman's Guide*, which observes that "there are really no safe

[26] This would have been a more appropriate undertaking for the long canoes of the Tainos that "travel wonderfully fast," according to the *Journal*. On October 28, the *Journal* records that it is a ten days' journey for the ships of the Grand Kahn from the mainland to his Cuban landfall. The actual distance is about two hundred miles, according to Morison's reconstruction.

harbors on [Watlings]" and that Graham's Harbor "always seems to carry a surge through it."[27] On October 14, 1492, Graham's Harbor would have almost certainly carried a surge, exposed as it was to the easterlies that blew with a vengeance on October 11 and were continuing to blow on October 15. Finally, are we to believe that Columbus would have failed to note that this fortress candidate was actually the mole of the harbor that he was planning to defend, and that some useful purpose would have been served by separating the mole from Watlings?

While the match of Sunday's clues with Egg and Royal islands leaves some troublesome questions, the basic congruence is very much better than for Watlings, and more sense can be made of the admiral's intentions. First, boats were the only sensible mode of exploration on the northern route, because the two hundred yards of wading between the two islands would have been inconvenient for a shore party an the uncharted shallows between his anchorage and the Royal Island harbor would have been dangerous for his ships. Thus restricted to exploration by boat, the admiral could have comfortably made the seven-mile circuit in less than five hours, leaving ample time to explore "the whole of that harbor."

From his Egg Island anchorage, Columbus could have sighted the course for his boats along the east coast of the island on exactly a north-northeast heading towards Royal Island, the "other part of the island," which swings out towards the east on the horizon as shown in Figure 2. The only question is whether Cecil Jane's translation of "la otra parte, que era de la parte del Leste," should be interpreted literally to mean "the other part" rather than just "the other side," as elected by the advocates of Watlings. Personally, I favor the rigid construction since Columbus describes the reef of rocks encircling the whole of "aquella isla" rather than "dicha isleta," as he would had he been referring to the islet that was his landfall. In fact, later this same day Columbus does use the expression, "junto a la dicha isleta" in describing the "loveliest groups of trees" "near the said islet." There is today on the south end of Royal Island a large grove of palm trees directly across the shallows from Egg Island, which I have claimed is the *isleta* of Columbus.

Two of the three harbor descriptors are apparently contradictory, for it would be impossible to have a harbor "large enough for all the ships of Christendom," while at the same time its surface was "no more disturbed than the water in a well." I can imagine both clues being almost satisfied simultaneously only if the harbor had a slender configuration, with its long dimension being oriented far enough from the wind direction to minimize wave buildup on its surface. Royal Island certainly meets these criteria, as it is one and a half miles long by a quarter mile wide at its extremities, with its long axis oriented at least forty-five degrees away from the prevailing trade winds. The *Yachtsman's Guide* enthuses over this harbor, describing it as "a beautiful and almost landlocked harbor which affords protection in almost any weather."[28] In January 1981 I examined and photographed this marvelous harbor, observing that its surface hardly had a ripple with a norther blowing across it. Having a smooth surface and the narrow entrance described by Columbus (actually there is a second and smaller one at the eastern end which might have escaped

[27] *Yachtsman's Guide*, p. 257.
[28] Ibid., p. 178.

his notice), the troublesome part of this clue for Royal Island harbor is the description of its size. At the most, the three miles of protected shoreline could be expected to handle three hundred ships, certainly far less than "all the ships of Christendom."[29] The northern route also offers a better explanation of why the Indians waited until Sunday to offer water to the thirsty Spaniards. The answer may be that there are no wells on Egg Island, while British admiralty charts from the mid-eighteenth century show a well on Royal Island, a few hundred yards from the peninsula that might have sheltered the six Arawak families. No such explanation exists for Watlings, an undivided and arid island, if we are to believe Didiez Burgos and the absence of wells on the British admiralty charts.

Finally, the northern route might explain why Columbus left his safe anchorage at San Salvador during the afternoon, as previously announced. If he had really been anchored at Watlings Island, what motivation would he have had for departing before Monday morning, choosing instead to risk his fleet in these uncharted waters, by simply standing offshore and waiting for sunrise? In contrast, there is strong motivation for an afternoon departure from Egg Island, because he could have used the half-knot tidal flow to help ease him off the bank and into Northeast Providence Channel. I measured that flow in October 1981 and determined that the maximum rate of outflow for Columbus would have occurred about 3:00 P.M. He realized on Saturday that if he waited for daybreak Monday, he would have had the tidal flow working against him most of the morning.

In summary, this day of personal exploration by the admiral gives the northern route a strong advantage over the central route. Not only does it have a beautiful harbor in the right direction and at a reasonable rowing distance from the anchorage, but it also has many islands within view, some of which are closer and some of which are farther than five leagues distant. It has a peninsula large enough for six families with a well conveniently nearby, and a tidal flow at the anchorage that would have explained why he chose to leave San Salvador in the afternoon.

Monday, October 15

Columbus "stood off that night, fearing to come to anchor before daylight," and at daybreak "hoisted sail. And as the island was more than five leagues distant, being rather about seven, and the tide was against me, it was about midday when I arrived at the island. I found that the side which lies toward the island of San Salvador runs north and south for a distance of five leagues, and that the other side, which I followed, runs east and west for more than ten leagues. And as from this island I saw another and larger to the west, I set sail to go all that day until night, since otherwise I should not have been able to have reached the westerly point [cabo]. To this island I gave the name Santa Maria de la Concepción, and about sunset, I anchored off the said point [cabo]." Not wishing "to pass any island without taking possession of it, . . . at dawn, I went ashore in the armed boats and landed."

[29] On the island of Cuba, Columbus describes the Mar de Nuestra Senora (Tanamo Bay?) as having "room for all the ships of Spain," and Rio del Sol (Puerto Sama?) as having "room for any ships whatever." These and other Cuban data points are currently questionable, as Tanamo Bay is actually several times larger than Puerto Sama.

As Columbus only sailed along one coast of this island, he must have derived its north-south dimension from Indian sketches, which would certainly have been more accurate in proportion than in scale. My candidate for this island, New Providence, has the exact east-west orientation, and is twenty-one miles long by seven miles wide, a closer congruence than any other island in the Bahamas, if it is assumed that Columbus used the same land league, 2.29 nautical miles, that his sovereigns used for their land grants. Although originally drawn to this argument by Morison's invention of an even shorter land league to rationalize his candidate, Rum Cay, I now believe that Columbus used the same league for both land and sea measurements. For the remainder of this paper, I will use the 3.18 nautical mile sea league described by Morison, while recognizing that a six percent shorter league actually fits the Atlantic crossing and the Bahama odyssey with greater precision.[30]

Figure 3 shows my reconstruction of Monday's voyage from Egg Island to the west end of New Providence, where Columbus anchored for the night. Safely off the anchorage with Sunday afternoon's tide, he established this morning's course to the southwest in accordance with Saturday's announced intention. This shortcut, actually on a heading of about 215 degrees, took him directly across the deep waters of the channel, returning him to the bank four miles north of the eastern end of Rose Island. Without adequate communication to distinguish the bank from the islands, he might have interpreted the eastern end of Rose Island as part of the Indian sketch of New Providence. He did not arrive here, exactly seven leagues from the Egg Island anchorage, until noon because of the countertides flowing off the bank and out of the Tongue of the Ocean. The *Yachtsman's Guide* shows a strong easterly set adjacent to the Egg Island anchorage which could well have impeded his headway through most of the morning.[31]

Rose Island is the easternmost of several long and overlapping cays that stretch out to the east from New Providence Island, along the south shore of North East Providence Channel. The major ones are Paradise Island, Salt Cay, Athol Island, and Rose Island. Although there are at least two anchorages on the north coast of Rose Island, a lookout in the rigging would have easily spotted the Blue Hills below Nassau from there, giving Columbus the preferred alternative of anchoring at "the larger island to the west."[32] Determined to make the anchorage at its west end by dark, he set sail for its westerly cape, arriving at sunset and giving this larger island the name Santa Maria.

The above scenario is in contradiction with the usual interpretation that the larger island to the west is actually his third discovery, Fernandina, viewed from the *eastern* end of his second discovery, Santa Maria. But careful reading of the paragraph extracted from his *Journal* makes it seem that the westerly cape where he anchored that Monday night was part of the larger island immediately to the west, Santa Maria and not Fernandina. One confirmation of this thesis is that Columbus recorded eighteen leagues from the sighting of the larger island at noon Monday until the landing at Fernandina on Wednesday morning. It is questionable whether noontime cumulus over Fernandina would have been so easy to interpret at a range

[30] Morison, *Admiral of the Ocean Sea*, p. 239.
[31] *Yachtsman's Guide*, p. 181.
[32] Ibid., map on p. 85.

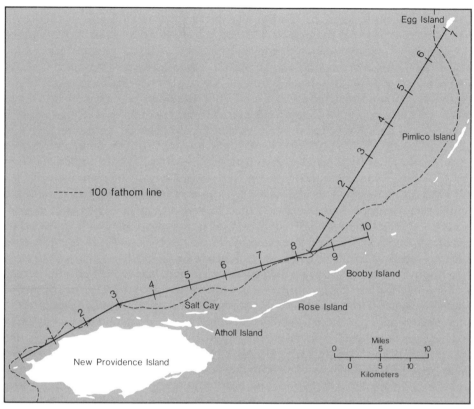

Figure 3: Journey between the San Salvador and Santa Maria anchorages on the northern route. Distances shown are based upon Morison's sea league of 3.18 nautical miles.

of 57 nautical miles. A second indicator that he recognized a multiple-island concept for Santa Maria is that the first *Journal* entry on Tuesday refers to "the islands of Santa Maria," clearly indicating their multiplicity.[33]

The total distance from the east end of Rose Island to his West Bay anchorage off the west end of New Providence Island is about eight and a half leagues. Once he decided to forego an anchorage at Rose Island, Columbus was committed to a late and risky anchorage at West Bay, for the *Yachtsman's Guide* tells us that "there are few anchorages around the coast of New Providence of interest to yachtsmen with the exception, perhaps, of West Bay."[34] The guide shows only this anchorage and two in the narrow channel between Paradise and New Providence islands, not a likely place for Columbus to attempt upwind in a tide that reaches two and a half knots.[35]

While the northern route offers a logical explanation for each of Monday's *Journal* entries, the central route is almost a total failure. The first problem occurs with Columbus's uncertainty as to which of the many islands he would visit first. Although Sunday's *Journal* entry clearly implied otherwise, Morison has this dilemma arise *after* the departure from the San Salvador anchorage, fully fifteen miles out to sea.[36] He would then have us believe that this experienced sailor somehow mistook the hillocks of Rum Cay for a string of six islands whose thirty-degree azimuth spread was sufficient to cause him mental anguish in the selection of a course! Even granting the above, we are now faced with the question of why it took Columbus six hours to traverse a distance that his ships had covered in little more than one on the day prior to the landfall, and at an average speed that was less than half that maintained by his awkward rowboats during the previous day's exploration of San Salvador. Morison implicitly attributes to Columbus the forbearance to endure this painfully slow progress without blaming it on what must have been very weak winds indeed, when Columbus was actually pointing his finger at the tide. The *Journal*'s mention of countertides is in fact the death knell for the central route, for there is no measurable tide in the open ocean between Watlings and Rum Cay, and the half-knot current that flows in that region would actually have been somewhat helpful in his course towards Rum Cay.[37]

Another major problem with the central route is that it falls far short of the *Journal* distance, being barely twelve leagues from the Fernandez Bay anchorage to the west end of Rum Cay. Even at that, Morison has Columbus making almost half that distance during the late afternoon of the preceding day, leaving only seven leagues for him to cover all day Monday. That seven leagues includes one and a half leagues along its south shore, far short of the dimensions described by Columbus. Morison attempts to rescue Rum Cay as a viable candidate for Santa Maria by inventing a "land league" of one and a half nautical miles.[38] Assuming this unjustified league

[33] Oliver Dunn has pointed out to me that, while Cecil Jane has translated the phrase as "the islands of Santa Maria," the holograph actually shows a plural article with a singular noun.

[34] *Yachtsman's Guide*, p. 76.

[35] Ibid., p. 76.

[36] Morison, *Admiral of the Ocean Sea*, pp. 238–39.

[37] U.S. Naval Hydrographic Office, *Sailing Directions for the West Indies*, vol. 1: *Bermuda, Bahamas, and Greater Antilles*, H. O. Pub. 21, 3d ed. (1958), p. 26.

[38] Morison, *Admiral of the Ocean Sea*, p. 239.

length would still leave Rum Cay less than two thirds the length described by Columbus.

Also, in order to avoid Pinder Reef at the northwest corner of Rum Cay, Morison assumes that Columbus sailed along the south coast. This detour introduces two new problems for the central route. First, it is now necessary to have Columbus sail along both the eastern and southern coasts of Rum Cay, while the *Journal* only mentions the latter. More importantly, this reconstruction has the admiral passing by the best anchorage on Rum Cay in the midafternoon, in order to barely reach a questionable anchorage at dusk. Why would Columbus, in his expressed intention to claim the islands for Spain, have sailed past protected Port Nelson, especially when he would have been laboring at one and a half knots in an (unmentioned) dying wind? While older editions of the *Yachtsman's Guide* show a "temporary anchorage" in seven fathoms of exposed water off the western end of Rum Cay, it has been deleted from recent editions because of "the nearby reefs and deep water so close at hand . . . [and] the persistent surge there."[39] The hazards of anchoring there in shifting winds would have been compounded for a fleet of three vessels. I suspect that the only reason that this exposed location was ever recognized as a "temporary anchorage" on late nineteenth-century British admiralty charts was because of the belief that Columbus had supposedly used it in 1492.

There is one more matter to consider here, and that is Cecil Jane's insistence on rendering *cabo* as "point" whenever it suits the needs of the central route. The correct translation as "cape" fits Lyford Cay at the West Bay anchorage of New Providence Island. If Rum Cay had been Columbus's Santa Maria, it is likely that he would have written "punta" for Sandy Point, or "cabo de isla" for the western end of the island.

In summary, New Providence Island is much closer to the size described by Columbus, logically explains "the larger island to the west," and has the distribution of anchorage locations implied by the *Journal* and the tidal flow that would have impeded his progress that morning. Rum Cay fails all of these tests, and imposes the need to assume that his ship's speed was half that of his rowboats that raced around Watlings the day before. I conclude that New Providence Island has an overwhelming advantage over Rum Cay as a candidate for the island of Santa Maria de la Concepción.

Tuesday, October 16

After meeting the Indians of Santa Maria, Columbus wrote, "the wind blew more strongly across from the south-east, [and] I was unwilling to wait and went back to the ship." To the caravel *Niña*, "there now came from another direction [*del otro cabo*] another small canoe. . . . I departed from the islands of Santa Maria de Concepción when it was already about midday . . . with a south-east wind that veered southerly, in order to pass over to the other island. It is very large." Before sailing he estimated that "from this island of Santa Maria to the other was some nine leagues, from east to

[39] *Yachtsman's Guide*, p. 259. Letter from Harry Kline (editor of *Yachtsman's Guide*) to A. B. Molander, 4 May 1980.

west, and all this side of the island runs from north-west to south-east. It seems that on this side the coast may extend for twenty-eight leagues or more." (These measurements were adjusted slightly the next day, following his firsthand observations.) On the crossing, he found a man in a canoe "in the middle of the channel [*golfo*] between these two islands, that of Santa Maria and this large island, to which I gave the name *Fernandina*. . . . Because I navigated all that day in a calm, . . . I could not arrive in time to see the bottom in order to anchor in a clear place . . . [and] I stood off and on all that night." Columbus also recorded that "the island is very flat, . . . and all the coasts are free from rocks, except that they all have some reefs near the land. . . . At a distance of two lombard shots from land, the water off all these islands is so deep that it cannot be sounded. These islands are very green and very fertile."

Not too much should be made of these distance estimates, since they were probably derived from Indian sketches or the interpretation of stationary cumulus by the admiral, and were refined by him after actually crossing over to Fernandina. Suffice it to say that the seven-plus leagues across the Tongue of the Ocean are a better fit to the estimate than the not quite six leagues from Rum Cay to Long Island along the central route. Also, Andros Island, my candidate for Fernandina, is almost twenty-nine leagues in length, while Long Island is barely eighteen, assuming Morison's value for the sea league. The preliminary bearing estimate for Fernandina's shoreline has helped analysts to correct an apparent transcription error in Columbus's refined bearing estimate.

In my view, the most significant clues have previously been masked by misleading and markedly inconsistent translations. When Columbus wrote "del otro cabo," I believe that he simply meant what he said, that is, "from the other cape." Having already camouflaged the first cape as a point, Cecil Jane was doubly constrained to render this phrase in an obtuse manner that would conceal reference to a second cape on the west end of Santa Maria. I have found the holograph to be written in very simple and direct Spanish, notably free from idiomatic expressions. It is interesting to note that of the twenty times that *cabo* appears during the Bahama odyssey, Cecil Jane chooses to translate it as "point" six times, while taking that liberty only four times out of its more than one hundred usages along the uncontested Cuba-Hispaniola route. It is truly remarkable that West Bay anchorage on New Providence Island is in fact embraced by two capes, Lyford Cay to the north and Clifton Point to the south, a unique configuration in the Bahamas.

The second dubious translation is *golfo*, which was used a total of nine times by Columbus, and in all other cases but one has always been precisely rendered as "gulf" by Cecil Jane. *Webster's Third New International Dictionary* defines a *gulf* as "a part of an ocean or sea extending into the land," and a *channel* as "a straight or narrow sea between two close land masses." A glance at a map must have convinced Cecil Jane that Columbus could not have meant "gulf" in describing the open ocean between Rum Cay and Long Island; hence he chose to render "golfo" as "channel." However, Columbus was familiar with the correct word for channel, having used the term "canal" five times in his *Journal*. While "channel" is still a weak description of the open area in question, it is far better than "gulf," so we have yet another illustration of how Cecil Jane distorted the translation in order to better accommodate the central route.

Along the northern route, the term *golfo* is quite appropriate in describing the Tongue of the Ocean that separates New Providence Island from Andros Island. Its dark blue waters are over a mile deep where Columbus would have crossed between the translucent shallows that make up more than ninety percent of its three-hundred-mile outline. Interestingly, Columbus was not the last explorer to so describe this waterway, for Ponce de León wrote how he "crossed the windward gulf of the Bahamas" after visiting San Salvador in 1513.[40] Additional support for the northern route is obtained from the other clues, particularly the references to large size, flatness, and verdant vegetation.

In summary, the northern route offers the second cape at its western end of Santa Maria, the multiple islands described there, the correct distance to Fernandina across a true gulf to a very large island having a coastline of the proper orientation and length, and is easily the largest while among the flattest and most verdant of the Bahama Islands. On the other hand, Rum Cay is singular with only one cape at its western end, too close to Long Island, and not separated by a gulf, while Long Island falls far short of the length cited by Columbus and is certainly not large, flat, or verdant by Bahama standards. Analysis of Tuesday's clues results in another substantial advantage for the northern route.

Wednesday, October 17 (Part 1 — Morning)

At daybreak, Columbus "came to a village, where I anchored.... And afterwards, at the hour of terce [9:00 A.M.], I sent the ship's boat ashore for water.... This island is very large, and I am resolved to round it.... [It] is distant from that of Santa Maria about eight leagues, almost from east to west, and this point [*cabo*], where I came, and all this coast runs north-north-west and south-south-east; I saw quite twenty leagues of it, but it did not end there.... This island is very green and flat and very fertile.... I saw many trees very unlike ours, and many of them had many branches of different kinds.... For example: one branch has leaves like those of a cane and another leaves like those of a mastic tree, and thus, on a single tree, there are five or six different kinds.... There are here fish, ... some shaped like dories, of the finest colours in the world, blue, yellow, red and of all colours, and others painted in a thousand ways.... There are also whales. I saw no land animals of any kind, except parrots and lizards.... If there had been any I could not have failed to see one.... A boy told me that he saw a large snake."

Long Island may have a marginal congruence with a few of these Fernandina clues, but for most of them it totally fails to match the recorded description. Not only does Burnt Ground, Morison's candidate for Columbus's Fernandina landfall, lie almost thirty percent short of the *Journal's* refined distance estimate, but there is also no place for his fleet to have anchored along this hostile shore. The *Yachtsman's Guide*

---

[40] Antonio de Herrera y Tordesillas, *Historia general de los hechos de los Castellanos en las islas i tierra firme del mar oceano*, trans. Thomas Frederick Davis (Jacksonville, 1935).

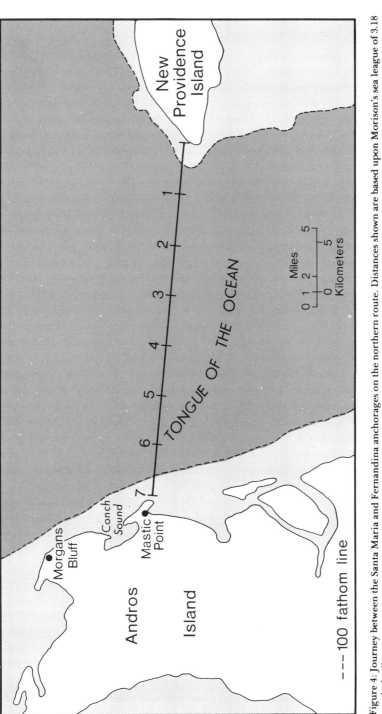

Figure 4: Journey between the Santa Maria and Fernandina anchorages on the northern route. Distances shown are based upon Morison's sea league of 3.18 nautical miles.

shows no anchorages north of Clarence Harbor, and U.S. Hydrographic Office *Sailing Directions* describes the stretch from Clarence Harbor north to Cape Santa Maria as "rocky and steep-to . . . exposed to the heavy sea which usually prevails on this side of the island."[41] As a sailor, Morison recognized the impossibility of anchorage on his central route, so he implied that it never happened with his misleading description: "Since the previous evening the fleet had been standing off-and-on, as the lee shore was so steep-to as to make anchoring unsafe. At noon October 17 the fleet got under way."[42] I also have evidence of physical contouring near Burnt Ground, possibly designed to enhance its congruence with the *Journal*. This evidence appears on a plat map specifying ownership of land parcels on northern Long Island about sixty years ago.[43] This map shows a narrow strip of crown land arcing out about two hundred yards into the Atlantic from Burnt Ground. Not evident on earlier British admiralty charts, this obviously man-made jetty might have temporarily given Burnt Ground the credentials described by Columbus, but it has long since been pounded into submission by the Atlantic surf.

Cecil Jane must have recognized that Burnt Ground does not have anything remotely resembling the "cabo" carefully described by Columbus, so he mistranslated the word as if it were "punta." Another physical shortcoming of Long Island is that it is barely eighteen leagues in length, in contrast to the expansive description recorded by Columbus after landing on Fernandina. Most importantly, Long Island totally fails to meet the verdant description of Columbus, particularly the mastic tree with its entwined and epiphytic vegetation, so common in the northern Bahamas. The rocky and windswept east coast of Long Island is devoid of lush vegetation, and its long annual dry spells make it more suitable to salt production, once a major industry there and on nearby Rum Cay.[44] Assuredly, the vegetation at Burnt Ground could not have been markedly different from the xerophytic growth observed by Shattuck near Clarence Town at the turn of this century. He wrote that "on this plain the conditions are extremely xerophytic . . . [and] on the north slope of the line of hills nearest town, the conditions are also extremely xerophytic."[45] However, the specific botanical failing of Long Island is that conditions are too dry to support the mastic tree, which Shattuck restricted to the northern islands of Eleuthera, New Providence, and Andros in 1903.[46]

Andros Island (figure 4), on the other hand, has a marvelously close congruence with the Fernandina described by Columbus (see figure 4). It is interesting that the *Yachtsman's Guide* indicats an anchorage at Mastic Point, almost 7.3 leagues due west from the postulated anchorage at West Bay on New Providence Island. It is noteworthy that Sharp Rock Point juts out several miles from the coast at a point exactly twenty leagues south of the northern end of Andros Island. It is remarkable that the eastern face of the candidate cape exactly parallels the east coast of Andros, both oriented precisely along a north-northwest–south-southwest bearing line.[47] It is

---

[41] *Yachtsman's Guide*, p. 242. U.S. Naval Hydrographic Office, p. 157.
[42] Morison, *Admiral of the Ocean Sea*, p. 243.
[43] Bahamas Lands and Surveys Department, *Long Island Plat Map*.
[44] Shattuck, p. 594.
[45] Ibid., p. 239.
[46] Ibid., p. 205.
[47] Since the holograph actually reads north-northwest–south-southwest, this is the one instance where I

extraordinary that this cape, where Columbus saw the marvelous mastic trees, should today carry the name of Mastic Point, and should be home to large numbers of mastic trees, many growing in closely packed thickets where they are intertwined with other vegetation and are festooned with the Bahamian "love-vine," an epiphytic aphrodisiac. It would be a truly amazing geographical coincidence if Columbus were actually describing some other location in the Bahamas, or for that matter, in the world.

Even the minor clues are in accord with Andros, since the island is large, green, flat, and fertile in relation to its neighbors, a statement that does not hold nearly as well for Long Island, whose "bold headlands" and "towering cliffs" are "an unusual treat for visitors."[48] Anchored behind the world's third longest reef off the east coast of Andros Island, it would not have been surprising for Columbus to have taken note of the reef fish, described in the *Yachtsman's Guide* as "brilliantly colored."[49] Neither Shattuck nor the guide make any reference to brightly colored fish off the steep-to east coast of Long Island. It is also not surprising that the admiral should mention lizards for the first time, as Andros Island has nineteen separate species, the most extensive listing in the Bahamas.[50]

In summary, Long Island is too close to Rum Cay, doesn't have the cape described by Columbus, would be impossible for anchoring, has too short a coastline (which runs closer to northwest-southeast than north-northwest–south-southeast), is far too dry for the mastic tree described in the *Journal*, and is clearly not very green and flat and very fertile. In contrast, Andros Island fits every description of Fernandina with near perfection, its only measurable failing being that it falls almost ten percent short of the specified distance from New Providence Island.

Wednesday, October 17 (Part 2 — Early Afternoon)

Columbus writes that he "set out from the village at midday from my anchorage and from where I had taken water in order to round this island of Fernandina, and the wind was south-west and south. It was my wish to follow the coast of this island, from where I was to the south-east, because it all trended north-north-west and

---

agree with Cecil Jane's contention that Las Casas must have made a transcription error. The *Journal* entries on Tuesday and Wednesday contain three explicit and three implicit references indicating that the shore trended to the southeast or south-southeast to the south of the cape. Simple laws of probability dictate a strong preference for the single, rather than the multiple, assumption of transcription errors necessary for consistency.

[48] *Yachtsman's Guide*, p. 243.

[49] Anchoring behind the reef at Andros would have presented serious problems to Columbus, as the reef opening north of Mastic Point now carries a low-water depth of five feet (*Yachtsman's Guide*, p. 157), which corresponds to a *maximum* depth of eight feet at high tide. Thus, the passage could have been made, if only very slowly, according to Morison's implication on page 120 of *Admiral* that the *Santa Maria* drew no more than 6.5 feet. On the other side of the question, Dr. Adey of the Smithsonian Reef Exhibit told me that Columbus might well have had three or four more feet of clearance back in 1492, due to the dynamics of reef structure. But, by the rules stated at the beginning of this paper, he also might have had three or four feet less clearance, so I would be more comfortable giving him a daytime anchorage on the gradually sloping reef itself, a tenuous location, but far safer than the Atlantic surf at Long Island. Paul Bartlett, an experienced contributor to the *Yachtsman's Guide*, told me he has no trouble accepting Columbus's day anchorage on the Andros reef. For the reference to fish, see *Yachtsman's Guide*, p. 289.

[50] Maclean et al., p. 13.

134

south-south-east, and I desired to take the route to the south-south-east, because in that direction . . . towards the south, lies . . . Samoet, where there is gold. . . . Pinzón . . . told me that one of them [the Indians] had very definitely given him to understand that the island could be rounded more quickly in a north-north-westerly direction. . . . I sailed north-north-west. And when I was about two leagues from the head of the island, I found a very wonderful harbour with a mouth, or rather it may be said with two mouths, since there is an islet [*isleo*] in the middle, and both mouths are very narrow, and within it is more than wide enough for a hundred ships, if it be deep and clear and there be depth at the entrance. . . . I anchored outside it, and went into it with all the ships' boats, and we saw that it was shallow. And as I thought, when I saw it, that it was the mouth of a river, I had ordered casks to be brought to take water, and on land I found . . . a village near there, where I sent the people for water. . . . And as it was some distance away, I was kept there for the space of two hours. . . . I walked among the trees, . . . the loveliest sight that I have yet seen, . . . green as those of Andalusia in the month of May, . . . as different from ours as day is from night. . . . Some trees were of the kind that are found in Castile, but yet there is a great difference. . . . There are here mastiffs and small dogs. . . . After the water had been taken, I returned to the ship and set sail."

Long Island does not fare any better with the early afternoon descriptions of Fernandina. The northernmost eighteen miles of its eastern coastline, which Burnt Ground is roughly centered on, runs along a bearing line which is thirty-five degrees west of north. This line is actually somewhat closer to northwest-southeast than it is to the north-northwest–south-southeast described by Columbus, and it is also evident that Long Island does not have the straight coastline described by the admiral. But the real difficulty with the early afternoon entries is in trying to understand how the Indians could have possibly thought it better to round Long Island in a counterclockwise direction. Morison puts it best when he writes, "very bad advice, or a misunderstanding, since nothing larger than a boat can pass around the leeward side of the island."[51] (Didiez Burgos, who challenges Morison on so much of his strained reconstruction, agrees that Long Island is Fernandina, but boldly asserts that the fleet sailed along this extremely shoal *western* coastline!)

Finding the wonderful harbor on Long Island is a curious problem. The 1851 British admiralty chart does not show any near the head of the island, but the current map from the *Yachtsman's Guide* clearly shows one with the exact proportions described in the *Journal* (figure 5). In 1940, Morison noted the deficiency of the admiralty charts when he wrote, "this *maravilloso puerto* is not shown on modern charts, but it is easily identified by those who have sailed there."[52] Well, Morison can rest in peace because it is now charted, although it fails to meet either of Columbus's quantitative measurements. First, the port is less than a league from Cape Santa Maria, the head of Long Island. Second, it is far too small, being about twenty-five hundred feet in its maximum dimension. In his reconstruction of the *Santa Maria*, Bjorn Landstrom estimates its beam at twenty-eight feet.[53] Employing the same

[51] Morison, *Admiral of the Ocean Sea*, p. 243.
[52] Ibid., p. 245.
[53] Bjorn Landstrom, *Columbus* (New York: Macmillan, 1967), p. 47.

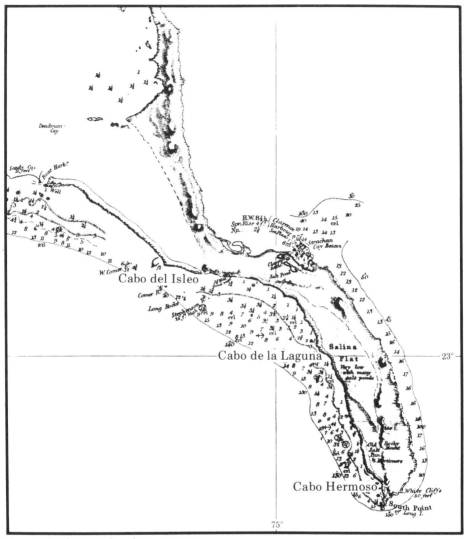

Figure 5: Southern portion of Long Island.

spacing criterion that I assumed in evaluating the size of Royal Island harbor would lead to this miniature basin having room for little more than forty ships. As for appearing to be the mouth of a river, we can again look to Morison, who writes that "Columbus rather stupidly assumed this shallow harbor to be the mouth of a great river."[54]

Another consideration about this wonderful port is that Columbus used the word *isleo* in describing the small island at its mouth. This word is normally used to describe a smaller island adjacent to a larger one, and does not necessarily imply an islet, as translated by Cecil Jane. It would be very difficult to ascertain Columbus's exact usage of this word, because it seems to appear only twice in the *Journal*—here and off the island of Isabela. But, we do know that when he saw the island of sixty or so acres in Samana Bay, he added the qualifier *pequenuela* to signify a "tiny" islet. On this basis, it is hard to imagine that he would have dignified the five-acre sandbar at the Seymours Inlet with the title of *isleo*.

As for the other clues, Morison would have us believe that Columbus made another impossible anchorage outside of Seymours Inlet, and then strolled through verdant forests when northern Long Island has only xerophytic growth, and that his men somehow found water where the British admiralty charts indicate there are no wells within dozens of miles.

In marked contrast the early afternoon *Journal* entries fit the northern coast of Andros with such exactitude that we must again wonder why the northern route has escaped the attention of analysts for so many years. From the Mastic Point anchorage it is easy to see why one of the Indians might have been concerned about the ability of the admiral's large vessels to pass over the shoal water south of the Tongue of the Ocean on a direct route to Cuba. With a southerly wind, they might have suggested the longer, but safer, deep-water route that would have carried the fleet counter-clockwise around Andros Island.

Sailing to the northwest, Columbus would have shortly come upon Conch Sound, which lies exactly two leagues south of Morgan's Bluff, the head of Andros Island (figure 4). This shallow sound is well over a mile in breadth and, when viewed from the reef, truly does give the impression of being the mouth of a river meandering off to the northwest behind its narrow opening. The single respect in which it fails to correspond to the *Journal* description is that it now has only one opening. Although I am reluctant to claim that minor changes might have occurred since 1492, it would be a lot easier to accept shifting sandbars in these shallows, than the basic alterations in vegetation and limestone rock so often imposed by advocacy of the central route. Mid-nineteenth-century admiralty charts of Conch Sound do in fact indicate an *isleo* in the rear central portion of the sound.

Shattuck continually refers to the large tree specimens found on Andros Island and, in describing Mangrove Cay at Andros, writes that "here for the first time we met with a forest in the Bahamas."[55] If Columbus actually strolled through the grove of towering trees that I saw near Conch Sound in October 1981, then it is likely that his men found the water with which to fill their casks, for wells near Morgan's Bluff

[54] Morison, *Admiral of the Ocean Sea*, p. 245.
[55] Shattuck, p. 223.

today supply water barges from Nassau with the excess requirements imposed by the winter tourist trade.[56]

In summary, this is an opportune time to recapitulate the analysis from Columbus's San Salvador departure up to his arrival at the north end of Fernandina. During this interval, the northern route almost perfectly matches the descriptions in the *Journal*. This precise fit is obtained without resorting to Morison's artifice of introducing a far shorter "land league," a distinction that does not appear in the verbatim *Journal*. Not only do the topography, flora, and fauna impressively match the details in the *Journal*, but we also develop a new respect for the admiral's bearing and distance measurements made while he coasted the Bahamas. The laws of probability involving three dozen or so independent *Journal* clues, make it virtually impossible that any other configuration of islands anywhere on the surface of the earth could come so close to matching this section of the *Journal*. The numerous discrepancies of the central route bear witness to that impossibility, and reasonable scholars must accept the fact that Columbus was almost surely describing a route along the Northeast Providence Channel, regardless of how poorly the northern route might fit subsequent portions of the *Journal*.

Wednesday, October 17 (Part 3 — Finale)

Columbus departed his second anchorage on Fernandina, "navigating so far to the north-west that I discovered all that part of the island until the coast runs east and west. And afterwards all these Indians repeated that this island was smaller than the island of Samoet and that it would be well to turn back in order to arrive at it sooner. There the wind presently fell and then began to blow from the west-north-west. . . . I therefore turned back and navigated all that night in an east-south-easterly direction, sometimes due east and sometimes south-east; this was done in order to keep clear from the land, because there were very thick clouds and the weather was very heavy. There was little wind and [*el era poco y*] this prevented me from coming to land to anchor. Then this night it rained very heavily from after midnight until near daybreak, and it is still cloudy with a threat of rain. We are at the end of the island to the south-east, where I hope to anchor until the weather clears. . . . So it has rained, more or less, every day. . . . This is the best and most fertile and temperate and level and good land that there is in the world."

The central route gives us an immediate problem, as it is unlikely that Columbus would have employed the imprecise expression "until the coast runs east and west" to describe Cape Santa Maria on Long Island, with his frequent (120 times) use of the clearly appropriate term *cabo*. In contrast, if Columbus had been two or three miles north of Morgan's Bluff at this time, he would have noted how the north coast of Andros does trend westerly from there.

After a long dry spell, the central route finally wins the next major clue, as its candidate for Isabela, Crooked-Acklins, is somewhat larger than Long Island, while the northern route's candidate for Isabela, Long Island, is very much smaller than

[56] The *Yachtsman's Guide* repeatedly warns boatsmen of the problems in obtaining fresh water in the Bahamas, taking care to note on page 154 that "there are two good fresh water wells on South Joulter," a small cay nine miles north of Morgan's Bluff and easily accessible to yachtsmen.

Andros Island. Even here, I must qualify the apparent advantage, for in a subsequent *Journal* entry describing Isabela, Columbus expresses doubts as to whether he has actually reached the Samoet described by the Indians.

The next clue is extremely important to the northern route since it involves consideration of whether it was even possible for Columbus to have sailed from the northern end of Andros to the southern end of Long Island with as much as thirty-six hours under sail. To answer this question we must first examine what kinds of winds were available to his fleet. We know that the winds had shifted around to southwest and south by midday Wednesday, and that the norther blew up sometime that afternoon. The rain and heavy weather continued until sometime Thursday, with the wind shifting around to north by Friday morning. On Saturday the wind was light, and by Tuesday there was a dead calm, with the strong easterly trades not reestablished until late Wednesday. See how well this pattern fits the one described by the *Yachtsman's Guide*, which states that winter "northers typically start with the wind veering to the south and southwest. When the coldfront arrives the wind shifts suddenly to NW, then works through north and blows itself out from the NE. In midwinter this cycle takes several days, in spring only 24 hours ... [with winds ranging] from brisk sailing breezes, through 20–25 knot winds, to anchor-rattlers."[57]

Considering how well the cited *Journal* entries correspond to the description of the typical Bahama norther, it is difficult to understand the single exception to the standard pattern, that is, the "little wind" that supposedly occurred sometime late Wednesday. As there is no noun associated with "el era poco," Jane assumed that Columbus was referring back to "viento," last entered in the *Journal* exactly sixty words earlier, while another masculine noun, "tiempo," appears only five words earlier. Wouldn't it have been just as reasonable for Columbus to have meant that there wasn't enough time to anchor, or for Las Casas to have omitted a noun describing some other limitation to an anchorage? It doesn't seem reasonable to scuttle the northern route because of a single tenuous translation by someone who previously has demonstrated his facility for warping the text to fit the existing "wisdom," especially when the weather pattern interpreted by Cecil Jane is not in accord with common knowledge about the behavior of weather fronts.

If it can be accepted that Columbus actually had a stiff breeze at his back for almost two full days, then the following argument shows that Long Island was within easy reach of his fleet. Eliminating the ninety or so leagues that Columbus made during the eight days of his transatlantic voyage that included some period of calm, we find that his overall average speed was an impressive one and a half leagues per hour. On his three best days he averaged a two-and-a-half-league rate around the clock, exceeding even this speed during the last eight hours prior to his landfall. Nowhere does the *Journal* imply that Columbus shortened sail during the tempest of October 17, suggesting that he had developed considerable confidence in the ability of his Indian pilots to guide him safely down the east coast of Fernandina. Thus the 70 leagues from Morgan's Bluff on Andros to the south end of Long Island might have been easily feasible for an aggressive sailor.

[57] *Yachtsman's Guide*, pp. 18–19.

In summary, the final major clue at the northern end of Fernandina again fits Andros Island perfectly, while it would have been a most quaint way of describing the north cape of Long Island. However, the size of Samoet is clearly in better congruence with the central route, although the importance of this clue is subsequently diminished by the admiral's doubts about the identity of Isabela. Neither route is really in accord with Columbus's sailing directions for this day. As for the distance traveled during approximately fourteen hours under sail (4:00 P.M.? to daybreak), my reconstruction places him near the south end of Andros Island at an average speed of two leagues per hour, well within his capability. The central route places him near Clarence Harbor at daybreak, at an average speed of only one league per hour, or the same speed that Morison assumed for the rowboats when they explored Watlings Island. This might have been a reasonable speed if Columbus had shortened sail for safety (not mentioned), or if the wind really had subsided. But, would Columbus have enthused about the "level" land while off the dramatic east coast of Long Island? Pending resolution of the "el era poco" uncertainty, I rate the third portion of Wednesday as a narrow win for the northern route.

Thursday, October 18

Columbus writes: "When the weather had cleared, I sailed before the wind and continued the circuit of the island when I could do so, and anchored when it was not well to navigate. But I did not land, and at dawn I set sail."

This complete entry for Thursday, far shorter than any other entry in the Bahamas, is as interesting for possible omissions as it is for content. In my reconstruction, Columbus makes it about halfway through the shoal water south of the Tongue of the Ocean, anchoring when lighting conditions prevent him from threading six to ten-foot keel depths through the channels that fan out across the shoals in the direction of Long Island.[58] I assume that he averaged two leagues per hour during the twelve or less hours available to him. I believe that he had good reason to keep this entry short, both exhausted by the difficult route and also having no land sightings for his sovereigns.

On the central route, Morison has Columbus making only about three leagues during the entire day! His fleet could have done this distance in little more than an hour when sailing before the wind. And, coming to anchor at Roses, Columbus would have had to bypass nearly Little Harbor, the finest harbor on his supposed central route. How uncharacteristic of Columbus to neither note nor utilize this sheltered harbor, and how foolish of him to select yet another nonexistent anchorage on the east coast of Long Island.[59] It seems likely that he would have extolled the dramatic beauty of Long Island's southeast coast, and would have utilized the waiting time by sending a shore party to explore the island.

In summary, the central route has much too short a sail "before the wind," doesn't explain how Columbus missed Little Harbor, and fails to account for his lack of

---

[58] According to the *Sailing Directions*, "white sand ridges, with depths of about 6 feet to 2 fathoms over their northern ends, show up in good contrast to the dark bottoms of the northern ends of the channels between them. . . . The principal passages between the sand ridges are . . . available to vessels of 14-foot draft."
[59] *Yachtsman's Guide*, p. 249.

interest in exploration. I think the northern route wins this meager collection of clues by default.

Friday, October 19

Columbus writes: "At dawn, I weighed anchor and sent the caravel *Pinta* to the east-south-east, and the caravel *Niña* to the south-south-east, while I in the ship went to the south-east. I gave orders that they should follow these courses until midday, and ... before we had sailed for three hours, we saw an island to the east, towards which we steered, and all the three vessels reached it before midday, at its northern point, where there is an islet [*isleo*] and a reef of rocks to its seaward side to the north and another between it and the main island. These men ... called this island 'Samoet,' and I named it *Isabella*. There was a north wind, and the said islet [*isleo*] lay on the course from the island of Fernandina, from which I had navigated from east to west [*yo habia partido Leste Oueste*] and extends for twelve leagues to a cape, which I named *Cape Hermoso*. It is on the west coast [*que es de la parte del Oueste*] and it is indeed lovely, round and in deep water, with no shoals off it. At first the shore is stony and low, and further on there is a sandy beach which is characteristic of most of that coast, and there I anchored this night, Friday, until morning. All this coast, and the part of the island which I saw, is mainly a beach; the island ... has many trees, very green and tall, and this land is higher than the other islands which have been discovered. There is in it one elevation, which cannot be called a mountain, but which serves to beautify the rest of the island, and it seems that there is much water there in the center of the island. On this north-eastern side the coast curves sharply [*De esta parte al Nordeste hace una grande angla*], and is very thickly wooded with very large trees. I wished to go to anchor there ..., but the water was of little depth and I could only anchor at a distance from the shore, and the wind was very favourable for reaching this point [*cabo*] where I am now lying at anchor, and which I have named Cape Hermoso.... I did not anchor within that curve [*no surgi en aquella angla*] and also because I saw this cape, so green and lovely, at a distance.... When I arrived here at this cape, there came from the land the scent of flowers or trees, so delicious and sweet.... In the morning ... I will land to see what is here at this point [*cabo*]. There is no village, except further inland.... To-morrow I wish to go so far inland to find the village.... I believe that it is an island separated from that of Samoet, and even that there is another small island between them."

The northern route assumes that Columbus sailed at daybreak from his shoal water anchorage at a speed of about two leagues per hour, with his fleet fanned out to cover a wide-open ocean area, far from the Guanahaní of his Indian guides. The *Pinta* detected land (the west end of the unnamed *isleo* stretching out to the west of Long Island in figure 5) four leagues west of the *isleo* after three hours of sail, giving the *Niña* a reasonable six leagues to cover by midday. I believe that Long Island is the larger island ("grande isla") adjacent to the "isleo," the twelve-mile-long sandbar that points back towards Andros Island, precisely as described, and also has the necessary rocks at both ends. From the west end of this *isleo*, the coast runs ten and a half leagues to South Point, a round cape in deep water, a welcome change from the shoal capes that Columbus had seen earlier this day. There is a 150-foot pinnacle four miles from South Point, the highest elevation he would have yet viewed along the

141

northern route. There are also many ponds and lagoons in this part of Long Island.[60]

On the central route, Morison has Columbus depart his phantom anchorage at dawn, unnecessarily spreading out his fleet to search for an island only nine leagues distant. Morison considers Bird Rock to be the "isleo," and Crooked Island to be the larger nearby island. While Cecil Jane's rendering of *isleo* as "islet" may make Bird Rock more acceptable, this tiny outpost still fails to lie on the course from Long Island, and it does not fit the distribution of rocks described in the *Journal*. A major problem with Morison's reconstruction is that the coast runs only six leagues to the south end of Fortune Island, where the cape is half in deep water and half in the shallow Bight of Acklins, hardly a noteworthy improvement over the northern cape.

It is Morison's position that this northern cape of Crooked Island is the "Cabo del Isleo" of Columbus, rather than the cape being part of the *isleo* itself. But this position is inconsistent with the *Journal's* use of the phrase *cabo de isla*, which always logically refers to the end of the island. However, it is clear why Morison chose to avoid trying to identify a cape on miniature Bird Rock. This problem doesn't exist with the northern route, where the "Cabo del Isleo" is clearly the eastern terminus of the twelve-mile sandbar.

A second related uncertainty here is the exact usage of the word *angla*, which Cecil Jane rendered here as "sharply curving coast," having already designated the more likely northwest corner of Crooked Island as the "Cabo del Isleo." But Jane is far from consistent in his handling of this term, rendering it as "promontory," "great bay," or "large bend," according to the requirements of the central route on Hispaniola.[61] Here on Isabela, Morison has designated the curving coastline on the western sides of Crooked and Fortune islands as the "angla" of Columbus. This leaves us wondering how Columbus could have sailed past French Wells (Morison's Cape de Laguna) without mentioning it, especially as it sits right in the middle of his supposed *angla*.

While figure 5 shows that the northern route fits the "curving coastline" interpretation of "angla" between Cabo de la Laguna and Cabo del Isleo, a more compelling congruence results from the more likely interpretation of angla as a wide cape (something intermediate between *cabo* and *punta*). It would then become the wide cape on Long Island directly across from the Cabo del Isleo, giving Columbus a stronger reason to write "Yo quise ir a surgir en ella"; for the shallow water at the entrance would truly have prevented him from anchoring within.

Despite its many difficulties, the central route does have some redeeming features that must be mentioned here. First, Columbus would indeed have passed within three miles of Blue Hill, an impressive two hundred feet in altitude, and the highest elevation that he would have seen along the entire central route. However, it is not that much higher than the 150-foot hill that he supposedly anchored under the previous night, without so much as a mention in his *Journal*. A second positive attribute is the Bight of Acklins, which easily meets the description of "much water."

---

[60] Ibid., map on p. 242.

[61] I was originally convinced of the accuracy of Jane's translation at this point in the *Journal*, and identified the "angla" on Long Island as the curving coastline between Cabo del Isleo and Cabo de la Laguna, as shown on figure 5. I now accept Robert Fuson's argument that *angla* is an additional term for "cape."

In summary, this day's *Journal* entries contribute substantial reasons for favoring the northern route. Long Island has the proper location and orientation of the "isleo," much closer agreement with the twelve-league estimate, precise agreement with the "angla" and the concept of anchoring within, and a cape that is truly all in deep water. Of lesser certainty, the northern route has a more distinctive hill, albeit of lower altitude, to warrant such heavy praise, and a more logical reason for fanning his fleet out over a forty-five-degree arc. One minor point in favor of the central route is its better explanation for the vegetation of Isabela.[62]

Saturday, October 20

Columbus writes: "Today, at sunrise, I weighed anchor from the place where I was with the ship, anchored off the south-west point [*cabo*] of this island of Samoet, to which point I gave the name *Cabo de la Laguna* and to the island that of Isabella, in order to steer to the north-east and east from the south-east and south [*de la parte del Sueste y Sur*]. For there . . . was the village and its king. I found the water everywhere so shallow that I could not enter or navigate to that point, and I saw that, following the route to the south-west, it would be a very great detour. Therefore I determined to return by the way which I had come, to the north-north-east from the west [*de la parte del Oueste*], and to round this island in that direction, and the wind was so light that I was unable to proceed along the coast except in the night, and as it is dangerous to anchor off these islands except in daytime, . . . I proceeded to stand off under sail all this Sunday night. The caravels anchored, because they found themselves near land earlier."

The first problem in interpreting Saturday's entry is that Columbus describes himself as being anchored at the previously unidentified Cabo de la Laguna, while Friday's had closed with him anchored at Cabo Hermoso. My explanation for this contradiction is that Laguna must have been a weakly formed cape in proximity to Hermoso. Thus, I propose that he never made it all the way to Hermoso on Friday, but rather anchored near Salina Flat, possibly the anchorage five miles south of the twenty-third parallel in figure 5. Such an argument does not hold for the central route, where Cabo de la Laguna is well formed and distinct from Hermoso, with no intervening anchorages.

Before continuing with the evaluation, it is necessary to examine Columbus's all-important sailing directions in some detail. The Cecil Jane translation is misleading in implying that Columbus steered "to the north-east and east from the south-east and south." It is clearly nonsensical to steer from one compass point to another unless those points are 180 degrees apart. That is, one does not sail to the northeast from the southeast, but from the southwest. For this reason I believe that the correct translation is that Columbus wished to sail two course legs, first to the northeast and then east, starting from the south-southeast *part* of Isabela. Similarly, when shallow water forced him to change plans, I think that he decided to retrace

---

[62] I hope to explore this area and verify that the wells shown in figure 5 are in fact indicative of better growing conditions on the sheltered western shore of Long Island.

Friday's course to the far end of the *isleo* (the western *part* of Isabela), from where he would sail in a north-northeasterly direction to his objective.

Unfortunately, the northern route does not have a very strong congruence with my proposed interpretation of the *Journal* sailing directions. His starting point, Cabo de la Laguna, is properly on the southeast portion of Long Island, and it is sensible that Columbus would have attempted to reach the northern part of Long Island by sailing through the entrance at Cabo del Isleo. While he would have been thwarted by the shallow water shown in figure 5, it is not possible to reconcile the northeast and east directions with figure 5 unless it assumed that the Indian sketch of northern Long Island was distorted. A major difficulty for the northern route now occurs with the admiral's observation that an alternative route to the southwest would be a very great detour. To fit this clue, it is necessary to assume that Las Casas incorrectly transcribed "southwest" in place of "southeast." It is my belief that Columbus now turned to his third alternative, which was to retrace his route to the west end of the *isleo*, from where he could sail north-northeast, as described in the *Journal*, towards the northern end of Long Island.

The initial weakness of the central route is that its starting point, Cabo Hermoso, is clearly not on the southeastern portion of Isabela. However, the proposed sailing directions fit perfectly with an entrance to the Bight of Acklins at the north end of Fortune Island and an objective at the east end of Crooked Island. Unable to enter the Bight, his rejection of the great detour to the southwest fits perfectly, although I am bothered by his failure to note that he would have been retracing his steps of that morning. When he finally does suggest retracing his route to Bird Rock in order to follow the third alternative, the north-northeast directions make no sense at all.

In summary, although there are some problems with the central route, I recognize its first advantage over the northern route in eleven *Journal* segments on this Saturday. It has a much better congruence with two out of the three alternative sailing directions, while the northern route has better explanations for the lesser clues regarding the anchorage confusion and the *parts* of Isabela. Both reconstructions have the shallow water described by Columbus.

Sunday, October 21

Columbus writes: "At ten o'clock I arrived here at this *Cape del Isleo* and anchored, as did the caravels. . . . I went ashore, and there was there no village but only a single house. . . . [I went] to examine the island . . . which is much more green and fertile than the others . . . and has large and very green trees. There are here very extensive lagoons, and by them and around them there are wonderful woods, . . . there are large and small birds of so many different kinds, . . . trees of a thousand types, all with their various fruits and all scented. . . . As I was thus going round one of these lagoons, I saw a snake, which we killed. . . . It is seven palms in length; I believe that there are many similar snakes here in these lagoons. Here, I recognized the aloe. . . . Going in search of very good water, we arrived at a village near here, half a league from where I am anchored. . . . I asked . . . for water; and, after I had returned to the ship, they came presently to the beach with their gourds full. . . . I was anxious to fill all the ship's casks with water here; accordingly, if the weather permit, I shall presently set out to go round the island. . . . After that I wish to leave for another

144

very large island, which I believe must be Cipangu . . .; they call it 'Colba.' . . . Beyond this island, there is another which they call 'Bofio,' which they say is very large. The others, which lie between them *.que son entremedio*], we shall see in passing. . . . But I am still determined to proceed to the mainland."

On the northern route, Cabo del Isleo is located at the western end of the *isleo*, directly across from the *angla* on Long Island. There are many extensive lagoons in the vicinity of this cape, and figure 5 shows a good well exactly one half league from there.[63] As there are no islands between Cuba and Hispaniola, Columbus must have been referring to the islands lying between Isabela and the Cuba-Hispaniola group. On the northern route, these islands are the Inaguas and the Crooked Island group. As to the snake that they killed, Morison believes that it was an iguana, even though the *Journal* specifies "sierpe" here after having used "lagarto" on Fernandina.[64] This is unfortunate, because neither the Smithsonian nor Shattuck lists any iguana on either Long Island or Crooked Island.[65] (I have not yet been able to ascertain the distribution of snakes in the Bahamas.)

One minor problem with the central route is that the Cabo del Isleo is a major topographical feature of Isabela, supposedly seen by Columbus on Friday, but not given a name until Sunday's revisit. Also, Morison sensibly has Columbus anchor off the north side of the cape, two miles from the well near Landrail Point.[66] This anchorage puts him out of convenient range of all lagoons on Crooked Island save the small one in the northwest corner.

In summary, while a final judgment must await further study of the flora and fauna on these two islands, as well as the character of their beaches and lagoons, I am inclined to give a slight edge to the northern route because of proximity to good water, multiple lagoons, and a better congruence with the description of multiple intervening islands.

Monday, October 22

Columbus writes: "All this night and to-day I have been here. . . . We took water for the ships in a lagoon which is here near Cape del Isleo, for so I have named it. And in the lagoon, Martin Alonzo Pinzón, captain of the *Pinta*, killed another snake, like that of yesterday."

The good well shown in figure 5 appears in some modern charts to be located right on the edge of a lagoon.[67] Without firsthand observation, I am inclined to call this day a draw.

Tuesday, October 23

Columbus writes: "I wished to-day to set out for the island of Cuba. . . . I did not delay longer here or . . . [there is a lacuna at this point in the text] round this island

[63] *Yachtsman's Guide*, p. 242.
[64] Morison, *Admiral of the Ocean Sea*, p. 249.
[65] Mclean et al., pp. 15–16 and 19. Shattuck, p. 238.
[66] Morison, *Admiral of the Ocean Sea*, p. 244.
[67] *Yachtsman's Guide*, p. 242.

to go to the village. . . . My impression, however, is that this is very rich in spices. . . . I recognize only the aloe. . . . I have not set nor am I setting sail for Cuba, because there is no wind, but a dead calm, and it is raining heavily and it rained heavily yesterday."

There is not enough new evidence here to make a judgment in favor of either route.

Wednesday, October 24

Columbus writes: "This night, at midnight, I weighed anchor from the island of Isabella, from Cape del Isleo, which is on the north side *. de la parte del Norte*] where I had stayed, for the island of Cuba, . . . and they indicated to me that I should steer west-south-west to go there. . . . I navigated until day to the west-south-west and at dawn the wind fell and it rained, and so it was almost all night. I was thus with little wind until after midday, and then it began to blow very gently, and I set all my sails on the ship. . . . So I went on my course until nightfall, when Cape Verde, in the island of Fernandina, which is on the south side in the western part, lay to my north-west, and was seven leagues distant from me. And as it now blew hard, . . . I decided to take in all sail, except the foresail, and to proceed under it. After a short while, the wind became much stronger and I made a considerable distance, at which I felt misgivings. . . . I ordered the foresail to be furled, and that night we went less than two leagues." So ends this verbatim portion of the *Journal*.

At first glance, the central route has a perfect congruence with this entry. A west-southwest course from Bird Rock would have brought Columbus to a point where a five-league sighting could be made to South Point of Long Island on the described northwest bearing. From that point on his course, an additional seven leagues to the west-southwest and eleven leagues due west would have brought him to within four leagues of the Columbus Bank: close enough to the five leagues reported in the next day's *Journal*! However, there are some basic questions with this reconstruction. In the first place, it should be noted that this is the first reference to Cabo Verde that appears in the *Journal*. How is it that, while supposedly anchored almost all day Thursday within easy viewing distance of that cape, Columbus failed to add its description to his meager entry of three dozen words? Secondly, in viewing South Point from its eastern side, he would have been struck by the dramatic beauty of its fifty-foot white cliffs (figure 5), rather than the greenery characteristic of most Bahama headlands, and would have given it some name other than Cabo Verde. Finally, how does Morison justify the description "on the south side in the western part"? South Point is on the southern end of Long Island, but in no way can it be considered to be in the western part of the island. Modifying the translation to read western "side" rather than "part" would make some sense, since it can be viewed from east or west. But, if we follow the Morison reconstruction, both of his viewings were from the *east* side of the cape.

The northern route has some major failings in trying to match this day's entry. First, there is really no good way to explain the description of Cabo del Isleo being "on the north side." While it is true that the cape is to the north of the areas explored since Friday, it had previously been described as westerly by the admiral. But my biggest problem is with the sighting of Cabo Verde seven leagues to the northwest. One possibility is that he was referring back to the cape with the mastic trees on Fernandina. It is an interesting coincidence that it is almost exactly seventy leagues on a northwest bearing from the south end of Long Island to Mastic Point on Andros. Could Las Casas have made a transcription error in recording this distance? If Columbus was not referring back to this heretofore unnamed cape (albeit the only verdant one of the two mentioned in the *Journal*) on Fernandina, then he must have been describing a cape on Isabela. But this hypothesis requires that Columbus incorrectly identify the island, confuse Cabo Hermoso with Cabo Verde, and reverse the direction of sighting from southeast to northwest. Although the central route is not without its defects, it clearly rates a substantial edge over the northern route. And well it should, for it is this single clue which has probably been responsible for misleading the analysts who backtracked from his landing place in Cuba.[68]

By taking a synoptic view of the admiral's journey through the Bahamas, rather than being locked into a distorted reconstruction by the Cabo Verde clue discussed above, I have arrived at a northern route which fits the *Journal* entries with much better overall precision than does Morison's central route. In order to cram the central route into congruence with the *Journal*, Morison has had to invent at least three nonexistent anchorages, pull a one-and-a-half-mile league out of thin air, ignore tidal, harbor, and foliage descriptions, and, when all else fails, accuse the admiral of negligent, hyperbolic, or illogical entries.

The final section of this article deals with the impact of contemporary sources known to me.

Independent Data Sources

The primary independent data source for reconstruction of Columbus's Bahama journey are those subsequent references in the *Journal* that might help determine the route between his landfall on San Salvador and Cuba. First, there is no certainty that Bahia Bariay was his Cuban landfall, and further study to positively identify this site would affect the Bahama reconstructions.[69] Second, I feel that the 1,142-league estimate of the distance from Hierro that Columbus entered in his *Journal* on November 2 cannot be related to either the northern or the central route with any degree of certainty. Third, while west-northwest of Great Inagua Island and twenty-five leagues from Puerto del Principe on November 20, Columbus describes himself as being twelve leagues from Isabela, which is a slightly better congruence with the central route. However, when he adds that he saw two islands to the south, the northern route can point to Crooked and Acklins, while the central route must resort to the Inaguas, far to the southeast of his projected position. On this same day he

---

[68] In his letter to me of 17 November 1972, Morison does in fact justify his reconstruction on the basis of backtracking from Cuba.

[69] Although it is beyond the scope of this paper, I have evidence to support the theory that the Cuban landfall was actually at Puerto Padre, rather than Bahia Bariay. This evidence was obtained by carefully correlating the *Journal* descriptions of the first two ports visited in Cuba with modern maps. Although a definitive answer will have to wait for verification of Columbus's entire Cuban transit, Puerto Padre would support a more westerly departure point from the Bahamas, such as Long Island rather than Crooked Island.

worries that his Indian guides might run away, since Isabela is only eight leagues from San Salvador. To make this claim fit the northern route, one must assume that Indian sketches blended all the islands running along the western shore of Exuma Sound into a single entity reaching to within ten leagues of Egg Island or eight leagues of Powell Point. To make this clue fit the central route, one must assume that Columbus forgot about his second and third discoveries. On January 5, he makes his final reference to San Salvador as an islet, which is certainly supportive of the northern route.

The major contemporary source is the biography by his son, Ferdinand. While obviously derived from the *Journal*, it contains at least four independent assessments. The first, that San Salvador is fifteen leagues in length, bears absolutely no relationship to Egg and Royal islands, and is almost four times as long as Watlings. The argument for the northern route is that Ferdinand, who never saw the Bahamas, recorded this estimate at a later date, after the Spanish had begun to accept the entire island of Eleuthera as San Salvador. The second addition by Ferdinand is the description of a peninsula on San Salvador which would have required at least three days of hard rowing to round. This clue is a total mismatch with Watlings, but it does add weight to the idea that the entire island of Eleuthera had somehow evolved into the landfall of his father. His third divergence from the holograph is that the direction taken by the rowboats on San Salvador was to the northwest rather than to the north-northwest. This clue points to the southern tip of Abaco, where one group could have taken the northwest direction, and the other followed the north-north-east direction in the *Journal*. The final important difference is that Ferdinand transfers many of the Isabela episodes onto Fernandina, suggesting that perhaps these two islands were close neighbors.

A second important contemporary source is Herrera's account of Ponce de León's exploration of the Bahamas in 1513. This source has generally been ignored by analysts because it doesn't fit the Watlings Island model. On his way to Florida, Ponce de León sailed northwestward along the eastern edge of the Bahamas. On the fourth day out of Puerto Rico he reached the Banks of Babueca at 22.5 degrees latitude, then an islet called Caycos before anchoring at an island called La Yaguna at 24 degrees (Watlings?), next stopping for repairs at Amaguayo on day seven before passing Manegua at 24.5 degrees, and finally reaching Guanahaní at 25 degrees and 40 minutes on day ten. This detailed listing of the islands, and a latitude measurement that is only twelve miles north of Egg Island, gives me some confidence that Ponce de León thought he knew the location of San Salvador. As a gentleman member of Columbus's second expedition, and later as governor of Puerto Rico, he must have been privy to detailed information about Bahamas geography. The accuracy of his latitude measurements is demonstrated by an error of only twelve miles in measuring what was obviously the latitude of Cape Canaveral. I believe that mislocation of the Columbus landfall and misinterpretation of the Herrera account have helped to contribute to an undeservedly negative reputation.

The final contemporary account is Las Casas's *Historia de las Indies* which contains the famous bean-shaped identification of San Salvador, the clue that turned my interest to this puzzle forty years ago. I fail to see now as I failed to see then why Columbus would have described Watlings Island as having the shape of a large bean. I would expect to see a pronounced concave shoreline such as the one described by the outline of Little Bahama Bank. But this secondhand clue does not seem so important to me now after reading Morison's account of how the Indians laid out the geography of the Bahamas with beans on a table in front of King John.[70] Isn't it possible that San Salvador was represented by a single bean, and that the story was garbled on the way to Las Casas? Also, consider the similarity of either the Egg and Royal island groups or the eastern portion of Eleuthera to a snap bean pod. (This description of Eleuthera appears in the September 1981 issue of *Skindiving Magazine*.) [Ed. note: See article by Robert Power in this volume.]

Of these contemporary sources, only the Ponce de León account is firsthand, and it gives strong quantitative support to the northern route.

Conclusions

Several conclusions and recommendations can be drawn from the results of this analysis. The primary conclusion is that the northern route has a much better congruence with the available data than the central route. This advantage occurs in the analysis of Columbus's transatlantic navigation, reconstruction of his Bahama odyssey, and in what little data are currently available from contemporary sources. The fit of the northern route to the admiral's *Journal* is especially close from his San Salvador departure through his exploration of the northern end of Fernandina. Over this interval the congruence is so precise as to raise questions about the possibility of a viable alternative.

There is a disturbing falloff in the quality of fit at Isabela that suggests the need for a study in greater depth. One requirement is the obvious need for an accurate translation of the *Journal*, free from the bias that has colored the Cecil Jane version in favor of the central route. In support of this effort, I have compiled a partial concordance of certain critical phrases that appear in the *Journal*. Another need is for reevaluation of portions of the route along the north coasts of Cuba and Hispaniola. I feel that his Cuban landfall and the Hispaniola coasting east of Monte Cristi are still questionable. Relocation of the admiral's Cuban landfall could have significant effect on the Bahamas reconstruction.

A definitive location of San Salvador is probably beyond the reach of a single analyst. Expert knowledge is required from many diverse disciplines, including fifteenth-century maritime capabilities and procedures, the Spanish language of that period, tidal flows in the Bahamas, detailed knowledge of flora and fauna throughout the islands, ranges of visibility under various lighting conditions, and the information content of cumulus cloud formations. Another area that will require international cooperation is the search for relevant data in the archives of Spain and the Vatican. Surely, in all the litigation that followed the discovery there must be some useful clues for the reconstruction, possibly even clues as strong as Ponce de León's that have been overlooked because they don't fit the prevailing wisdom.

Finally, on the basis of my reconstruction through Northeast Providence Channel, we must conclude that Christopher Columbus was both a more proficient explorer and also a more accurate journalist than he is generally given credit for by advocates of the central route.

---

[70] Morison, *Admiral of the Ocean Sea*, pp. 345–47.

The Discovery of Columbus's Island Passage to Cuba, October 12–27, 1492

Robert H. Power

Christopher Columbus's arrival in the Americas on 12 October 1492 is the most celebrated historical event in the Age of Discovery. However, historians still debate among themselves exactly which island was the Admiral of the Ocean Sea's landing place. The search for that elusive island that the native inhabitants called Guanahaní and Columbus named San Salvador is limited to about eight islands that face the Atlantic Ocean on the northeastern face of the Bahamian archipelago.

The purpose of this paper is to identify Columbus's arrival island and to establish an original solution for the subsequent route to Cuba during the fortnight following the landfall. The methods used will be a careful compliance with the text of Columbus's *Journal* and the development of a series of geographic diagrams from this text that can be closely matched with the geographic diagrams based on the islands in the Bahamas.[1] This paper will establish the identity of Columbus's islands with their modern counterparts as follows: (1) Guanahaní, renamed San Salvador by Columbus[2] — Grand Turk Island; (2) the island of Santa Maria de la Concepción — Providenciales Island (one of the Caicos Islands); (3) the island of Santa Maria de la Concepción — the Caicos Islands; (4) the island of Fernandina — Mayaguana, Plana Cays, and Acklins islands; (5) the island of Isabela — Great Inagua Island; (6) the *isleo* next to Isabela — Little Inagua Island; and (7) the Islas de Arena — Ragged Islands.

Grand Turk Island is not a new candidate for Columbus's Guanahaní. It was so identified by the famous Columbus scholar, Fernández de Navarrete, in 1825; in that year, he edited and published a long-lost extract of Columbus's *Journal* made by

---

[1] The Columbus *Journal* referred to in this paper is the extract from Christopher Columbus's *Diario* as transcribed by Bartolomé de Las Casas. This long-lost abstract was discovered by Martín Fernández de Navarrete in 1790. A new transcript of the document was completed in 1982 by Oliver Dunn. The translation utilized in this paper was completed in 1983 by Michael Mathis of the University of San Francisco.

[2] The name of this island was changed by the Bahamian legislature in 1926 from Watlings Island to San Salvador island to reflect the consensus of historical opinion that Columbus had landed there and so named it San Salvador on October 12, 1492. Today, all modern maps of the region identify this island by its legislated name of San Salvador and this paper follows this policy. Columbus's discovery island, to avoid confusion, is therefore identified by its Arawak Indian name of Guanahani.

Bartolomé de Las Casas.[3] This document has been generally accepted by historians as the definitive source of information about Columbus's first voyage to the New World. However, Navarrete's identification of Grand Turk as the discovery island was largely ignored by subsequent historical writers, among them Washington Irving, who favored the then traditional solution of Cat Island in his *Life and Voyages of Christopher Columbus*, published in 1828.[4]

My interest in the Columbus landing debate was originally kindled by the late Commodore Pieter Verhoog of the Netherlands, who authored a paper titled "Columbus landed on the Caicos." Excerpts from this paper were read on behalf of Commodore Verhoog by John Parker at the November 1980 annual meeting in Columbus, Ohio, of the Society for the History of Discoveries. Verhoog's 1980 paper was an abridgment of an article that had appeared in the October 1954 issue of the U.S. Naval Institute *Proceedings*.[5] That article was intended as an open challenge to Samuel Eliot Morison, the Columbian authority for the twentieth century. Morison, in his writings, augmented the already prevailing historical consensus that San Salvador Island (formerly Watlings Island) was the island where Christopher Columbus landed on October 12, 1492.[6]

Morison ignored Verhoog's article until 1963 when he dismissed the whole matter by a short footnote in his *Journals and Other Documents on the Life and Voyages of Christopher Columbus*. In part, he declared that "another Dutch master mariner, Captain E. Roukema, has demolished . . . Verhoog's . . . arguments in 'Columbus Landed on Watling Island'. . . and the question can be considered settled."[7] Verhoog's plea was for the members of the Society for the History of Discoveries to give fair consideration to his theory because he still believed it gave a better solution to Columbus's route through the Bahamas than that advocated by Morison.[8] It appeared to me that Verhoog had made a reasonable case for his identification of East Caicos as Columbus's Guanahaní. I made a quiet resolve to visit the little-known Caicos Islands and personally evaluate whether the physical evidence on East Caicos could be paired with Columbus's description of Guanahaní.

With the assistance of Harold Russell, the proprietor of Turks Head Inn in Cockburn Town on Grand Turk Island, I arranged a two-day excursion to the Turks and Caicos Islands.[9] Russell advised me that the authority in the Turks and Caicos

---

[3] Martín Fernández de Navarrete, *Colección de las viages y descubrimientos que hicieron por mar los españoles desde fines del siglo quince* (Madrid, 1825).

[4] Washington Irving, *The Life and Voyages of Christopher Columbus*, John Harmon McElroy, ed. (Boston, 1981).

[5] Pieter Verhoog, "Columbus Landed on Caicos," *Proceedings of the U.S. Naval Institute* 80 (1954): 1101–11. Verhoog had first advanced the Caicos landing theory in a pamphlet, *Guanahaní Again* (Amsterdam, 1947).

[6] Samuel Eliot Morison, *Admiral of the Ocean Sea: The Life of Christopher Columbus* (New York, 1942); this work was awarded the Pulitzer Prize for biography in 1942. *Christopher Columbus, Mariner* (Boston, 1942). An example of this strong twentieth-century bias for Watlings Island is the work of John Boyd Thacher, *Christopher Columbus: His Life, His Work, His Remains* (1902; reprint, New York: Kraus, 1962).

[7] Samuel Eliot Morison, trans., *Journals and Other Documents on the Life and Voyages of Christopher Columbus* (New York, 1963), p.66, n.3.

[8] After consideration of the previously proposed routes for Columbus through the Bahamas, the closest match to Columbus's actual route was the one identified by Verhoog.

[9] It is coincidence that Cockburn Town is both the site selected by Morison and the landing site in this paper for Columbus; one, however, is on San Salvador and the other on Grand Turk. Cockburn Harbor is

Islands on Columbus was H. E. Sadler, in whose opinion neither Morison nor Verhoog was correct in identifying Columbus's arrival island. In Sadler's opinion, the true island of Guanahaní was the island of Grand Turk.[10] Sadler introduced me to the complexity of the Columbus landing riddle by acquainting me with the extensive investigations by boat and plane for both Verhoog's and Morison's Columbus theory by Edwin and Marion Link and P. V. H. Weems in 1958.[11] Their conclusion favored Verhoog's identification of East Caicos but differed with him on Columbus's subsequent route to Cuba, which merged with Morison's route at the southern end of Long Island. Sadler also shared with me an article by Robert Fuson on the Columbus landing question, which likewise supported Verhoog's landing site.[12]

It was significant to me that two famous navigators, Edwin Link and Weems, as well as Fuson had all favored Verhoog's identification of Columbus's landing site at the entrance to Turks Island Passage. Among living historians, Sadler alone believed that the evidence favored the island of Grand Turk, which forms the eastern shore of this same passage. For different reasons, Verhoog, the Links, Weems, Fuson, and Sadler all found Morison's theory invalid and opted instead for an anchorage within Turks Island Passage. In October 1981, my continuing interest took me back to Grand Turk Island, and this time I chartered a twin-engined Piper aircraft and flew over Turk and Caicos Islands. I also made a ground tour of Grand Turk. Finally, local journalist John Houseman arranged for William Everstein to fly me clockwise around Grand Turk Island at what he termed "mast height" of the *Santa Maria*. (However, for part of the flight, the Cessna aircraft was only the height of the *Santa Maria's* forecastle!)

Later, as I reflected on these experiences and reviewed my photographs of the Turks and Caicos Islands, I reached a summary judgment: If Columbus had anchored in the Turks and Caicos Islands, then the island of arrival was Grand Turk, as advocated by H. E. Sadler, and not East Caicos, as advocated by Verhoog. Subsequently, I developed significant evidence to support that judgment, which will be reviewed in greater detail later in this paper. That preliminary report identifying Grand Turk Island as a viable candidate for Columbus's Guanahaní was presented to the 1981 Annual Meeting of the Society for the History of Discoveries in

---

the port for South Caicos. Cockburn was a distinguished Scotch family. James Cockburn was governor of the Bermudas. Admiral George Cockburn was co-commander of the British forces that burned the U.S. Capitol in 1814 and he was made admiral of the fleet in 1851.

[10] H. E. Sadler, *Turk Island Landfall* (Grand Turk, 1981), pp. 3–7. In Sadler's opinion, Columbus discovered Grand Turk Island from the southeast and landed within Hawks Nest Anchorage. His route to Cuba identifies the Caicos Islands as the islands of both Santa Maria and Fernandina. He then accepts Verhoog's route from Great Inagua to Cuba.

[11] Edwin Link and Marion C. Link, "A New Theory on Columbus's Voyage through the Bahamas," *Smithsonian Miscellaneous Collections*, 135 (1958). Associated with the Links was their friend P. V. H. Weems. Their respective skills in navigational matters was established in World War II by the Link Trainer for pilots and the Weems Navigational System used in aircraft. Morison dismissed their solution in the same footnote he used to dismiss Verhoog's theory by merely utilizing the conjunction "and." See note 7 above.

[12] The compatibility between Grand Turk and Guanahaní is additionally demonstrated by the events of 14 October. On that date, Columbus "took the small boats and went along the island on a course 'el Camino del' north-north-east to see the other part, which was . . . the east side." The phrase "el Camino del" usually means "the road towards," but it can also be translated as "the road from."

Athens, Georgia. Once Grand Turk Island was tentatively established as the most logical Columbus landing site within Turks Island Passage, it was then necessary to evaluate Grand Turk, 21°30′ N latitude, versus San Salvador Island, 24° N latitude, in comparison with all the traits known about Columbus's island of Guanahaní.

The general issues to be explored in comparing Grand Turk Island and San Salvador to Columbus's Guanahaní are as follows: (1) identification of Columbus's "course made good" from the Canary Islands to the Bahamian archipelago; (2) the evaluation of the environmental, geographical and other specific evidence related in Columbus's *Journal* and other related documents describing Guanahaní; and (3) the relationship of Grand Turk Island and San Salvador Island to routes toward Cuba that compare favorably with the text in Columbus's *Journal* describing the route from Guanahaní to Cuba.

Identification of Columbus's "Course Made Good" from the Canary Islands to the Bahamian Archipelago

Columbus sailed west from the island of Hierro on 11 September, 1492, "directing his voyage towarde the west following the falling of the sunne, but declining somewhat towarde the left hande, sailed on forwarde . . . [and] he discovered, VI, islandes."[13] This statement from Peter Martyr's *Decades* suggests that Columbus used the sun as his principal directional guide for keeping a westerly course, but allowed the currents to carry him southward. The entire Bahamian archipelago is in the southern segment of the west sector of a compass rose when the island of Hierro is at its center; therefore, all of the Bahamas are west "towards the left hand" to a lesser or greater extent from the Canary Islands.

There is evidence that Columbus's fleet sailed farther "toward the left hand" than even Columbus realized because most of the early maps of Cuba and Hispaniola place these islands two degrees too far north. Therefore, 22° N latitude was thought by Columbus to be 24° N latitude, which is the average latitude in which Guanahaní appears on these same maps.

However, there are some geographical surprises in the relationship between the Canaries and the Bahamas. The axis of the Bahamas runs more east and west than north and south, making Grand Turk Island the closest Bahamian island to Hierro. Measuring by direct rhumbline, Grand Turk is 2,933 nautical miles from Hierro, 108 miles closer than San Salvador, which lies 3,041 nautical miles from the island. Using a J-curve rhumbline, Grand Turk is 3,171 nautical miles from Hierro, 151 miles closer than San Salvador, which would then lie 3,322 nautical miles from the island.

Today, of course, the currents and winds of the Atlantic Ocean are well known,

---

[13] Peter Martyr of Anghiera, *Decades of the Ocean*, ed. Richard Eden and Richard Willes in *The History of Travel in the West and East Indies*, (London, 1577), fol. 9.

and they cause sailing ships to follow a rather tightly prescribed route from the Mediterranean area to North America. This average transit for sailing vessels is termed the southern route on modern navigational charts and is located in 23° ± 1° N latitude.

Yachtsman Bennett Bibel, after reviewing the *Journal*, came to the conclusion that it would be impossible, based on the evidence available, to prescribe the precise course for Columbus's crossing of the Atlantic Ocean in 1492.[14] Bibel, therefore, suggests that the midline of the southern route on a chart of the world sailing ship routes is very likely the route Columbus unknowingly sailed to the New World.[15]

This route is heavily influenced by the southerly flow of the Canary Current, which curves at about 24° N latitude into the westward-flowing, southward-arcing north Equatorial Current. Columbus probably followed this standard route until October 7 when he saw birds flying from the north to the southwest, headed for what he presumed was an island sanctuary over the horizon. Columbus noted in the *Journal* that this method of following birds had been used by the Portuguese to discover many of their islands. If Columbus was following the southern route and had followed those birds to the southwest, he would have discovered the island of Hispaniola. However, because he did not want to sacrifice his westward progress, he compromised with a course of south-southwest from 7 October to 11 October, at which point he resumed his westerly sailing. At 2 A.M., 12 October, Columbus saw Grand Turk's north point two leagues from the *Santa Maria*. By the light of day he turned into Turks Island Passage and came to anchor in one of two possible areas on the western shore of Grand Turk near either Cockburn Town or English Point.

The experience of mariners over the past five centuries has established that the winds and currents create a natural route from the Canary Islands to the Bahamas in 23° ± 1° N latitude. If Columbus unknowingly followed this natural southern route until he decided to follow the birds towards the south-southwest, he would have dipped towards 21° N where he would then have encountered Grand Turk on 12 October. The only Bahamian islands south-southwest of the southern route's median line in 23°30′ N latitude on the Atlantic side of the archipelago are Maya-guana and the Turks and Caicos Islands.

As realistic as this assumption is that the southern route was Columbus's actual route, the evidence available does not allow a definite conclusion to be drawn unless other evidence is established that Grand Turk Island was the destination Columbus reached on 12 October 1492. However, if the other evidence is definitive in identifying Grand Turk Island as Columbus's Guanahaní, then we can accept Bennett Bibel's assumption that the most likely course made good by Columbus was what is known as the southern route, because it is the only route by which Columbus could have arrived at Grand Turk Island from the Canaries.

[14] Personal communications on Columbus's route from Bennett Bibel, letters dated 19 August 1982 and 6 May 1983.
[15] *The World Sailing Ship Routes* [chart], comp. Rear Admiral Boyle T. Somerville, C.M.G., hydrographer for the Navy, (Taunton, 14 June 1974).

The Evaluation of the Environmental, Geographical, and Other Specific Evidence Related in Columbus's "Journal" and Related Documents Describing Guanahaní

The most famous summary description of *Guanahaní* appears in Las Casa's *Historia*, in which he states that San Salvador had the form of a *haba*, a "bean pod."[16] It has been alleged that San Salvador Island has the form of a bean pod, but no one has ever graphically illustrated this comparison. Only if the reef of that island is incorporated into the design of the island does it remotely take the form of a bean pod. In contrast, Grand Turk Island is uniquely like the form of the pod of the Old World's "great garden beane" or the wild "Greek beane," as they were illustrated in Gerard's *Herbal* (London, 1636).[17] The comparison of the pod of a Greek bean in Gerard's *Herbal* to Grand Turk Island is clearly the best comparison available between an Old World bean pod and a New World island. In contrast, the comparison of the old *Herbal* illustration to San Salvador requires considerable imagination to find a similarity of form.

Columbus's *Journal* records an unusual demographic statistic among the native inhabitants who greeted Columbus on 12 October: they were "all youths, and none more than thirty years of age . . . and . . . I saw no more than one [woman] who was just a girl."[18] Apparently, Columbus found no settlement in his explorations on 12 and 13 October, because at sunrise on 14 October he set out in the small ship's boats "to see the settlements," and he later "saw two or three of them," one of which consisted of six houses. In association with these settlements he reported seeing both men and women who shouted that the seamen should go ashore. All indications in the *Journal* are that no significant village was encountered on the island of Guanahaní and that there was an abundance of young males.

Recent archeological investigations in the Turks and Caicos Islands have revealed that Grand Turk was only a fishing outpost for the Arawak Indians who lived on the Caicos Islands. No permanent village sites have been discovered on Grand Turk, marked by piles of conch shells left from pre-Columbian times. A single flaked stone and no pottery shards have been recorded from Grand Turk. Therefore, the young male population Columbus found on the day of discovery and the absence of a significant village conforms to the demographic pattern of Grand Turk revealed through archeology.[19] In contrast, San Salvador Island has the large, well-developed Arawak Indian cultural site near Pigeon Point, where hundreds of

---

[16] Bartolomé de Las Casas, *Apologetica Historia Sumaria* (Mexico City: Universidad Nacional auto noma de Mexico Instituto de Investigaciones Historicas, n.d.), vol. 1, chap. 1, p. 9, "Iisla forma de una haba." This is not part of Las Casa's journal of original transcripts for Columbus's *Journal*, but Las Casas's father was a participant in the voyage of 1492, and therefore privy to certain oral information concerning the voyage of discovery.

[17] John Gerard, *The Herbal or General Historie of Plantes* (London, 1636), p. 1209.

[18] Michael Mathis's translation of Las Casas's abstract. All references in this paper, unless otherwise noted, are from unpublished translations from Oliver Dunn's transcription.

[19] Shawn Sullivan, "Pre-Historic Caicos," *Turk and Caicos Current* (July-August, 1982), p. 34.

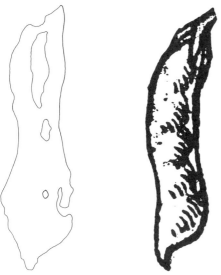

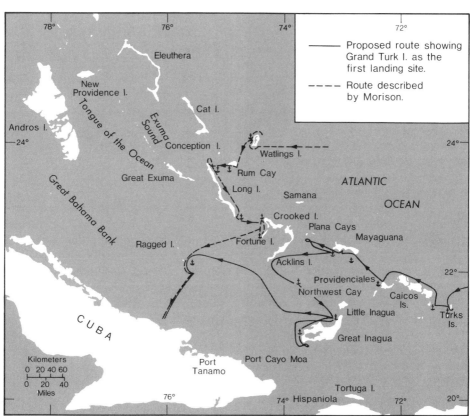

Figure 1: Outline of Grand Turk Island and an enlargement of a bean pod from Gerard's *Herbal*.

Figure 2: Comparison of routes from Turks Islands landfall and from Watlings Island landfall.

artifacts have been excavated. Columbus did not report seeing a significant village on Guanahaní. The demographic information in Columbus's *Journal* favors Grand Turk over San Salvador.

The events of 14 October additionally establish that Grand Turk is a good fit for Columbus's Guanahaní. "At sunrise he took the small ship's boats and set out to explore the other part which was the other part of the east side" of Guanahaní. Their course followed "el Camino del [north-northeast]," that is, "the road of the north-northeast." This is usually assumed to indicate a course towards the north-northeast, but it can also be translated as the "route *from* the north-northeast [to the south-southwest]." However, the island of Grand Turk gives room for either interpretation because the southeastern shore where Columbus apparently explored also trends north-northeast.

Eastward of Small Cut in the coral reef at the south end of Grand Turk, Columbus found "a port which would serve for all of the ships of all Christian nations." The sea in that port was "as calm as the inside of a well." This is an overzealous description of Hawks Nest Anchorage, which is a pane of calm water within the Turk Island reef. Hawks Nest is an unusual anchorage east and southeast of the island protected by a nearly submerged rim of coral. The north part of Hawks Nest Anchorage extends a mile and a half up the southeastern side of Grand Turk to South Creek. It is there that the final discoveries on 14 October were made.

The *Journal* states that Columbus wrote "I . . . know where I could place a fort . . . [on] a piece of land which is like an island, but which is not . . . which would take two days of work" to make it a true island. This matches the "sand flat" marked on the modern map at the mouth of South Creek.[20] Next to this peninsula, Columbus describes "Tree gardens . . . so green . . . and there is much water." This precisely fits the description of the mangrove swamp in South Creek. Columbus then declares: "I looked at all of this port." From the hill on the north side of South Creek, Columbus could easily survey "all of this port" and note "many islands" such as Salt Cay, Cotton Cay, Pear Cay, Long Cay, and East Cay.

Then Columbus returned to the *Santa Maria* and prepared to depart Guanahaní for another island. The elapsed time for the small boat exploration can be estimated at nine hours, and the distance round trip was about eleven miles if Guanahaní was Grand Turk. Grand Turk is a proper size to match the requirements of Guanahaní.

Morison's solution for the events of 14 October is to take Columbus northward along San Salvador and then eastward into Graham's Harbor. Without comment, he blends these two directions to equal the north-northeast given by Columbus. Morison seems to be oblivious to the fact that Graham's Harbor is on the north side of San Salvador Island, not the east side where Columbus declared he was going. Morison designates Rocky Point as the "almost an island," but he notes that it has been cut by the sea into an island just as Columbus declared he could do in two days' time. Morison found no very green tree gardens in much water, and in a footnote he projects how the Bahamas were cleared for cotton in the eighteenth century and alleges that "hurricanes felled the remaining trees."[21]

[20] "Bahama Islands, Grand Turk Island," Defense Mapping Agency Hydrographic Center, Chart No. 26262 (Washington, D.C.).

[21] Morison, *Journals and Other Documents*, p. 66, n.3.

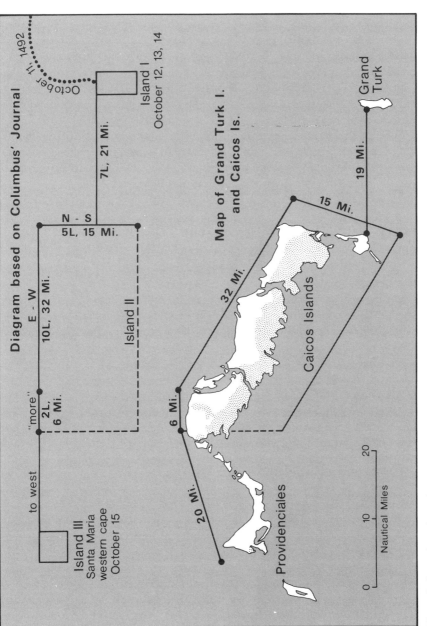

Figure 3: At top is a schematic representation of the journey Columbus describes between Guanahani and Santa Maria. At bottom is a chart of the Turks and Caicos Islands, showing the match between the data of the *Journal* and the author's proposed route.

Graham's Harbor is a very poor anchorage, not the large, safe, calm harbor discovered by Columbus. In this regard, the *Yachtsman's Guide to the Bahamas* (1982) undercuts Morison's whole theory. It declares, "There are really no safe natural habors in San Salvador"; the best is in the bight off Cockburn Town and an alternate "is the open Graham's Harbor in the northeast corner where a draft of 7 ft. can be carried in." It further declares that it is only legend that Graham's Harbor is the one Columbus described as able to "hold all the ships of Christendom."[22]

Grand Turk in shape, size, cultural history, and geographical features is a far better fit to the known facts about Guanahaní than San Salvador. Morison, however, was correct in finding that San Salvador was a better fit with Columbus's Guanahaní than any of the islands in the Commonwealth of the Bahamas.

The Routes to Cuba from Grand Turk Island and San Salvador Island Compared with the Text in Columbus's "Journal" Describing the Route from Guanahaní to Cuba

Columbus wrote to his financial patron Luis Santangel while at sea off the Canaries on his return voyage and identified the islands that he had discovered on his route to "Juana" (Cuba):

> The first that I discovered I named San Salvador, in remembrance of that Almighty Power which had so miraculously bestowed them. The Indians call it Guanahaní. To the second I assigned the name of Santa Marie de Conception; to the third, that of Fernandina; to the fourth, that of Isabella; to the fifth, Juana; and so on to every one a new name.[23]

14 October 1492 — Midafternoon

After returning from exploring Guanahaní in midafternoon, Columbus raised sail and "saw so many islands that I was not able to decide to which I should go first. . . . I looked for the largest, and decided to go there."

Turks Islands consist of Grand Turk, Salt Cay, Cotton Cay and several smaller cays, but the Caicos Islands are not visible from Grand Turk. The *Journal* indicated, however, that the fleet set sail and *then* saw "the largest [island] . . . and decided to go there. . . . It would be five leagues distant from this island of San Salvador and others would be more and others less." The next day the *Journal* states that "the island would be farther than five leagues, it will be seven first" [i.e., six to seven leagues]." The distance from Grand Turk to South Caicos is nineteen miles, which is more than six and less than seven leagues. It is less to Cotton and Salt Cays — South Caicos could

[22] The *Yachtsman's Guide to the Bahamas*, 32d ed. (1982), pp. 316–18.
[23] William Elroy Curtis, *The Relics of Columbus*, (Washington, D.C., 1983), p. 140.

be seen on 14 October once Columbus was ten miles from Grand Turk. This was a possible sailing distance between middle to late afternoon and sunset, as called for in the *Journal*.

In contrast to this reasonable fit with Columbus's *Journal*, there are no islands whatsoever visible from San Salvador, and Rum Cay does not come into view until more than sixteen miles are sailed from San Salvador Island. Morison explains the "many islands" as the hills on Rum Cay, which upon the horizon appear as separate islands. It is unlikely that an experienced seaman like Columbus would report this transitory illusion as "many islands" in the day's entry into the *Journal*.

15 October 1492—An Unnamed Island and Santa Maria de la Concepción

Columbus "passed time" through the night of 14 October and sailed on towards island II at sunrise on 15 October. By midday, he arrived at island II, which had a "face, which is towards the island of San Salvador, runs north-south, and there are five leagues to it [15 miles]." South and East Caicos have a fifteen mile (five league) north-south shoreline that faces Grand Turk nineteen miles (six leagues) distant, forming Turks Island Passage. This geographic pattern of land and water perfectly fits the diagram in Columbus's *Journal*, based on the assumption that Columbus's leagues consisted of 3.18 nautical miles. This is the length of Morison's "sea league," and this paper adopts this measurement as Columbus's league.[24]

Morison utilizes a footnote to cover the most controversial call of his career concerning the matching of Rum Cay to Columbus's Santa Maria:

> This orientation of Rum Cay is correct, but is only 10 miles long by 5 wide. This is the first instance of Columbus' using a different league, equivalent to between 1 and 1.5 nautical miles, for distances along shore.[25]

The orientation of Rum Cay is incorrect because its north-south shoreline does not face San Salvador but is situated at a forty-five-degree angle eight leagues southwest of San Salvador. It is not ten miles long and five miles wide: it is a nine- by four-mile island. In addition, Morison had no justification whatsoever for his "along-shore" league. This controversial claim was required to justify his conclusion that Rum Cay matched Columbus's description of Santa Maria. In contrast to the perfect fit between the features of Turks Island Passage and Columbus's *Journal*, there is no fit whatsoever of the passage from San Salvador Island to Rum Cay with the *Journal*.

There is still another critically important interpretation of the text in Columbus's *Journal* concerning the events of 15 October. This has to do with the names of the islands discovered on this date. Traditionally, it was assumed that only Santa Maria was discovered, but in 1958 Edwin and Marion Link decided that a close interpretation of the *Journal* indicated that there was an unnamed island measuring five by

---

[24] All miles in this paper are nautical miles and all leagues are computed at 3.18 nautical miles. There are many opinions about the length of the leagues, but I believe that Morison's computation of 3.18 for his "sea leagues" is the best fit with Columbus's *Journal*.

[25] Morison, *Journals and Other Documents*, p. 71, n.1.

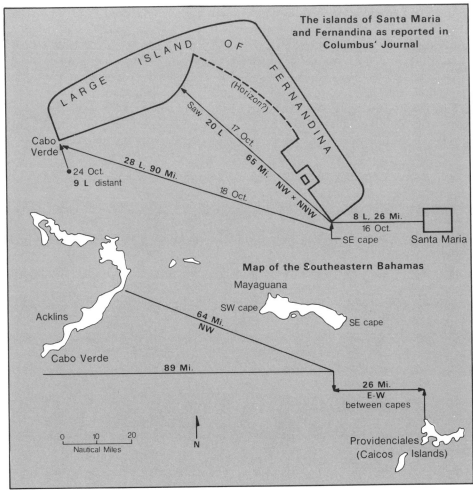

Figure 4: At top is a schematic representation of the journey Columbus describes for the period October 16–18, as well as a sketch of the shoreline on Fernandina. At bottom is a chart of Providenciales, Mayaguana, and Acklins islands, showing the match between the data of the *Journal* and the author's proposed route.

tation of the *Journal* indicated that there was an unnamed island measuring five by ten leagues—island II.[26] This interpretation was the principal reason they rejected Verhoog's route to Cuba, which did not allow for an unnamed island II. Morison's theory, of course, predated this interpretation. Robert Fuson has strongly defended the Links and Weems interpretation of Columbus's *Journal* that island II was not named by Columbus.[27]

After observing that the north-south face of island II was five leagues, the *Journal* states that the "the other [face] that I followed ran east-west, and there were more than ten leagues [32 miles] to it. Since from this island [island II] I saw another larger one [island III] to the west, I put on more sails to run all that day until night . . . to the West Cape. To this island [island III] I gave the name of Isla de Santa Maria de la Concepción and at almost sunset I anchored near the aforesaid cape." The Caicos Islands have a north-south face of fifteen miles and a northwest-southeast face of thirty-eight miles (twelve leagues), and then a southwest-northeast face for twenty miles (seven leagues), with the higher, Blue Hills on Providenciales Island forming a westerly cape.

The relationship of the islands of the Turk and Caicos archipelago is very compatible with Columbus's *Journal*, strongly indicating that Grand Turk is Guanahaní. It appears that Columbus's second landing in the New World was on Providenciales in the Caicos archipelago. The Caicos Islands remained unnamed except as indicated below.

In contrast, Morison was only able to make Rum Cay match Columbus's description of the island of Santa Maria by reducing the measurement of Columbus's league by seventy percent and designating this new measurement an "along-shore league."

16 October 1492 — De las Isla[s] de Santa Maria de la Concepción and the Route to Fernandina

The next day, 16 October, Columbus went ashore and saw naked natives and did not find any aspect to compliment, which is in conformance with the unattractive tropical scrub that grows on semi-arid Providenciales Island. In contrast, Rum Cay, according to Morison, is "one of the prettiest" Bahamian islands he explored, "particularly interesting in flora and/or fauna and for landscape forms." Columbus recorded no such beauty, reserving those adjectives for 17 October on the island of Fernandina and 19 October for the island of Isabela.

After Columbus finished his uneventful visit with natives on the island of Santa Maria, the *Journal* states that he set sail from "delas ysla de Scta maria de Concepcion." On the day following the original naming, in which he used the singular form, Columbus has ow mutated towards a pluralized form with the utilization of "delas." This suggests that Columbus's island of Santa Maria de la Concepción was part of an archipelago, as is Providenciales Island, which is part of the Caicos archipelago; and it suggests that Columbus was expanding the use of the name to include all of the Caicos islands that he had seen the previous day. This interpretation is consistent with the concept that there were at least two islands discovered on

[26] Link and Link, *Christopher Columbus's Voyage*, p. 3.
[27] Robert Fuson, "Grand Turk Was Guanahaní," *Turk and Caicos Current* (July/August 1982), pp. 21–30.

15 October. In contrast, Rum Cay is a solitary island that would not have inspired the use of the plural form "delas."

The distance given in Columbus's *Journal* from the islands of Santa Maria de la Concepción to the large island of Fernandina is noted in one place as eight leagues and in another as nine leagues. In both instances, however, the distance is stated as the east-to-west distance between the two islands. This converts into twenty-five–twenty-nine miles of longitude between Santa Maria and Fernandina. Conveniently, there are twenty-seven miles of longitude between the north cape of Providenciales and the southeast cape of Mayaguana.

In midchannel between those two islands, Columbus "found a lone man in a canoe" that he "recognized . . . [had] come from the island of San Salvador [via] . . . of Santa Maria" and now was headed for Fernandina. The evidence that he had followed this route was "a strand of glass beads and two castilian coins" Columbus had traded for friendship after arrival on 12 October. If this circumstance is applied to the Grand Turk Island route to Cuba, it places the Arawak Indian eighty-three miles from San Salvador, indicating a steady pace of twenty-eight miles per day for three days across the shallow and quiet water on the south side of the Caicos archipelago. If the canoe route is the one selected by Morison, the Indian only needed to paddle an easy twenty miles per day, but if the route is the one selected by the Link theory, the lone Indian had to paddle forty miles per day. Morison's route is the most plausible of the three. However, the Grand-Turk-to-Cuba route also provides a possible solution to this piece of evidence, while it tends to mitigate against the longer route plan developed by the Links. The Indian and canoe were released off Fernandina on the evening of 16 October, according to Columbus's *Journal*, so that he could give good reports about the expeditiion to those on that island.

17 October — The Island of Fernandina (I)

At sunrise, Columbus made an anchorage off a native coastal village, and many canoes set off to visit and trade with the Columbian fleet. Three hours later, he went ashore and found a level island where maize was grown all year. There were many trees and wondrous fish. The trees he found especially interesting for they had "branches of many kinds, all on one trunk . . . one branch had leaves like cane, another like sumac, and thus on a single tree there were five or six varieties." The fish were "like roosters of the finest colors of the world, blues, yellows, reds, and others painted in a thousand ways."

According to the *Yachtsman's Guide*, there is a safe anchorage just to the west of the southeast cape of Mayaguana. The text in this same guide gives a condensed description that mirrors amazingly well the description in Columbus's *Journal* of woods, crops and fish. It specifically states that "for the most part it is 'thickly wooded (and) its inhabitants . . . exist by raising crops and fishing.' "[28] In contrast, Long Island, which is the island Morison identifies as the island of Fernandina, "lacks the south sea flavor found elsewhere in the Bahamas" and has "towering cliffs and rolling hills."[29] It is an open island used for stock raising and crops.

[28] *Yachtsman's Guide to the Bahamas*, p. 335.
[29] Ibid.

At midday, he left the settlement where he had anchored and followed the shoreline towards the north-northeast.

The description in Columbus's *Journal* for the afternoon of 17 October is a perfect fit with the features still in existence along the southeastern shore of Mayaguana Island, except the shoreline running northeast instead of north-northeast. Columbus states that when "I was near the cape of the island, at two leagues, I found a very marvellous port with one entrance, although it can be said of two entrances, because it has a rock island in the middle, and inside it is very wide, for a hundred ships if it were deep and clear." The *Yachtsman's Guide*, in part, says of Mayaguana: "Abrahams Bay on the south coast is best. There are two entrances through the reef which forms the southern side of the harbor. The easiest [entrance] is that at the southwest corner of the reef; ... this is good for twelve feet craft. The second entrance ... carries seven feet at L[ow] W[ater]."[30] Abraham Bay is a precise seven miles (two leagues) from the southwest cape of Mayaguana.

Columbus went ashore with his men to secure fresh water, presuming Abraham Bay to be a river mouth, but found it only a saltwater lagoon. Therefore, Columbus sent his men with the local inhabitants to the nearby village to fill their casks. The *Journal* tells how Columbus waited two hours for their return and in that time he went to the trees, "which were the most beautiful to be seen ... [the] greennesss in such a degree as in the month of May in Andalucia." The chart of Abraham Bay carries three legends on the island shoreline denoting "densely wooded." Mayaguana Island remains a timber island where mahogany and lignum vitae are commercially harvested.

Morison makes an unfounded claim that Santa Maria Harbor on Long Island "perfectly fits" the description given in Columbus's *Journal* of the harbor discovered and explored on the afternoon of 17 October. Santa Maria Harbor does not match the geographical descriptions in the *Journal*. It is not two leagues from any cape because it is part of the north cape of Long Island. It has only one entrance channel, as there is no division caused by a reef of rock. The island's shoreline is bold and without large trees such as those admired by Columbus when his men went for water. Columbus's *Journal* then says that after the water was secured, he set sail and "went so far out to the north-west that I discovered all that part of the island up to the coast that runs east-west." This has no fit at all with Long Island, as there is no farther land to the north or west of Santa Maria Harbor. It is clear that Morison failed to find or identify Columbus's island of Fernandina.

However, the Grand-Turk-to-Cuba route also has its difficulties in fitting a route to these sailing directions in the *Journal*. There is a coast "up," or north of the southwest cape of Mayaguana, but there is no coast that runs east-west except for the Plana Cays in Mayaguana Passage. Apparently, on this stormy evening Columbus thought that Mayaguana, the Plana Cays, and north-east Acklins islands were all one island. Instead of realizing that he was in a passage between two islands, he believed he was in the gulf of one large island that had a coast that ran east-west. This concept that both Mayaguana and Acklins are part of the island of Fernandina is consistently supported by all the passages that deal with Fernandina after the afternoon of 17

[30] Ibid.

165

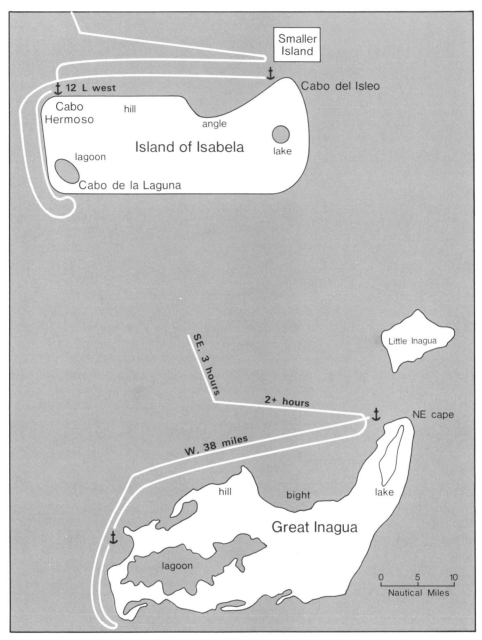

Figure 5: At top is a schematic representation of the journey Columbus describes in the vicinity of Isabela, as well as a sketch of Isabela. At bottom is a chart of Great Inagua, showing the match between the data of the *Journal* and the author's proposed route.

October. It also explains why Columbus thought he had seen twenty leagues (sixty-four miles) of the island of Fernandina, for it is exactly twenty leagues from the southeast cape of Mayaguana and the most easterly cape of Acklins Island.

As strained as this solution appears to be, it is immeasurably more palatable than any explanation for this evening in the San Salvador-to-Cuba route. Morison did not even attempt to make the facts in Columbus's *Journal* fit this evening: he just ignored this part of the route.

18 October — Island of Fernandina (I and II)

The only entry for this date in Columbus's *Journal* gives no course or distance or geographic detail. It merely states: "After it cleared,I followed the wind and went as far around the island as I could, and I anchored at the time when it was no longer proper to sail. However, I did not go ashore, and at sunrise I set sail." The lack of information in Columbus's *Journal* for this day allows it to be used as a wild card day where any possible course can be declared as a probable course.

On the Grand-Turk-to-Cuba route, the course for this day begins at the southwest cape of Mayaguana and arches toward the west to within sight of southwestern Acklins Island and ending at Hogsty Reef, located between Acklins Island and Great Inagua. This proposed course has a track of about eighty-five miles, which is within the range of a day's sailing. This anchorage was first identified by Robert Fuson in 1982.[31]

Columbus speculated in two places that the large island of Fernandina had a face of twenty-eight leagues, or about eighty-nine miles. This is the exact distance from the southeast cape of Mayaguana, where Columbus anchored on the morning of 17 October, to the southwest cape of Acklins, which Columbus apparently saw from the sea on the afternoon of 18 October. This additional information supports the concept that Columbus thought Mayaguana and Acklins were all one island with a combined southern face of twenty-eight leagues (eighty-nine miles).

The San Salvador Island route, as designated by Morison, takes Columbus from the northern tip of Long Island to the southern part of Long Island, a distance of about fifty miles. This is plausible if, in fact, Columbus had found himself at Long Island on 18 October. Long Island is only about eighteen leagues long, and there is no explanation by Morison for what Columbus meant when he said that the island of Fernandina had a face of twenty-eight leagues unless a two-mile along-shore league is Morison's unit of measure for this island. If he had applied his along-shore league, Long Island is double the size given in the *Journal*, and if he applied his sea league measurement, it was one-third too small.

19 October — The Island of Isabela, Cabo Hermosa

At sunrise, Columbus set out in search of the island his native guides called *Saomete*, which he was to rename Isabela. To increase the probability of discovery, the three ships formed a forty-five-degree wedge with Columbus's *Santa Maria* sailing

---

[31] Fuson, "Grand Turk Was Guanahaní."

the central tangent to the southeast. Before they had sailed three hours, they saw a large island and converged upon its north cape where there is a smaller island to the north.

Columbus turned westward without landing and coasted the island for twelve leagues (thirty-eight miles). This island, as seen from the sea, was the most beautiful he had seen and was higher than the other islands. It was not enough to be called a mountain, but something that made it more beautiful. Columbus also describes a great angle or bight and then comes to anchor near a beautiful cape that he calls *Cabo Hermosa*, which appears to him to be almost an island, and he notes that there is a small island between his anchorage near this cape and the main part of the island.

This is a perfect description of sailing from Hogsty Reef to Great Inagua and then coasting the northern shore of that island. The small island to the north is Little Inagua, the great angle is Ocean Bight, the hill that is not a mountain is James Hill, the final anchorage on the western side of the northwest cape of Great Inagua. Little Sheeps Cay lies between this cape and the main part of the island. The northwest cape of Great Inagua has a lagoon that almost severs the headland from the main island. The modern chart indicates why Columbus named the northwest cape of Great Inagua, Cabo Hermosa ("Cape Beautiful"), for it says "low with coconut trees."

In contrast to this point-by-point compatibility between Columbus's *Journal* and the geographical features on the north face of Great Inagua, the route that Morison plots for Columbus on this day has no compatibility whatsoever with the *Journal*. Morison, by this time hopelessly lost, displays his frustration with the 17 October entry by declaring, "The only way to make sense out of this passage . . . is to read *Sueste* (southeast) for *Gueste* (west) and to reduce the distance." Morison then, with these selected interpretations, has Columbus sail seven miles south-southeast coasting Crooked Island, passing by the narrow and shallow entrance to the bight of Acklins, and then sailing another seven miles south-southwest to the southern cape of Fortune Island. Morison, without comment, combines Crooked and Fortune islands into a single island that extends almost due south rather than west as called for in Columbus's *Journal*. The total distance in Morison's route is five leagues rather than the twelve leagues called for in Columbus's *Journal*. However, Morison's contention that Columbus would perceive Crooked and Fortune to be all one island is reasonable because the entrance to the bight of Acklins is obscured by the Goat and Rat Cays. Morison matches Fortune Hill to the small hill in the *Journal* but has no explanation of how the southern tip of Fortune Island fits the description in the *Journal* of being "almost an island."

20 October — Island of Isabela, Cabo Hermosa to Cabo de la Laguna and Back towards Cabo del Isleo

At sunrise, Columbus sailed from the northwest cape to the southwest cape of the island and named this corner of the island Cabo de la Laguna. Columbus then tried to proceed around this cape towards the southeast to return to the northeast cape, but he found the water too shallow for safe navigation. Therefore, the decision was made to return to the northeast by the route they had come.

The track of Columbus on 20 October is fully compatible with the geographical characteristics existent today on the western side of Great Inagua. The northwest and southwest capes are only eighteen miles apart. The southwest cape of Great Inagua has a large lagoon close to the shoreline and thus was appropriately named Cabo de la Laguna by Columbus. The water on the south side of the southwest cape of Great Inagua is too shallow for safe sailing, and the prevailing wind blows toward the shore.

In contrast, Morison continues to be hopelessly lost in his attempt to follow Columbus's track through the Bahamas. It is clear that one sails southward to reach a southwest cape from a northwest cape, but Morison—once again at land's end—is forced to have Columbus sail northward to reach the southwest cape. Morison achieves this remarkable feat by now dividing Crooked and Fortune into two islands, leaving Fortune unnamed and restricting the identification of Columbus's Isabela Island to Crooked Island. Therefore, this allows Morison to have Columbus sail from the south cape of Fortune northward to the south cape of Crooked Island. This assumption by Morison requires that Columbus begin to return by the way he had come on 19 October, but the *Journal* states that this turnaround did not take place until the southwest cape was reached midday on 20 October.

Morison offers no explanation of why, in his scenario, Columbus thought Fortune and Crooked were all one island, but on 20 October he suddenly changed his mind and decided that the true southwest cape of the island was towards the north and that Fortune Island was not a part of the island of Isabela. Fortune Island is the same length as Crooked Island and therefore, is too large to be the cape that was "almost an island." Crooked and Fortune Islands have no fit whatsoever with Columbus's island of Isabela. However, the similarities between Great Inagua and the island of Isabela continue as Columbus explores this island farther.

21–23 October—Island of Isabela, Cabo del Isleo

The two caravels reached the north cape of the island on 20 October, but Columbus waited until the next morning at 10:00 A.M. to bring the *Santa Maria* into the anchorage at the north cape of the island of Isabela. He named the north cape Cabo del Isleo for the reef island to the north of the cape. Columbus, continuing his environmental interests, describes the great forests, large lakes, and singing of little birds, "parrots that darken the sun . . . and birds . . . of so many kinds."

Great Inagua is now a bird refuge for the Commonwealth of the Bahamas. There is also a large lake near the northeast cape of the island. The reef island to the north of the northeast cape is Little Inagua.

24 October—Under Sail

"This night, at midnight, I raised the anchors from the island of Isabela and from Cabo del Isleo which is on the north . . . to go to the Island of Cuba. . . . I sailed until daylight to the west-south-west . . . the wind calmed and it rained . . . until past midday. . . . [the wind] began to blow very lovingly." Columbus's decision to sail at

169

midnight was apparently undertaken because he had twice sailed off the northern shore of Isabela and found it to be safe. However, the route Morison selects for Columbus's nighttime sailing is an unexplored tract of sea, which seems to be a risk Columbus would not have taken.

When the loving wind filled Columbus's sails at midday, the Grand-Turk-to-Cuba route requires that he ran with that wind towards the northwest, even though no change of direction is noted in the *Journal*. This course brought him within what Columbus calculated to be seven leagues from the southern cape of the island of Fernandina, which, on this assumed route, would have been Acklins Island. The distance sailed from past midday 24 October to dawn 25 October is approximately seventy miles, which does not exceed the maximum amount Columbus could have sailed in a sixteen-hour period. Morison's route allows for a course to the west-southwest for all of 24 October, as called for in the *Journal*.

25–26 October — Sailing to the Islas de Arena

From sunrise until 9:00 A.M., Columbus sailed west-southwest for five leagues and then changed course to the west. After sailing "44 Roman miles," they sighted land and "there were seven or eight islands strung out, all north to south" that Columbus named Islas de Arena. These islands are universally identified as the Ragged Islands. At this point, the San Salvador route to Cuba, as identified by Morison, and the Grand-Turk-to-Cuba route identified in this paper converge into a single track across shallow water well named the Columbus Bank.

27 October

By evening on 27 October, Cuba was sighted and a landing was made the next day.

Conclusion

The only major point of incompatibility between the geography, tracks, and distances of this new route and the one described in Columbus's *Journal* is our assumption that Columbus incorrectly considered Mayaguana and Acklins islands to be one and the same island. Accepting this assumption, however, Columbus's *Journal* becomes consistent with the geography of the area. With this single exception, this route of discovery through the Bahamas from Grand Turk to the Ragged Islands north of Cuba has a better fit with Columbus's *Journal* than any route yet identified (see table 1).

I have carefully considered the evidence in Columbus's *Journal* and matched it to a route not yet previously identified. The discovery island is Grand Turk at what is now Cockburn Town in the Turk and Caicos Islands, a British dependency. In the fortnight that followed 12 October 1492, Columbus crossed the Turks Island Passage to South and East Caicos and followed the shore of the same British dependency to Providenciales, which forms the northwest cape for the Caicos Islands. Then he

TABLE 1
Distances in Columbus's *Journal* Compared with Actual Distances in Turks Islands Route through the Bahamas to Cuba

| Date | Turks Islands Route | *Journal* Route | Actual Distances | | *Journal* Distances |
			Nautical Miles	Columbian Leagues (3.18 nau. mi.)[a]	Columbian Leagues
Oct. 14/15	Grand Turk to South Caicos	Guanahaní to shore of island II	19	6	Less than 7
Oct. 15	South and East Caicos	N-S shore of island II	15	5	5
Oct. 15	Northeast shore of Caicos Bank	E-W shore of island II	32	10	More than 10
Oct. 15	Northeast cape of Caicos Island	E-W shore of island II	6	2	
Oct. 16	E-W from Providenciales to Mayaguana	E-W from Santa Maria to Fernandina	26	8	8
Oct. 17	Cape of Mayaguana to Abraham Bay	Cape of island to harbor of two mouths	7	2	2
Oct. 17	Southeast cape of Mayaguana to northeast cape of Acklins Island	To the northeast as far as coast goes E-W[b]	62	20	20
Oct. 18	Southeast cape of Mayaguana to southwest cape of Acklins Island	Southeast cape of Fernandina to southwest cape of Fernandina	89	28	28
Oct. 19	Northeast to northwest cape of Great Inagua	Northeast to northwest cape of Isabela	38	12	12

[a] The numbers below demonstrate that S. E. Morison was precisely correct in assuming 3.18 nautical miles to the Columbian league. Of nine assumed courses and distances comprising 170 nautical miles, there are no measurable errors. This compatibility rating of ninety-six percent between the distances in the *Journal* and the actual distances of the southern route from Grand Turk to Great Inagua is definitive evidence that Columbus's route has been identified.

[b] There is no east-west coast; this was an error in observation by Columbus.

proceeded across Caicos Passage to Mayaguana Island in the Commonwealth of the Bahamas. He explored the south side of Mayaguana and discovered Abraham Bay. Confused as to the nature of Mayaguana Passage, believing it was a gulf formed by Mayaguana and Acklins islands, he turned southward and discovered Little Inagua and Great Inagua. Then he sailed west and north until he reached the Ragged Islands, crossed the shallow Columbus Banks, and finally on 27 October anchored off Cuba.

The tiny bean pod island of Grand Turk, which was first designated as Columbus's landing site by Navarrete in 1825, should in light of this review of the evidence in Columbus's *Journal* be the focal point of the quincentenary celebration of Columbus's discovery of the New World.

The Diario, or Journal, of Columbus's First Voyage: A New Transcription of the Las Casas Manuscript for the Period October 10 through December 6, 1492

Oliver Dunn

This partial transcript of the *Diario*, or *Journal*, of Columbus's first voyage is derived from the facsimile of the Las Casas manuscript published by Carlos Sanz in 1961. The portion transcribed begins with the entry for October 10, 1492, and continues through that for December 6. It thus covers the events of the voyage from the day preceding the first landfall through the day on which the fleet arrived at Puerto de San Nicolas on the island of Hispaniola. This is the text most critical for reconstructing Columbus's route through the West Indies, the determination of which seems to offer the best prospect of pinpointing the location of San Salvador, the island on which Columbus first landed.

A number of Spanish editions of the *Diario* have been published previously. The most important of these are mentioned, with their bibliographic details, in my paper, "Columbus's First Landing Place: The Evidence of the *Journal*" (included in this volume), and so will not again be listed here. However, none of these editions attempts to do what is attempted in the version that follows: to present a text as close to that of the manuscript as can be produced on an ordinary typewriter equipped with an almost standard keyboard. In the version printed here, punctuation and capitalization have been left as they appear; words obviously misspelled have not been corrected, nor have words mistakenly substituted for others of similar sound ("un nombre" for un hombre," for example) been changed to the words probably intended; words compressed for speed in writing have not been expanded, and the marks indicating the omission of letters have been reproduced as closely as possible.

Compromises have been necessary in representing manuscript letter forms that have no typing analogs. The word "que" is usually compressed to " *⌐* ," but has been typed as "q̄." The combination of "c" and "h" is usually written " *ʄ* ." In this case I have expanded the contraction to "ch." The combination of letters "ver" is often written "Vᵒ." In the typed version, this is indicated by "Vr."

Insertions are another problem. In the manuscript most are set off from the original text by a pair of quotation marks preceding the insertion, one mark above the line of original text, the other below. In the typed transcript insertions are separated from the original text by quotation marks preceding and following the insertion. Words in the manuscript are often joined. I have separated words written without a space between if no letters have been omitted and if in modern usage the words are two, not one. But if, as in the case of "adonde," the *Diccionario* of the Academy gives "a donde" as an alternative form, I have allowed separations to remain.

Uncertainties and difficulties in reading the manuscript include those of deciding whether certain letters are intended to be capitals or lower case; those of deciphering words that at first sight seem a hopeless scrawl; and those of distinguishing between letters similarly formed, for example, "e" and "o," "a" and "n." In resolving such difficulties I have relied regularly and often on two of the printed Spanish editions of the *Diario*, namely the *Raccolta* and the Arce–Gil Esteve versions, but have occasionally consulted also those of Navarrete, Guillén, and Sanz. If the difficulties are so great that any reading is conjectural, I have put my conjecture, followed by a question mark, between brackets. In the very few instances in which a word or part of a word has been supplied to complete the manuscript text, the addition is also enclosed within brackets, but without a question mark.

Miercoles .10. de otubre

Fol. 8
(cont.)

Navego al guesudueste: anduvie
ro a diez millas por ora y a ratos
.12. y algu rato a .7. y entre dia y noche
5[9] leguas: conto a la gēte .44. leguas no
mas /. Aqui la gente ya no lo podia
çufrir: quexavase del largo viaje: ̩po el
almi^e. los esforço lo mejor q̃ pudo dādoles
buena esperāça de los provechos q̃ podrian
aver /. y añidia q̃ por demas era quexar
se pues q̃ "el" avia venido a las Yndias
y q̃ asi lo avia de proseguir hasta hallar
las / con el ayuda de nr̄o señor /.

Jueves .11°. de otubre

Fol. 8
(cont.)

Navego al guesudueste tuvierō mucha
mar mas q̃ en todo el viaje avian te
nido /. vierō pardelas y vn junco verde
junto a la nao /. vierō los dla caravela pin
ta vña caña y vn palo: y tomaro otro
palillo labrado a lo q̃ pareçia con hyerro
y vn pedaço de caña: y otra yerva q nace
en tierra: y vna tab[l?]illa /. los dla carave

la niña tābien vierō otras señales de
tr̄ra y vn palillo cargado descaramojos: cō
estas señales respiarō y alegrarōse todos /.
Anduvierō en este dia hasta puesto el sol
.27. leguas /.
despues dl sol puesto navego a su primer
camino al gueste: andarian doze millas
cada ora y hasta dos oras despues de media
noche andariā .90. millas q̄ son .22. leguas
y media /. y porq̄ la caravela pinta era
mas velera e yva delante dl almirāte
hallo tierra y hizo las señas q̄l almiᵉ. avia
mādado /. esta tr̄ra vido primero vn mari
nero q̄ se dezia rodrigo de triana: puesto q̄
el almiᵉ. a las diez dla noche estando enl
castillo de popa vido lūbre avnq̄ fue cosa
tan çerrada q̄ no quiso affirmar q fuese
tr̄ra /. pero llamo a pero gutierrez repostero

Fol. 8v   destrados dl Rey e dixole q̄ parecia lūbre: q̄
mirasse el y asi lo hizo y vidola: dixolo tābiē
a rodrigo sanches de segovia q̄l Rey y la Rey
na enviavā en el armada por veedor el qual
no vido nada porq̄ no estava en lugar do la
pudiese ver /. despues q̄l almiᵉ lo dixo se
vido vna vez /o dos: y era comō vna candeli
lla de cera q̄ se alçava y levātava lo qual
a pocos pareçiera ser indiçio de tr̄ra /. pero el al
mirāte tuvo por çierto estar junto a la
tierra /. por lo qual quādo dixerō la salve
q̄ la acostūbrā dezir e cantar a su māra
todos los marineros y se hallan todos: "rogo y" a
monestolos el almiᵉ q̄ hiziesen buena guar
da al castillo de proa y mirasen bien por la
tr̄ra: y q̄ al q̄ le dixese primero q̄ via tr̄ra
le daria luego vn jubon de seda: sin las
otras mds que los reyes avian prome
tido que erā diez mill m̄ı̄s de juro a quien
primero la viese /. a las dos oras despues
de media noche pareçio la tr̄ra dla qual esta
rian dos leguas /. amaynarō todas las velas
y quedarō con el treo que es la vela grade
sin bonetas y pusierōse a la corda tempo
rizādo hasta el dia "viernes" q̄ llegarō a vna isleta
dlos lucayos q̄ se llamava en lengua de
yndios guanahani /. luego vierō gente ds

175

nuda: y el almi͡e͡ salio a t͞rra en la barca arma
da: y martin alonso pincon y viçeynte anes
su hr° q̃ era capitan dla niña /. Saco el almi͡e
la vandera real: y los capitanes con dós
vanderas dla cruz verde: q̃ llevava el al
mir͞ate en todos los navios por seña: co
vna .f. y vna .y. ençima de cada letra
su corona vna de vn cabo dla ✝. y otra
de otro/. "[y]" puestos en t͞rra vieron
arboles m͞y verdes: y aguas m͞uchas
y frutas de diversas mañeras /. el almi͡e
llæmo a los dos capitanes y a los demas
q̃ saltar͞o en t͞rra y a rodrigo descobedo
escrivano de toda el armada y a rodrigo
sanches de segovia: y dixo q̃ le diesen [p]or
fe y testimonio: co͞mo el por ante todos toma
va como de hecho tomo possession dla dc͞ha

Fol. 9 ysla por el rey e por la reyna sus señores
hazi͞edo las protestaciones q̃ se requirian co
m͞o mas largo se contiene en los testimo
nios q̃ alli se hizier͞o por escripto / luego
se ayunto alli mucha gente de la ysla
esto q̃ se sigue son palabras formales dl
almi͡e en su libro dsu primera nave
gacion y dscubrimi° destas yndias /. yo di
ze el porq̃ cognosci q̃ era gente q̃ mejor se
libraria y conVrteria a n͞ra s͞acta fe con a
mor q̃ no por fuerça: les di a algu
nos dllos vnos bonetes colorados y vnas
cuentas de vidro q̃ se ponian al pescueç[o]
y otras cosas m͞uchas de poco valor c͞o que
ovier͞o mucho plazer y quedar͞o tanto nro[s?]
q̃ era maravilla /. los quales despues
venian a las barcas dlos navios adonde
nos estavamos nad͞ado: y nos trayan papa
gayos y hylo de algodon en ovillos y
azagayas y otras cosas m͞uchas y nos las
trocavan por otras cosas q̃ nos les dava
mos co͞mo cuentezillas de vidro y casca
veles /. en fin todo tomav͞a y dav͞a de aq̃llo
q̃ tenian de buena vol͞utad ./. mas me
pareçio q̃ era gente m͞y pobre de todo /. ellos
andan todos desnudos co͞mo su madre los pa
rio: y t͞abien las mugeres: avnq̃ no vide
mas de vna farto moça /. y todos los que

176

yo vi eran todos manc[e]bos q̃ ninguº vide
de edad de mas de .xxx. añoſ /. m̄y biē
hechos de m̄uy fermosos cuerpos y m̄uy
buenas caras: los cabellos gruessos quasi
com̄o sedas de cola de cavallos e cortos /.
los cabellos traen por encima dlas çejas sal
vo vnos pocos detras q̃ traen largos q̃
jamas cortan. dllos se pintan de prieto: y
ellos son dla color dlos canarios ni negros
ni blancos: y dellos se pintan de blanco: y dellos
de colorado: y dllos dlo q̃ fallan /. y dllos se pin
tan las caras: y dllos todo el cuerpo: y dllos
solos los ojos: y dllos solo el nariz /. ellos
no traen armas ni las cognosçen: porq̃ les
amostre espadas y las tomavan por el filo: y

se cortavā con ignorāçia /. no tienē algun
fierro: sus azagayas son vnas varas
sin fierro y algunas dellas tienen al cabo
vn diente de peçe y otras de otras cosas /. ellos
todos a vna mano son de buena estatura de
grandeza y buenos gestos biēn hechos /. yo vide
algunos q̃ tenian señales de feridas en sus
cuerpos y les hize señas q̃ era aq̃llos: y ellos
me amostrarō com̄o alli venian gente de
otras yslas q̃ estavā açerca y los querian tomar
y se defendian y yo crey e creo q̃ aqui vienē
de t̄r̄ra firme a tomarlos por captivos /. ellos
dever ser buenos suidores y de buē ingenio
q̃ veo q̃ m̄uy presto dizē todo lo q̃ les dezia:
y creo q̃ ligeram̄ete se harian x̄rianos q̃ me
pareçio q̃ ninguᵃ secta tenian /. yo plaziendo
a n̄r̄o señor levare de aqui al t̄p̄o de mi parti
da seys a .v.al. pa q̃ deprendā fablar /. nin
guna bestia de ninguᵃ m̄ār̄a vide salvo papa
gayos en esta ysla /. todas son palabras del
almirāte /.

Sabado .13. de otubre

luego q̃ amaneçio vinierō a la playa m̄uchos
destos hōbres todos m̄āçebos com̄o dicho tengo:
y todos de buena estatura / gente m̄y fermosa:
los cabellos no crespos salvo corredios y grues

177

sos como seda[s] de cavallo: y todos dla frēte
y cabeça mūy ancha mas q̃ otra generaçion
q̃ fasta aqui aya visto /. y los ojos mȳ
fermosos y no pequeños: y ellos ninguᵒ
prieto salvo dla color dlos canarios /. ni se
deve esperar otra cosa pues esta leste gueste cō
la ysla dl fierro en canarias so vna linea /.
las piernas mūy derechas todos a vna mano:
y no barriga salvo mūy bien hecha /. Ellos
vinierō a la nao con almadias q̃ son hechas
del pie de vn arbol comō vn barco luēgo
y todo de vn pedaço y labrado mūy a maravilla
segū la tīrra y grādes en q̃ en alguᵃ venian
40. y .45. hōbres /. y otras mas pequeñas
fasta aver dllas en que venia vn solo hobre /.
remavā con vna pala comō de fornero y

Fol. 10
anda a maravilla /. y si se le trastorna luego
se echan todos a nadar y la enderecan y va
zian con calabaças q̃ traen ellos . trayan ovi
llos de algodon filado y papagayos [y] azaga
yas y otras cositas q̃ seria tedio de escrevir
y todo davā por qualquiera cosa q̃ se los diese
y yo estava atento y trabajava de saber si avia
oro: y vide q̃ algunos dellos trayan vn
pedaçuelo colgado en vn agujero q̃ tienen
a la nariz /. y por señas pude entender
q̃ yendo al sur o bolviendo la ysla por el
sur q̃ estava alli vn rey q̃ tenia grādes vaso[s]
dllo y tenia mūy mūcho /. trabaje q̃ fuesen
alla: y despues vide q̃ no entendian en la yda /.
determine de aguardar fasta maña"na" en la
tarde y despues partir pa el subdueste q̃
segū muchos dllos me enseñarō dezian
q̃ avia tīrra al sur y al sudueste y al norue
ste: y q̃stas dl norueste les venian a cō
batir mūchas vezes /. y asi yr[e?] al sudueste
a buscar el oro y piedras preciosas /. Esta ysla
es bien grāde y mȳ llana y de arboles mȳ
verdes y mūchas aguas y vna laguna en
medio mūy grāde sin ninguᵃ montaña y toda
ella verde q̃s plazer de mirarla /. y esta gēete
farto māsa y por la gana de aver de n̄ras
cosas y teniendo q̃ no se les a de dar sin que
den algo y no lo tienen: tomā lo q̃ pueden
y se echan luego a nadar /. mas todo lo q̃ tiene

178

lo dan por qualquiera cosa q̃ les den / que fasta
los pedaços dlas escudillas y dlas taças de
vidro rotas rescatavan fasta q̃ vi dar 16
ovillos de algodon por tres çeotis de portu
gal q̃ es vna blanca de Castilla / y en ellos
avria mas de vn arrova de algodon filado /.
esto defendiera y no dexara tomar a nadie
salvo q̃ yo lo mādara tomar todo p̱a v. al
si oviera en cantidad /. aqui nace en esta ysla [/?]
mas por el poco t̄p̄o no pude dar asi del todo
fe /. y tambien aqui nace el oro q̃ traen colga

Fol. 10v   do a la nariz mas por no perder t̄p̄o quiero
yr a ver si puedo topar a la ysla de çipan
go /. agora com̄o fue noche: todos se fue
r̄o a tierra con sus almadias /

Dom̄igo .14 de otubre

Fol. 10v   En amaneçiendo mād̄e adereçar el batel
(cont.)   dla nao y las barcas dlas caravelas
y fue al lueḡo dla ysla en el camino del
nornordeste p̱a ver la otra p̱te que era de
la p̱te del leste q̃ avia /. y tābien p̱a ver
las poblaçiones y vide luego dos /o tres:
y la gente q̃ veniā todos a la playa llamā
donos y dando g̃ras a dios /. los vnos nos
trayan agua: otros otras cosas de comer:
otros quād̄o veyan q̃ yo no curava de yr
a t̄r̄ra se echavā a la mar nadād̄o y venian
y entēdiamos q̃ nos pregutavan si eramos
venidos dl çielo /. y vino vno viejo en el
batel dentro y otros a bozes grād̄es llamavā
todos h̄obres y mugeres: venid a ver los
hobres que vinierō del çielo traedles de
comer y de bever /. vinierō mūchos y
mūchas mugeres cada vno con algo dād̄o
g̃ras a dios / echandose al suelo / y levātavā
las manos al çielo y despues a bozes
nos llamavā q̃ fuesemos a tierra mas
yo temia de ver vna grād̄e restinga de pie
dras q̃ çerca toda aq̃lla ysla al rededor /.
y entremedias queda hondo y puerto
p̱a quātas naos ay en toda la xr̄iandad
y la entrada dello mūy angosta /. Es verdad

179

q̃ dentro desta cintha ay algunas baxas:
mas la mar no se mueve mas que dē̄tro
en vn pozo /. y p̲a̲ ver todo esto me movi
esta mañana porq̃ supiese dar de todo rela
cion a vr̄as aletezas /. y tambien a donde
pudiera hazer fortaleza y vide
vn pedaço de tr̄ra q̃ se haze co͞mo ysla avnq̃
no lo es en q̃ avia seys casas /. el qual se
pudiera atajar en dos dias por ysla avnq
yo no veo ser neçessario / porq̃ esta gente
es mui simplice en armas co͞mo veran v. al

Fol. 11

de siete q̃ yo hize tomar p̲a̲ l[e?] llevar y
deprender nr̄a fabla y bolvellos /. salvo
que.v.al quā̄do mā̄darē̄ pueden los
todos llevar a castilla /o tenellos en la misma
ysla captivos /. porq̃ con çinquē̄ta hobres los
terna todos sojuzgados: y les hara hazer todo
lo q̃ quisiere /. y despues junto con la dc̄ha ysle
ta estan guertas de arboles las mas her
mosas q̃ yo vi e tan verdes y con sus hojas
co͞mo las de castilla en el mes de abril y
de mayo // y mū̄cha agua /. yo mire todo
aq̃l puerto y despues me bolvi a la nao y
di la vela y vide tantas yslas que yo no
sabia determinarme a qual yria primero /.
y aq̃llos hō̄bres q̃ yo tenia tomā̄do me dezian
por señas q̃ erā̄ tantas y tantas q̃ no avia
numero /. y anō̄brarō̄ por su nombre
mas de çiento /. por ende yo mire por
la mas grā̄de y aq̃lla determine andar
y asi hago y sera lexos desta de sant salvador
çinco leguas y las otras dellas mas dellas
menos /. todas son mū̄y llanas sin mon
tañas y mū̄y fertiles y todas pobladas
y se hazē̄ guerra la vna a la otra / avnq̃stos
son mū̄y simplices y mū̄y lindos cuerpos de hō̄bres /.

Lunes .15. de otubre

Fol. 11
(cont.)

avia temporejado esta noche con temor
de no llegar a tr̄ra a sorgir antes dla
mañana por no saber si la costa era limpia
de baxas: y en amaneçiendo cargar velas /
y como la ysla fuese mas lexos de çinco

leguas antes sera siete y la marea me
detuvo seria medio dia quãdo llegue a la dh̄a
ysla y falle q̃ aq̃lla haz que es dla parte
dla ysla de san salvador se corre norte sur
y an en ella .5. leguas: y la otra que yo
segui se corria leste gueste: y an en ella mas de
diez leguas /. y comõ desta ysla vide otra mayor al
gueste: cargue las velas por andar todo aq̃l dia
fasta la noche: porq̃ avn no pudiera aver anda
do al cabo del gueste: a la qual puse nõbre la
ysla de sancta maria dla concepçion y quasi al
poner del sol sorgi acerca del dho cabo por saver

Fol. 11v

si avia alli oro porq̃ estos que yo avia hecho
tomar en la ysla de san salvador me dezian
q̃ ay trayan manillas de oro mũy grandes
a las piernas y a los braços /. yo bien crey q̃
todo lo que dezian era burla pa se fugir /
con todo mi volũtad era de no passar por
ninguª ysla de que no tomase possessiõ /.
puesto que tomado de vna: se puede dezir
de todas /. y sorgi e estuve hasta oy mar
tes q̃ en amaneçiendo fue a tr̄r̄a con las bar
cas armadas: y sali y ellos que erã mũchos
asi desnudos y dla misma condiçion dla otra ysla
de sant salvador nos dexarõ yr por la ysla y
nos davan lo q̃ les pedia /. y porq̃ el viento
cargava a la traviesa sueste: no me quise
detener y parti pa la nao: y vna almadia
grande estava a bordo dla caravela niña /. y vno
dlos hõbres dla ysla de sant salvador que en ella
era: se echo a la mar y se fue en ella /. y la
noche de antes a medio echado el otro
y fue atras la almadia: la qual fugio q̃ jamas
fue barca que le pudiese alcançar puesto q̃ le
teniamos grãde avante /. Con todo dio en tr̄r̄a
y dexarõ la almadia y algunos dlos de mi
compañia salierõ en tr̄r̄a tras ellos: y todos
fugerõ comõ gallinas /. y la almadia q̃ avian
dexado la llevamos a bordo dla caravela ni
ña adonde ya de otro cabo venia otra almadia
pequeña con vn hõbre q̃ venia a rescatar vn
ovillo de algodon: y se echaro algunos marine
ros a la mar porq̃ el no queria entrar en la
caravela y le tomarõ y yo q̃stava a la popa
dla Nao q̃ vide todo enbie por el y le di vn

181

bonete colorado y vnas cuētas de vidro
verdes pequeñas q̃ le puse al braço y dos casca
veles q̃ le puse a las orejas y le mãde bol
ver su almadia que tambien tenia en la barca
y le enbie a tr̄ra /. y di luego la vela p̲a̲ yr a
la otra isla grāde q̃ yo via al gueste /. y mãde
largar tãbien la otra almadia q̃ traya
la caravela niña por popa /. y vide des
pues en tr̄ra al tp̄o de la llegada del otro a quien yo
avia dado las cosas susodichas y no le avia que
rido tomar el ovillo dl algodon // puesto q̃l me
lo queria dar /. y todos los otros se llegarō a el
y tenia a grā maravilla e bien le parecio que

eramos buena gente /. y q̃ el otro [que?] se avia
fugido nos avia hecho algun daño y q̃
por esto lo llevavamos /. y a esta razon u̲s̲e̲ esto
con el de le mãda alargar y le di las dh̄as
cosas // porq̃ nos tuviese en esta esti
ma /. porq̃ otra vez quā
do vtr̄s altezas aqui tornē a enviar no hagā
mala compañia /. y todo lo q̃ yo le di no valia
quatro m̄is /. y asi parti q̃ serian las diez
oras con el viento sueste y tocava de sur p̲a̲
passar a estotra ysla /. la qual es grandissima y
adonde todos estos hōbres q̃ yo traygo dla
de san salvador hazen señas q̃ ay mūy mū
cho oro / y q̃ lo traen en los braços en ma
nillas y a las piernas y a las orejas y al na
riz y al pescueço /. y avia desta isla de sancta
maria a esta otra nueve leguas leste gueste /
y se corre toda esta parte dla isla norueste
sueste /. y se pareçe q̃ bien avria en esta costa
mas de veynte ocho leguas en esta faz /. y
[es?] mūy llana sin mōtaña ninguᵃ: asi comõ a
q̃lla de sant salvador y de sancta maria /. y
todas playas sin roquedos: salvo q̃ a todas
ay algunas peñas açerca de tr̄ra debaxo del
agua por donde es menester abrir el ojo
quādo se quiere surgir e no surgir mūcho a
çerca de tr̄ra avnq̃ las aguas son siempre
m̄y claras y se vee el fondo /. y desviado
de tr̄ra dos tyros de lōbarda: ay en todas estas
islas tanto fondo q̃ no se puede llegar
a el /. son estas islas m̄y Vrdes y fertiles y
de ayres m̄y dulçes: y puede aver muchas

182

cosas q̃ yo no se porq̃ no me quiero dete
ner por calar y andar mūchas islas p̲a
fallar oro /. y pues estas dan asi estas senas
q̃ lo traen a los braços y a las piernas y es
oro porq̃ les amostre algunos pedaços del q̃
yo tengo: no puedo errar con el ayu
da de nro señor q̃ yo no le falle adonde
naçe /. y estando a medio golpho destas dos
islas es de saber de aq̃lla de sancta maria
y desta grāde a la qual pongo nōbre la ferna
dina: falle vn nōbre solo en vna almadia q̃ se
passava dla isla de sancta maria a la fernādina
y traya vn poco de su pan q̃ seria tanto como

el puño y vna calabaça de agua y vn peda
ço de tierra bermeja hecha en polvo y des
pues amassada: y vnas hojas secas: q̃
deve ser cosa mūy apreçiada entrellos: porq̃
ya me truxerō en sā salvador dellas en
presente /. y traya vn çestillo a su guisa
en q̃ tenia vn ramalejo de cuentezillas de
vidro y dos blancas: por las quales cogno
sci q̃l venia dla isla de sant salvador
y avi passado a aq̃lla de sācta maria y se
passava a la fernādina /. El qual se llego
a la nao y le hize entrar q̃ asi lo demā
dava el y le hize poner su almādia en la
nao y guardar todo lo q̃ el traya y le mā
de dar de comer pan y miel y de bever
y asi le passare a la fernādina y le dare todo
lo suyo: porq̃ de buenas nuevas de nos
por a n̄ro señor aplaziendo quādo v̄trs alte
zas enbien aca que aq̃llos q̃ vinierē
resçiban honrra y nos den de todo lo q̃ oviere /.

martes y miercoles .16. de otubre

parti dlas isla de Sc̄ta maria de Concepçiō
q̃ seria ya çerca de medio dia p̲a la isla
fernādina: la qual amuestra ser grādissima
al gueste y navegue todo aq̃l dia con cal
meria no pude llegar a t͞po de poder ver
el fondo p̲a surgir en limpio porq̃ es
en esto mūcho de aver grā diligençia por
no perder las anclas y asi temporize toda

183

esta noche hasta el dia q̃ vine a vna pobla
çion a donde yo surgi e adonde avia veni
do aq̃l hōbre q̃ yo halle ayer en aq̃lla alma
dia a medio golfo /. El qual avia dado tātas
buenas nuevas de nos: q̃ toda esta noche
no falto almadias abordo dla nao q̃ nos
trayan agua y dlo q̃ tenian /. yo a cada
vno le mādava dar algo es a saber algu
nas cuentezillas diez /o doze dllas de vidro
en vn filo y algunas sonajas de laton
destas q̃ valen en castilla vn maravedi
cada vna: y algunas agujetas: de que todo
tenian en grādissima exçelençia . y tambiē
los mādava dar <u>pa</u> q̃ comiesen quādo ve

nian en la nao y miel de acucar /. y despues
a oras de tercia embie el batel de la nao en
tr̄ra por agua: y ellos de muȳ buena gana
le enseñavā a mi gente adonde estava el agua
y ellos mesmos trayan los barriles llenos
al batel y se folgavā mūcho de nos hazer
plazer /. Esta isla es grādissima y tengo deter
minado dla rodear: porq̃ segū puedo entēder
en ella /o açerca della ay mina de oro /.
esta isla esta desviada dla de sācta maria .8º
leguas quasi leste gueste y este cabo adonde
yo vine y toda estas costa se corre nornorueste
y sursudueste: y vide bien veynte leguas dlla
mas ay no acabava /. agora escriviendo esto di la
vela cō el viento sur <u>pa</u> pujar a rodear toda la
isla / y trabajar hasta q̃ halle samoet q̃ es la
isla /o ciudad adonde es el oro q̃ asi lo dizen
todos estos q̃ aqui vienē en la nao y nos lo
dezian los dla isla de san salvador y de sancta
maria /. Esta gente es semejāte a aq̃lla
dlas dhas islas y vna fabla y vnas costūbres
salvo q̃stos ya me pareçen algū tanto mas
domestica gente y de tracto "y" mas sotiles /.
porq̃ veo q̃ an traydo algodon aqui a la nao
y otras cositas q̃ saben mejor refetar el
pagamēto q̃ no hazian los otros /. y a
vn en esta isla vide paños de algodon
fechos comō mātillos: y la gente mas dis
puesta y las mugeres traen por delante
su cuerpo vna cosita de algodon q̃ escassa
mēte les cobija su natura /. ella es isla

184

mūy verde y llana y fertilissima y no pon
go duda q̃ todo el año siembrā panizo
y cogen y asi todas otras cosas /. y vide
mūchos arboles mūy diformes dlos nr̄os /.
y dllos mūchos q̃ tenian los ramos de mū
chas maneras: y todo en vn pie /. y vn
ramito es de vna mañra y otro de otra: y
tan disforme: q̃ es la mayor maravilla
dl mūdo quāta es la diversidad dla vna
mañra a la otra // verbigracia: vn ramo
tenia las fojas de mañra de cañas: y otro

Fol. 13v

de mañra de lantisco /. y assi en vn solo arbol de
cinco /o seys destas mañra: y todos tan diversos /.
ni estos son enxeridos porq̃ se pueda dezir que el
enxerto lo haze: antes son por los mōtes ni cura
dellos esta gente /. no le cognozco secta ninguᵃ
y creo q̃ mūy presto se tornarian xr̄ianos: porque
ellos son de mūy buen entender /. aqui son los
peçes tan disformes de los nr̄os q̃s maravilla /.
ay algunos hechos comō gallos dlas mas finas colo
res del mūdo / azules amarillos colorados y de
todas colores y otros pintados de mill māras /. y las
colores son tan finas q̃ no ay hōbre q̃ no se ma
raville y no tome grā descanso a verlos /. tam
bien ay vallenas bestias en tr̄ra no vide ninguᵃ
de ninguna māra / salvo papagayos y lagartos
vn moço me dixo q̃ vido vna grāde culebra:
ovejas ni cabras ni otra ninguᵃ bestia vide
avnq̃ yo e estado aqui mūy poco q̃ es medio dia
mas si las oviese no pudiera errar de ver alguᵃ /.
El çerco desta isla escrivire despues q̃ yo la oviere arrodeada /.
arrodeada /.

miercoles .17. de otubre

Fol. 13v
(cont.)

A medio dia parti dla poblaçion adonde yo estava
surgido y adonde tome agua pa "yr" rodear esta isla
fernādina y el viento era sudueste y sur: y comō
mi volūtad fuese de seguir esta costa desta isla adonde
yo estava al sueste porq̃ asi se corre toda norno
rueste y sursueste: y queria llevar el dh̄o camino
dl sur y sueste: porq̃ aq̃lla pte todos estos yn
dios que traygo y otro de quien ove señas en esta
parte del sur a la isla aq̃llos llamā samoet a

donde es el oro: y martin alonso pinçon capitan
dla caravela pinta / en la qual yo m͞ade a tres destos
yndios vino a mi y me dixo q̃ vno dellos m͞uy
çertificadam͞ete le avia dado a entender q̃ por la
p͟te dl nornorueste m͞y mas presto arrodearia
la isla: yo vide q̃ el viento no me ayudava por
el camino q̃ yo queria llevar y era bueno por
el otro: di la vela al nornorueste y qu͞ado fue a
çerca dl cabo dla isla a dos leguas: halle vn m͞uy ma
ravilloso puerto con vna boca avnq̃ dos bocas se le
puede dezir porq̃ tiene vn isleo en medio y son
ambas m͞uy angostas y dentro m͞uy ancho pareçian
navios si fuera fondo y limpio y fondo al entrada:
pareciome raz͞o del ver bien y sondear y asi sur
gi fuera del y fuy en el con todas las barcas de los
navios y vimos q̃ no avia fondo /. y porq̃ pense
qu͞ado yo le vi q̃ era boca de alg͞u rio: avia m͞adado
llevar barriles p͟a tomar agua y en t͞rra halle vnos
ocho /o diez h͞obres q̃ luego vinier͞o a nos y nos
amostrar͞o [muy?] çerca la poblaçion adonde yo enbie
la gente por agua / vna parte con armas / otros
con barriles y asi la tomar͞o. y porq̃ era lexuelos
me detuve por espaçio de dos oras en este t͞po andu
ve asi por aq̃llos arboles q̃ er͞a la cosa mas fer
mosa de ver q̃ se aya visto / veyendo tanta
verdura en tanto grado com͞o en el mes de mayo
en el andaluzia /. y los arboles todos estan tan disfor
mes dlos n͞ros com͞o el dia dla noche: y asi las
frutas y asi las yervas y las piedras y todas las
cosas /. verdad es q̃ algunos arboles er͞a dla na
turaleza de otros q̃ ay en castilla: por ende avia
m͞y gr͞a difer͞eçia /. y los otros arboles de otras ma
neras er͞a tantos q̃ no ay p͟sona q̃ lo pueda dezir
ni asemejar a otros de castilla /. la gente toda
era vna c͞o los otros ya d͞hos dlas mismas condi
çiones y asi desnudos y dla misma estatura y
dav͞a dlo q̃ tenian por qualquiera cosa q̃ les diesen /.
y aqui vide q̃ vnos moços dlos navios les
trocar͞o azagayas vnos pedaçuelos de escudillas
rotas y de vidro /. y los otros q̃ fuer͞o por el agua
me dixer͞o com͞o avi͞a estado en sus casas / y q̃
er͞a de dentro m͞y barridas y limpias: y sus
camas y param͞etos de cosas q̃ son com͞o redes
de aldogon /. ellas "sc las casas" son todas a m͞ara de alfane
ques y m͞uy altas y buenas chimeneas / mas

no vide entre mūchas poblaçiones q̃ yo vide [que?]
ninguᵃ q̃ passasse de doze hasta quinze casas /. aqui
fallarō q̃ las mugeres casadas trayan bragas de
algodon: las moças no sino salvo algunas que erā
ya de edad de diez y ocho años /. y ay avia
perros mastines y branchetes: y ay fallarō vno
q̃ avia al nariz vn pedaço de oro q̃ seria comō
la mitad de vn castellano: en el qual vierō letras /.
reñi yo c̄o ellos porq̃ no se lo resgatarō y die
rō quatō pedia por ver q̃ era y cuya esta mone
da era: y ellos me respōdierō q̃ nūca se lo oso
resgatar /. dspues de tomada la agua bolvi
a la nao y di la vela y sali al norueste tanto q̃
yo descubri toda aq̃lla pte dla isla hasta la
costa q̃ se corre leste gueste /. y despues todos
estos yndios tornarō a dezir q̃sta isla era
mas pequeña q̃ "no" la isla samoet: y q̃ seria biē
bolver atras por ser en ella mas presto /. El
viento alli luego nos calmo y comēço a vētar
guesnorueste /. El qual era contrario pa donde
aviamos venido /. y asi tome la buelta y navegue

Fol. 14v

toda esta noche passada al leste sueste y quādo
al leste todo y quādo al sueste / y esto pa
apartarme dla tr̄ra porq̃ hazia mȳ grā çerra
zon y el tp̄o mȳ cargado /. el era poco y no
me dexo llegar a tr̄ra a surgir /. asi que esta
noche llovio mūy fuerte despues de media
noche hasta quasi el dia y avn esta nūblado
pa llover y nos al cabo dla isla dla pte
dl sueste adonde espo surgir fasta
q̃ aclaresca pa ver las otras islas / adonde
tengo de yr /. y asi todos estos dias
despues q̃ en estas yndias estoy a llovido
poco /o mucho ./. creā .v.al. que es esta
tr̄ra la mejor e mas fertil y temperada y llana
y buena q̃ aya en el mūdo /.

Jueves .18. de otubre

dspues q̃ aclarescio segui el viento y fui en
derredor dla isla quāto pude y surgi al
tp̄o q̃ ya no era de navegar: mas nō fui
en tr̄ra y en amaneçiendo di la vela /.

187

viernes . 19. de otubre

En amaneçiendo levante las anclas y enbie
la caravela pinta al leste y sueste: y la caravela
ninā al sursueste: y yo con la
nao fui al sueste y dado orden q̃ llevasen a
q̃lla buelta fasta medio dia y despues q̃ am
bas se mudasen las derrotas y se recogierō
p̃a mi/. y luego antes q̃ andassemos tres oras
vimos vna isla al leste sobre la qual descar
gamos y llegamos a ella todos tres los navios
antes de medio dia a la punta dl norte adonde
haze vn isleo y vn restinga de piedra fuera del
al norte: y otro entre el y la isla grāde: la
qual anōbrarō estos hōbres de Sā salvador q̃ yo
traygo la isla saomete: a la qual puse nōbre
la islabela/. El viento era norte y quedava
el d̄ho ysleo en derrota dla ysla fernā
dina de adonde yo avia p̃tido leste gueste
y se corria despues la costa desde
el ysleo al gueste y avia en ella doze leguas
fasta vn cabo/. y aqui yo llame el cabo
hermoso que es dla parte dl gueste/. y asi
es fermoso redondo y mūy fondo sin baxas
fuera del y al comīeço es de piedra y baxo
y mas adentro es playa de arena comō quasi

la d̄ha costa es y ay surgi esta noche viernes
hasta la mañana/. Esta costa toda y la parte
dla isla q̃ yo vi: es toda quasi playa y la isla
la mas fermosa cosa q̃ yo vi/. q̃ si las otras
son mȳ hermosas esta es mas/. es de mu
chos arboles y mūy Vrdes y mūy grādes/. y esta
tr̄ra es mas alta q̃ las otras islas falladas /
y en ella alguno altillo no q̃ se le pueda llamar
mōtaña mas cosa q̃ afermosea lo otro y parece
de mūchas aguas /. alla al medio dla isla desta
parte al nordeste haze vna grāde angla y
a mūchos arboledos y mūy espessos y muy grā
des /. yo quise yr a surgir en ella p̃a salir
a tr̄ra y ver tanta fermosura: mas era el
fondo baxo y no podia surgir salvo largo de
tr̄ra y el viento era mȳ bueno p̃a venir a
este cabo adonde yo surgi agora: al qual pu
se nōbre cabo fermoso porq̃ asi lo es /. y asi
no surgi en aq̃lla angla y avn porq̃ vide

188

este cabo de alla tan verde y tā fermoso: asi
como todas las otras cosas y tr̄ras destas islas
q̃ yo no se adonde me vaya primero / ni
me se cansar los ojos de Vr tan fermosas
verduras y tan diversas dlas nr̄as /. y avn
creo q̃ a en ellas mūchas yervas y mūchos ar
boles q̃ valen mūcho en españa pa tinturas
y pa medicinas de espeçeria mas yo no
los cognozco de q̃ llevo grāde pena /. y llegā
do yo aqui a este cabo vino el olor tan bueno
y suave de flores /o arboles dla tierra q̃ era la
cosa mas dulçe dl mūdo /. de mañana antes
q̃ yo de aqui vaya yre en tr̄ra a ver q̃ es aqui
en el cabo /. no es la poblaçion salvo alla
mas dentro adonde dizē estos hōbres q̃ yo
traygo q̃sta el rey y q̃ trae mucho oro /. y yo
de mañana quiero yr tanto avante q̃ halle la po
blaçion y vea /o aya lengua con este rey q̃ se
gū estos dan las señas: el señorea todas estas
islas comarcanas: y va vestido y trae sobre si
mucho oro /. avnq̃ no doy mūcha fe a sus dezi
res: asi por no los entender yo bien: como
en cognoscer q̃llos son tan pobres de oro
que qualquiera poco q̃ste rey trayga les pare
çe a ellos mucho /. Este aqui yo digo cabo fer

Fol. 15v

moso creo q̃ es isla apartada de saometo y avn
ay ya otra entremedias pequeña /. yo no
curo asi de ver tanto por menudo porq̃ no
lo podria fazer en çinquenta años: porq̃ quiero
ver y descubrir lo mas q̃ yo pudiere pa bolver
a vr̄as altezas a nr̄o señor aplaziendo en abril/
verdad es que fallando adonde aya oro o espeçeria
en cantidad me deterne fasta q̃ yo aya dello quā
to pudiere /. y por esto no fago sino andar pa
ver de topar en ello /.

Sabado .20. de otubre

Fol. 15v
(cont.)

Oy al sol salido levante las anclas de donde
yo estava con la nao surgido en esta isla de
saometo al cabo del sudueste adonde yo puse
nōbre el cabo dla laguna y a la isla la Isabe
la pa navegar al nordeste y al leste de la pte
dl sueste y sur: adonde entendi destos hōbres
q̃ yo traygo q̃ era la poblacion y el rey della y

189

falle todo tan baxo el fondo q̃ no pude entrar
ni navegar a ella y vide q̃ siguiendo el camino del
sudueste era mūy grā rodeo /. y por esto determi
ne de me bolver por el camino q̃ yo avia traydo
dl nornordeste dla p̱te del gueste y rode
ar esta isla p̱az y /. y el viento me fue tan
escasso q̃ yo no nūca pude aver la tr̄ra al lon
go dla costa salvo en la noche /. y porq̃s peligro
surgir en estas islas salvo en el dia q̃ se vea
con el ojo adonde se echa el ancla porq̃ es to
do mānchas: vna de limpio y otra de non: yo
me puse a temporejar a la vela toda esta noche
dl domīgo /. las caravelas surgierō porque
hallarō en tr̄ra temprano y pensarō q̃ a sus
señas q̃ erā acostūbradas de hazer / yria a sur
gir mas no quise /.

Domīgo .21. de otubre

Fol. 15v
(cont.)
A las diez oras llegue aqui a este cabo del
isleo y surgi y asi mismo las caravelas:
y despues de aver comigo fui en tr̄ra: adōde
aqui no avia otra poblacion q̃ vna casa /.
En la qual no falle a nadie q̃ creo q̃ con te
mor se aviā fugido / porq̃ en ella estavā to
dos sus adereços de casa /. yo no le de
xe tocar nada salvo q̃ me sali cō estos
capitanes y gente a ver la isla: que si las
otras ya vistas son mūy fermosas y verdes

Fol. 16
y fertibles: esta es mucho mas y de grādes
arboledos y mȳ verdes /. aqui es vnas gra
des lagunas y sobre ellas y a la rueda es el
arboledo en maravilla /. y aqui y en toda la isla
son todos Vrdes y las yervas comō en el abril
en el andaluzia /. y el cantar dlos paxaritos
q̃ pareçe q̃l hōbre nūca se querria partir de
aqui /. y las manadas dlos papagayos q̃ ascu
reçen el sol: y aves y paxaritos de tantas
mar̃as y tan diversas dlas nr̃as: q̃ es ma
ravilla /. y despues ha arboles de mill mār̃as
y todos de su mār̃a fruto y todos guelen q̃s
maravilla /. que yo estoy el mas penado dl mu
do de no los cognosçer /. porq̃
soy bien çierto q̃ todos son cosa de valia y de

llos traygo la demuestra / y asimismo dlas
yervas /. andādo asi en çerco de vna destas
lagunas: vide vna sierpe: la qual matamos
y traygo el cuero a vr̄as altezas /. Ella co
mo nos vido se echo en la laguna y nos le
seguimos dentro: porꝗ no era m̄y fonda fasta
ꝗ con lanças la matamos /. es de siete pal
mos en largo /. creo ꝗ destas semejantes ay
aqui en estas lagunas / muchas /. aqui cognos
çi dl lignaloe y mañana "e" determinado de ha
zer traer a la nao diez quintales porꝗ me di
zen ꝗ vale m̄ucho /. tambien andādo en
busca de m̄y buena agua: fuimos a vna pobla
çion aqui çerca adonde estoy surto media
legua: y la gente della com̄o nos sintier̄o
dier̄o todos a fugir y dexar̄o las casas y es
condier̄o su ropa y lo ꝗ tenian por el m̄ote /.
yo no dexe tomar nada ni la valia de vn
alfilel /. despues se llegar̄o a nos vnos
h̄obres dellos y vno se llego aqui /.
yo di vnos cascaveles y vnas cuentezillas
de vidro y quedo m̄uy contento y m̄uy alegre /.
y porꝗ la amistad creciese mas y los requirie
se algo le hize pedir agua /. y ellos des
pues ꝗ fui en la nao vinier̄o luego a la pla
la con sus calabaças llenas y folgar̄o m̄ucho de

Fol. 16v   darnosla y yo les m̄ade dar otro ramalejo
de cuentezillas de vidro y dixer̄o ꝗ de mañana
vernian aca /. yo queria henchir aqui toda la
vasija dlos navios de agua: por ende si el
tp̄o me da lugar luego me p̲tire a rodear
esta isla fasta ꝗ yo aya lengua con este rey y
ver si puedo aver dl el oro ꝗ oyo ꝗ trae /. y des
pues partir p̲ar otra isla gr̄āde m̄ucho ꝗ creo
ꝗ deve ser cipango segū las señas ꝗ me dan
estos yndios ꝗ yo traygo a la qual llam̄a
Colba /. en la qual dizen ꝗ a naos y marc̄a
tes m̄uchos y m̄uy gr̄ādes /. y desta isla otra ꝗ
llam̄a bofio ꝗ tanbien dizen ꝗs m̄uy gr̄āde /.
y a las otras ꝗ son entremedio vere asi de pas
sada: y segū yo fallare recaudo de oro /o espe
çeria determinare lo ꝗ e de fazer /. mas toda
via tengo determinado de yr a la tr̄ra firme
y a la çiudad de quisay y "dar" las C̄tas de vr̄as
altezas al gr̄a Can y pedir respuesta y venir
con ella /.

191

lunes .22. de otubre

toda esta noche y oy estuve aqui aguar
dando si el rey de aqui /o otras psonas
traherian oro /o otra cosa de sustançia y vinie
rō mūchos desta gente semejantes a los otros
dlas otras islas asi desnudos y asi pintados
dellos de blanco / dellos de colorado / dellos de
prieto / y asi de mūchas mār̄as /. trayan aza
gayas y algunos ovillos de algodon a res
gatar /. el qual trocavā aqui cō algunos ma
rineros por pedaços de vidro de taças quebra
das: y por pedaços descudillas de barro /. al
gunos dllos trayan algunos pedaços de oro
colgado al nariz /. el qual de buena gana
davan por vn cascavel destos de pie de gavi
lano / y por cuētezillas de vidro // mas es
tan poco q̃ no es nada /. Que es Vrdad q̃ qual
quier poca cosa q̃ se les de: ellos tabiē
teniā a grā maravilla nr̄a venida y creyan
q̃ eramos venidos dl çielo /. tomamos
agua pa los navios en vna laguna q̃ aqui
esta açerca dl cabo dl isleo q̃ asi anōbre / y en
la dh̄a laguna martin aloso pinçon capitan dla pin
ta mato otra sierpe tal cōmo la otra de ayer de siete
palmos y fize tomar aqui del liñaloe quāto se fallo /

martes 23. de otubre

Quisiera oy ptir pa la isla de cuba q creo q̃ deve ser
çipango segun las señas q̃ dan esta gente dla grāde
za della y riqueza y no me detorne mas aqui ni
　　　　esta isla al rededor pa yr a la poblacion
cōmo tenia determinado pa aver lengua con este rey
o señor /. q̃ es por no me detener mūcho pues veo
q̃ aqui no ay mina de oro y al rodear destas islas
a menester mūchas maneras de viento y no
vienta asi cōmo los hōbres querrian /. y pues es
de andar adonde aya trato grāde: digo q̃ no es
razō de se detener salvo yr a camino y calar
mūcha tr̄ra fasta topar en tr̄ra mūy provechosa avnq̃
mi entender es q̃sta sea mūy provechosa de espeçe
ria mas q̃ yo no la cognozco q̃ llevo la major pena
dl mūdo q̃ veo mill mar̄as de arboles que

tienē cada vno su mar̄a de fruta y verde agora
comō en españa en el mes de mayo y junio y mill
mar̄as de yervas: eso mesmo con flores y de todo
no se cognoscio salvo este liñaloe de q̃ oy māde tā
biēn traer a la nao mūcho pa levar a .v.al /. y no
e dado ni doy la vela pa cuba porq̃ no ay viento
salvo calma muerta y llueve mūcho y llovio ayer
mucho sin hazer ningū frio antes el dia haze calor
y las noches temperadas comō en mayo en españa
en el andaluzia /.

miercoles 24. de otubre

esta noche a media noche levante las anclas dla
isla Ysabela dl cabo del isleo q̃s dla pte del norte
adonde y estava posado pa yr a la isla de Cuba a
donde oy desta gente q̃ era mūy grāde y de gran
trato y avia en ella oro y especerias y naos
grādes y mercaderos y me amostro q̃ al gues
sudueste yria a ella /. y yo asi lo tēgo
porq̃ creo q̃ si es asi comō por señas q̃ me
hizierō todos los yndios destas islas y aqllos
q̃ llevo yo en los navios porq̃ por lengua
no los entiendo: es la isla de cipango de q̃
se cuētan cosas maravillosas /. y en las esperas
q̃ yo vi y en las pinturas de mapamūdos es
ella en esta comarca /. y asi navegue fasta el dia
al guesudueste y amaneçiendo calmo el viē
to y llovio y asi cassi toda la noche y estuve asi
cō poco viento fasta q̃ passava de medio dia y
estonçes torno a ventar mūy amoroso y llevava
todas mis velas dla nao maestra y dos bone
tas y triquete y çevadera y mezana y vela de
gavia y el batel por popa /. Asi anduve al ca
mino fasta q̃ anocheçio: y estonçes me quedava

el cabo verde dla isla fernādina el qual es dla pte
de sur a la pte de gueste me quedava al norueste
y hazia de mi a el siete leguas /. y porq̃ venta
va ya rezio y no sabia yo cuāto camino ovie
se fasta la dha isla de cuba y por no la yr a
demādar de noche: porq̃ todas estas islas
son mȳ fondas a no hallar fondo todo ende
rredor salvo a tyro de dos lōbardos y esto es todo
māchado vn pedaço de rrquedo y otro de arena

y por esto no se puede seguramēte surgir salvo
a vista de ojo /. y por tanto acorde de amaynar
las velas todas salvo el triquete y andar c̄o
el y de a vn rato creçia mūcho el viento y hazia
mūcho camino de q̃ dudava y hera mūy gran
çerrazō y llovia: māde amaynar el trinquete
y no anduvimos esta noche dos leguas etc̃ /.

Jueves .25. de otubre

Navego dspues dl sol salido al gueste
sudueste hasta las nueve oras andarian .5.
leguas / despues mudo el camino al gueste
andavā .8. millas por ora hasta la vna dspues
de medio dia y de alli hasta las tres y andariā
.44. millas / entōçes vierō tr̄ra y erā siete /o ocho
islas en luēgo todas de norte a sur distavan
dllas .5. leguas etc̃.

viernes .26. de otubre

estuvo dlas dh̄as islas dla ₚte dl sur era todo
baxo çinco /o seys leguas surgio por alli /. dixe
ro los yndios q̃ llevava q̃ avia dllas a cuba
andadura de dia y medio con sus almadias
q̃ son navetas de vn madero adonde no
llevā vela /. estas son las canoas /. ₚtio de alli
ₚa cuba . porq̃ por las señas q̃ los yndios
le davā dla grādeza y dl oro y ₚlas dlla
pensava q̃ era ella conviene a saber çipango /.

Sabado .27. de otubre

levāto las anclas "salido el sol" de aq̃llas islas q̃ llamo las
islas de arena por el poco fondo q̃ tenian dla ₚte
dl sur hasta seys leguas / anduvo ocho millas
por ora hasta la vna del dia al sursudueste y
avrian andado .40. millas / y hasta la noche an
darian 28 ∴ millas al mesmo camino
y antes de noche vierō tr̄ra / estuvierō la noche
al reₚaro c̄o mūcha lluvia q̃ llovio anduvierō
el sabado fasta el poner dl sol .17. leguas al sur sudueste /

194

Domīgo 28 dias de otubre

fue de alli en demāda de la isla de cuba al sursudueste
a la tr̄ra dlla mas çercana y entro en vn rio
mȳ hermoso y mȳ sin peligro de baxas ni
de otros inconvenientes y toda la costa q̃ anduvo por
alli era mȳ hōdo y mȳ limpio fasta tr̄ra / te
nia la boca del rio doze braças y es bien ancha
p̲a̲ barloventear / surgio dentro diz q̃ a tyro de lo
barda /. dize el almiᵉ q̃ nūca tan hermosa
cosa vido / lleno de arboles todo "çercado el rio"
                                        fermosos y ver
des y diversos de los nr̄os c̄o flores y con su
fruto cada vno dsu mār̄a /. aves mūchas y pa
xaritos q̃ cantavā mūy dulçemēte /. avia grā
cantidad de palmas de otra mār̄a q̃ las de guinea
y dlas nr̄as: de vna estatura mediana y los
pies sin aq̃lla camisa y las hojas mȳ
grādes c̄o las quales cobijan las casas y la
tierra mȳ llana /. salto el almiᵉ en la barca y
fue a tierra y llego a dos casas q̃ creyo ser de
pescadores y q̃ c̄o temor se huyerō en
vna dla q̃les hallo vn perro q̃ nūca ladro. y en
ambas casas hallo redes de hilo de palma y cordeles
y anzuelo de cuerno y fisgas de guesso y otros
aparejos de pescar y muchos huegos dentro
y creyo q̃ en cada vna casa se ajuntan muchas p̲sonas /.
mādo q̃ no se tocase en cosa de todo ello y asi se
hizo /. la yerva era grāde com̄o enl andaluzia por
abril y mayo: hallo verdolagas mūchas y bledos /.
tornose a la barca y andubo por el rio arriba vn buē
rato y era: diz q̃ grā plazer ver aq̃llas Vrduras
y arboledas y dlas aves q̃ no podia dexallas
p̲a̲ se bolver /. dize q̃ es aq̃lla isla la mas hermo
sa q̃ oyos ayā visto: llena de mȳ
buenos puertos y rios hondos y la mar q̃ pa
reçia q̃ nūca se devia de alçar: porq̃ la yerva
dla playa llegava hasta quasi el agua . la qual
no suele llegar donde la mar es brava /.
hasta entonces no avia experimentado en todas aq̃llas
islas q̃ la mar fuese brava /. la isla dize q̃s
llena de mōtañas mȳ hermosas avnq̃ no son mȳ

195

grādes en lōgura salvo altas y toda la
otra tr̄ra es alta de la mar̄a de çeçilia /. llena es de
mch̄as aguas segū pudo entēder dlos
yndios q̃ cosigo lleva q̃ tomo en la isla de gua
nahani /. los quales le dizē por señas q̃ ay diez rios
grādes: y q̃ cō sus canoas no la pueden çercar en
.xx. dias /. quādo yva a tr̄ra cō los navios
salierō dos almadias /o canoas / y comō vierō q̃ los
marineros entravā en la barca y remavan pa yr

Fol. 18v

a ver el fondo del rio pa saber donde avian de
surgir: huyerō las canoas /. dezian los yndios
q̃ en aq̃lla isla avia minas de oro y perlas
y vido el almi\e lugar apto pa ellas y almejas
q̃s señal dellas / y entendia el almi\e q̃ alli ve
nian naos del grā can y grādes / y q̃ de alli a
tr̄ra firme avia jornada de diez dias lla
mo el almi\e aq̃l rio y puerto de san salvador /.

Lunes .29. de otubre

Fol. 18v
(cont.)

alço las anclas de aq̃l puerto y navego al poniente
pa yr diz q̃ a la çiudad donde le pareçia q̃ le
dezian los yndios q̃stava aq̃l rey /. vna punta
dla isla le salia al norueste seys leguas de
alli /. otra punta le salia al leste diez leguas /.
andada otra legua vido vn rio no tā grāde entrada
al qual puso nōbre el rio dla luna /. anduvo
hasta ora de bisperas: vido otro rio m̄y mas
grāde q̃ los otros y asi se lo dixerō por señas
los yndios y açerca del vido buenas poblaçio
nes de casas: llamo al rio el rio de "mares" /.
enbio dos barcas a vna poblaçion por aver len
gua y a vna dllas vn yndio dlos q̃ traya porq̃
ya los entēdian algo y mostravā estar contentos
co los xr̄ianos /. dlas quales todos los hōbres
y mugeres y criaturas huyerō desm̄aparādo
las casas cō todo lo q̃ tenian / y mādo el almi\e q̃
no se tocase en cosa /. las casas diz q̃ erā ya mas
hermosas q̃ las q̃ aviā visto y creya q̃ cuāto mas
se allegase a la tr̄ra firme serian mejores /. erā
hecha a mar̄a de alfaneques m̄y grādes y pare
çian tiendas en real sin cōcierto de calles
sino vna aca y otra aculla y de dentro m̄y
barridas y linpias y sus adereços m̄y compuestos

todas son de ramos de palma m̄y "hermosas" /.
hallar̄o m̄uchas estatuas en figura de mugeres
y m̄uchas cabeças en m̄ara de caratona m̄y
bī e labradas /. no se si esto tienē por hermo
sura /o ador̄a en ellas /. avia perros q̃ jamas
ladrar̄o: avia avezitas salvajes m̄asas por sus
casas: avia maravillosos adereços de redes
y anzuelos y artifiçios de pescar /. no le tocar̄o
en cosa dello /. creyo q̃ todos los dla costa devī a
de ser pescadores ∴q̃ llev̄a el pescado la t̄r̄ra dē tro:
porq̃ aq̃lla isla es m̄y gr̄ade y tan hermosa
q̃ no se hartava dezir bien dlla /. dize q̃ hallo
arboles y frutas de m̄y maravilloso sabor
y dize q̃ deve aver vacas enlla y otros gana
dos: porq̃ vido cabeças en guesso q̃ le pareciero
de vaca /. Aves y paxaritos y el cantar dlos gri

llos en toda la noche c̄o q̃ se holgava todos / los
aryes sabrosos y dulçes de toda la noche ni
frio ni callente /. mas por el camino dlas otras
islas aq̃lla diz q̃ hazī a gr̄a calor y alli
no / salvo tē plado c̄omo en mayo / atrivuye
el calor dlas otras islas: por ser m̄y llanas
y por el viento q̃ trayan hasta alli ser levate
y por eso calido / el agua de aq̃llos rios
era salada a la boca: no supier̄o de donde
bevian los yndios avnq̃ tenī a en sus casas
agua dulçe /. en este rio podia los navios bolte
jar p̲a̲ entrar y p̲a̲ salir y tienē m̄y buenas
señas /o marcas: tienē siete o ocho braças de
fondo a la boca y dentro çinco /. toda aq̃lla mar
dize q̃ le peçe q̃ deve ser siemp^r m̄asa c̄omo el rio
de sevilla: y el agua aparejada p̲a̲ criar per
las /. hallo caracoles gr̄ades sin sabor no c̄omo
los despaña /. señala la disposiçion dl rio y dl
puerto q'arriba dixo y n̄obro san salvador: q̃
tiene sus m̄otañas hermosas y altas c̄omo
la peña dlos enamorados y vna dllas tiene
en çima otro m̄otezillo a m̄ara de vna hermosa
mezquita /. estotro rio y puerto en q̃ agora estava
tiene dla p̲t̲e̲ del sueste dos m̄otañas: asi red̄odas
y dla p̲t̲e̲ del gueste norueste vn hermoso cabo lla
no q̃ sale fuera /.

martes .30. de otubre

salio dl rio de mares al norue
ste y vido cabo lleno de palmas y pusole cabo
de palmas dspues de avia andado quinze le
guas /. los yndios q̃ yvā en la caravela pin
ta dixerō q̃ detras de aq̃l cabo avia vn rio y dl
rio a cuba avia quatro jornadas . y dixo el capi
tā dla pinta q̃ entendia q̃ esta cuba era çiudad
y q̃ aq̃lla tr̄ra era tr̄ra firme mȳ grāde q̃ va
mūcho al norte . y q̃l rey de aq̃lla tr̄ra tenia
guerra c̄o el gra can al qual ellos llamavā cami
y a su tr̄ra /o çiudad faba y otros mūchos nōbres
determino el almiᵉ de llegar a aq̃l rio y en
biar vn presente al rey dla tr̄ra y enbiarle la Cta
dlos reyes /. y pa ella tenia vn marinero q̃ a
via andado en guinea en lo mismo: y çiertos
yndios de guanahani q̃ querian yr con el con
q̃ dspues los tornasen a su tr̄ra /. al pareçer
dl almiᵉ distava dla linea equinocial .42 gra
dos hazia la vāda dl norte . sino esta corrupta
la letra de donde treslade esto / y dize q̃ avia
de trabajar de yr al grā can y pensava q̃stava
por alli /o a la çiudad de cathay q̃s del gra
can / q̃ diz q̃ es mȳ grāde segū le fue "dicho"
antes q̃ p̱tiese despaña /. toda aq̃sta tr̄ra dize ser
baxa
y hermosa y fonda la mar

miercoles 31.º de noviēbre

toda la noche martes anduvo
barloventeando y vido vn rio donde no pudo
entrar por ser baxa la entrada y p̄esarō los
yndios q̃ pudierā entrar los navios cōmo entrava
sus canoas: y navegādo adelante hallo vn cabo q̃
salia mȳ fuera y çercado de baxos y vido
vna concha /o baya donde podian estar navio peque
ños y no lo pudo encabalgar porq̃l viento se
avia tyrado dl todo al norte y toda la costa se cor
ria al nornorueste y sueste y otro cabo q̃ vido
adelante le salia mas afuera /. por esto y
por q̃l çielo mostrava de ventar rezio: se ovo de
tornar al rio de mares /.

Jueves .1º de noviẽbre

En saliendo el sol enbio el almi.ᵉ las barcas
a tr̄ra a las casas q̃ alli estavan y hallarō q̃ erā
toda la gente huida . y desde a buẽ rato pa
reçio vn hōbre / y mādo el almi.ᵉ q̃ lo dexasen
asegurar y bolvierōse las barcas /. y despues
de comer, torno a enbiar a tr̄ra vno de
los yndios q̃ llevava: el qual dsde lexos le dio
bozes diziẽdo q̃ no oviesen miedo porq̃ erā bue
na gẽte y no haziā mal a nadie "ni erā delg can" /
antes dava
de lo suyo en mūchas islas q̃ aviā estado /.
y echose a nadar el yndio y fue a tr̄ra: y dos
dlos de alli lo tomarō de braços y llevarō
lo a vna casa donde se informarō del /. y co
mō fuerō çiertos q̃ no se les avia de hazer
mal: se asegurarō y vinierō luego a los
navios mas de diez y seys almadias /o cano
as cō algodon hylado y otras cosillas suyas
dlas quales mādo el almi.ᵉ q̃ no se tomasse
nada: porq̃ supiesen q̃ no buscava el almi.ᵉ
salvo oro a que ellos llamā nucay /.
y asi en todo el dia anduvierō y vinieron de
tr̄ra a los navios: y fuerō dlos xr̄ianos a tr̄ra
mȳ seguramẽte /. el almi.ᵉ no vido a
alguno dllos oro / p̱o dize el almi.ᵉ q̃
vido a vno dllos vn pedaço de plata labra
da colgado a la nariz: q̃ tuvo por señal q̃ en
la tr̄ra avia p̱lata /. dixerō "por señas" q̃ antes de
tres dias vernian mūchos mercaderes dla
tr̄ra dentro a cōprar dlas cosas q̃ alli llevan
los xrianos: y darian nuevas del rey de aq̃lla
tr̄ra: el qual segū se pudo entender por las
señas q̃ davā q̃stava de alli quatro jornadas
porq̃ ellos avian enbiado mūchos por toda la

tr̄ra a le hazer saber dl almi.ᵉ /. Esta gẽte dize
el almi.ᵉ es dla misma calidad y costūbre dlos
otros hallados: sin ningū secta q̃ yo cognozco
q̃ fasta oy aquestos q̃ traygo no e visto hazer
ninguᵃ oraçion /. antes dizẽ la salve y
el ave maria cō las manos al çielo comō le
amuestran / y hazẽ la señal dla cruz /.
toda la lengua tābien es vna y todos ami
gos y creo q̃ sean todas estas islas: y q̃ tengā

guerra con el gr̄a chan a q̃ ellos llamā cavi
la y a la provinçia ba[s]an /. y assi andā tābiē
desnudos comō los otros /. Esto dize el almiᵉ.
El rio dize q̃s mūy hōdo: y en la boca pueden
llegar los navio c̄o el bordo hasta tr̄ra: no llega
el agua dulçe a la boca con vna legua / y es
mȳ dulçe /. y es çierto dize el almiᵉ q̃sta es
la tr̄ra firme /. y q̃stoy dize el ante zayto y
quīsay ciē leguas poco mas
/o poco menos lexos dlo vno y de lo otro y
bien se amuestra por la mar q̃ viene de otra
suerte q̃ fasta aqui no a venido y ayer que
yva al norueste falle q̃ hazia frio /.

Viernes 2. de noviēbre

Fol. 20
(cont.)

Acordo el almiᵉ enbiar dos hōbres españoles
el vno se llamava rodrigo de xerez q̃ bivia
en ayamōte: y el otro era vn luis de
torres y avia bivido con el adelātado de mur
çia y avia sido judio y sabia diz q̃ ebrayco y
caldeo y avn algo aravigo /. y con estos enbio
dos yndios: vno dlos q̃ c̄osigo traya de gua
nahani: y el otro de aq̃llas casas
q̃ en el rio estavā poblados /. dioles
sartas de cuētas p̲a c̄oprar de comer
si les faltase: y seys dias de termino p̲a q̃
bolviesen /. dioles muestras de espeçeria
p̲a ver si alguna della topasen /. dioles
instruçion / de comō aviā de pregūtar por
el rey de aq̃lla tr̄ra y lo q̃ le aviā de hablar
de p̲tes dlos reyes de castilla / comō enbiavan
al almiᵉ p̲a q̃ les diese de su p̲te sus ctas y
vn presente / y p̲a saber dsu estado y cobrar
amistad con el: y favoreçelle en lo q̃ oviese
dllos menester etc̃. y q̃ supiesen de çier

Fol. 20v

tas provinçias y puertos y rios de q̃ el almiᵉ
tenia noticia y quāto distavā de alli etc̃.
Aqui tomo el almiᵉ el altura c̄o vn quadrā
te esta noche y hallo q̃stava .42. grados dla
linea equinoçial /. y dize q̃ por su cuēta ha
llo q̃ avia andado dsde la isla del hierro
mill y çiento y quarēta y dos leguas /. y to
davia afirma q̃ aq̃lla es tr̄ra firma /.

200

Sabado .3. de noviēbre

Fol. 20v
(cont.)

en la mañana entro en la barca
el almi.ᵉ y porꝗ haze el rio en la boca vn
grā lago el qual haze vn singularissimo puer
to mȳ hōdo y limpio de piedras mȳ buena
playa p̲a poner navios a mōte y mūcha le
ña: entro por el rio arriba hasta llegar al agua
dulce ꝗ seria çerca de dos leguas: y subio en vn
motezillo por dscubrir algo dla tr̄ra
y no pudo ver nada por las grādes arboledas
las quales mȳ frescas /o odoriferas /. por lo qual
dize no tener duda ꝗ no aya yervas aromati
cas /. dize ꝗ todo era tan hermoso lo ꝗ via: ꝗ
no podia cansar los ojos de ver tanta lindeza /
y los cantos dlas aves y paxaritos /. vinie
rō en aꝗl dia mūchas almadias /o canoas a los
navios a resgatar cosas de algodon filado y redes
en ꝗ dormian ꝗ son hamacas

Domīgo .4. de noviēbre

Fol. 20v
(cont.)

luego en amaneçiendo entro el almiᵉ en la
barca y salio a tr̄ra a caçar dlas aves ꝗl dia
antes avia visto /. despues de buelto vino
a el martin alōso pinçon c̄o dos pedaços
de canela: y dixo ꝗ vn portugues ꝗ tenia
en su navio avia visto a vn yndio ꝗ traya
dos manojos della grādes: p̲o ꝗ no se la oso
resgatar por la pena ꝗl almiᵉ tenia puesta
ꝗ nadie resgatase /. dezia mas ꝗ aꝗl yndio
traya vnas cosas bermejas com̄o nuezes /.
el contramaestre dla pinta dixo ꝗ avia halla
do arboles de canela: fue el almi.ᵉ luego alla
y hallo ꝗ no erā /. mostro el almi.ᵉ a vnos
yndios de alli canela y pimienta parez que
dla ꝗ llevava de castilla p̲a muestra: y co
gnoscierōla dizꝗ: y dixerō por señas
ꝗ çerca de alli avia mucho de aꝗllo al camino
dl sueste /. mostroles oro "y perlas" y respōdieron
çier

Fol. 21

tos viejos ꝗ en vn lugar ꝗ llamarō bohio
avia infinito y ꝗ lo trayan al cuello y a las

201

orejas y a los braços y a las piernas: y tābiē
perlas /. Entendio mas q̃ dezian q̃ avia
naos grādes y mercaderias y todo esto era
al sueste /. entēdio tābien q̃ lexos de alli avia
hōbres de vn ojo / y otros con hoçicos de perros
q̃ comian los hōbres: y q̃ en tomādo vno
lo degollavā y le bevian la sangre: y le corta
van su natura /. determino de bolver a la nao
el almi.ᵉ a esperar los dos hōbres q̃ avia en
biado: pa determinar de partirse a buscar a
q̃llas tr̄ras: sino truxesen aq̃llos alguna
buena nueva dlo q̃ dseavan /. dize mas el
almi.ᵉ esta gente es mȳ māsa y mūy teme
rosa desnuda comō dcho tengo / sin armas y sin
ley /. estas tr̄ras son mȳ fertiles: ellos las
tienē llenas de mames q̃ son somō çanahorias
q̃ tienē sabor de castañas: y tienē faxones y fa
vas mȳ diversas dlas nr̄as y mucho algodon
el qual no siembrā y nace por los mōtes arbo
les grādes: y creo q̃ en todo tpo lo aya pa coger
porq̃ vi lo cogujos abiertos y otros q̃ se abrian y
flores todo en vn arbol y otras mill mar̄as de
frutas q̃ "me" no es possible escrevir y todo deve ser
cosa provechosa /. todo esto dize el almi.ᵉ

lunes .5. de noviēbre

Fol. 21
(cont.)
en amaneziendo mādo poner la nao a'mōte
y los otros navios po no todos juntos sino q̃
quedasen siempʳ dos en el lugar donde estavan
por la seguridad / avnq̃ dize q̃ aq̃lla gente era mȳ
segura y sin temor se pudieran poner todos los na
vios junto en mōte /. Estando asi vino el contra
maestre dl niña a pedir albriçias al almiᵉ
porq̃ avia hallado almaçiga mas "no" traya la mue
stra porq̃ se le avia caido /. prometioselas el almiᵉ
y enbio a rodrigo sanches y a mastre dg a los
arboles y truxerō vn poco dlla: la qual guar
do pa llevar a los reyes y tambiē del arbol y dize
q̃ se cognoscio q̃ [era?] almaçiga avnq̃ se a de coger
a sus tpos: y q̃ avia en aq̃lla comarca pa sacar
mill quintales cada año /. hallo dizq̃ alli mucho
de aq̃l palo q̃ le pareçio lignaloe /. Dize mas
q̃ aq̃l puᵉʳto de mares es dlos mejores dl mun̄do
y mejores ayres y mas māsa gēte /.

202

y porq̃ tiene vn cabo de peña altillo / se puede h̄azer̄
vna fortaleza: pa q̃ si aq̃llo saliese rico y cosa
gr̄āde: estaria alli los mercaderes seguros "de
        qualquiera otras naçiones:" y dize
n̄ro señor en cuyas manos estan todas las victorias
aderezca todo lo q̃ fuere su svi° / dizq̃ dixo vn yndio
por señas q̃ el almaciga era buena pa quādo les dolia
        el esto [mago]

martes 6. de noviēbre

Fol. 21v   ayer en la noche dize el almiᵉ. vinierō los dos
h̄ōbres q̃ avia embiado a ver la tr̄ra dentro y le
dixerō como avian andado doze leguas q̃ avia
hasta vna poblaçion de çinqũeta casas: donde diz q
avria mill vezinos porq̃ biven m̄uchos en vna casa /.
estas casas son de mar̃a de alfaneques gr̄ādissimos /
dixerō q̃ los avian resçibido cō gr̄a solenidad segū
su costūbre /. y todos asi h̄ōbres como mugeres los
venian a ver̃ / y aposentarōlos en las mejores casas /.
los quales los tocavā y les besavā las manos y
los pies maravillandose y creyēdo q̃ venian del
çielo y asi se lo davā a entender /. davāles de
comer dlos q̃ tenian /. dixerō q̃ en llegādo los
llevarō de bracos los mas h̄ōrrados del pueblo a la
casa principal: y dierōles dos sillas en q̃ assenta
rō: y ellos todos se assentarō en el suelo en derre
dor dellos /. el yndio q̃ con ellos yva les notifi
co la mar̃a de bivir dlos xr̄īanos y como er̄ā bue
na gente /. despues salierōse los h̄ōbreo = y entra
rō las mugeres y sentarōse dla misma mar̃a
en derredor dellos beysandoles las manos y los pies
        palpādol[os]
atentandolos si er̄ā de carne y de guesso como ellos /.
Rogavāles q̃ se estuviesen alli con ellos al menos
por çinco dias /. mostrarō la canela y pimienta
y otras espeçias q̃l almiᵉ les avia dado: y
dixerōles por señas q̃ mucha dlla avia çerca de alli
al sueste: po q̃ en alli no sabian si la avia /.
visto como no tenian recaudo de çiudad se bolvierō:
y q̃ si quisierā dar lugar a los q̃ con ellos se queriā
venir q̃ mas de quinientos h̄ōbres y mugeres vinie
rā cō ellos: porq̃ pensavā q̃ se bolvian al çielo /.
        vino
enpo cō ellos vn principal dl pueblo y vn su hijo y

203

vn hōbre suyo /. hablo co ellos el almiᵉ hizoles
mūcha hōrra: señalole mūchas tr̄ras e islas q̃ avia
en aq̃llas ꝑtes /. penso de traerlo a los reyes:
y diz q̃ no supo q̃ se le antojo parez q̃ de miedo: y
de noche escuro quisose yr a tr̄ra: y el almiᵉ diz q̃
porq̃ tenia la nao en seco en tr̄ra: no le queriēdo
enojar le dexo yr Diziendo q̃ en amaneçiendo
tornaria el qual nūca torno /. hallarō los dos
xrianos por el camino mūcha gente q̃ atravesava a sus
pueblos mugeres y hōbres con vn tizon en la mano
yervas ꝑa tomar sus sahumerios q̃ acostūbravan /.
no hallarō poblaçion por el camino de mas de çinco
casas: y todos les hazian el mismo acatamiᵒ /. viero
muchas mar̃as de arboles e yervas y flores odoriferas /
viero aves de muchas mīr̄as diversas dlas despaña salvo

Fol. 22

perdizes y ruysenores q̃ cantava y ansares
q̃ destos ay alli hartos /. bestias de quatro pies
no vierō : salvo perros q̃ no ladravā /. la tr̄ra
mȳ fertil y mȳ labrada de aq̃llos manēs
y fexoes y habas mȳ diversas dlas nr̄as /. eso
mismo panizo: y mūcha cantidad de algodon cogi
do y filado y obrado: y q̃ en vna sola casa avian
visto mas de quinientas arrovas: y q̃ se pudiera
aver alli cada año quatro mill quintales /. dize el
almiᵉ q̃ le ꝑeçia q̃ no lo sembravā y q̃ da fruto
todo el año: es mȳ fino tiene el capillo grāde /. to
do lo q̃ aq̃lla gente tenia: diz q̃ dava por mȳ vil
preçio: y q̃ vna grā espuerta de algodon: dava por
cabo de agujeta /o otra cosa q̃ se le de /. Son gente
dize el almiᵉ mȳ sin mal ni de guerra: dsnudos
todos hōbres y mugeres comō sus madres los pa
rio /. Vrdad es q̃ las mugeres traen vna cosa de
algodon solamēte tan grāde q̃ le cobija su natura
y no mas /. y son ellas de mȳ buē acatamiēto
ni mȳ negros salvo menos q̃ canarias /. tengo
por dcho serenissimos prinçipes (dize aqui el almiᵉ)
q̃ sabiendo la lengua dispuesta suya personas devo
tas religiosas q̃ luego todos se tornarian xr̄ianos /.
y asi esꝑo en nr̄o señor q̃ vr̄as altezas se determi
narā a ello con mūcha diligençia ꝑa tornar a la igle
sia tan grādes pueblos y los conVrtirā: asi comō
an destruydo aq̃llos q̃ no quisierō confessar el
padre y el hijo y el esꝑu sancto: y dspues de sus
dias (q̃ todos somos mortales dexarā sus reynos
en mȳ tranquilo estado: y limpios de heregia y

maldad: y serā bien resçibidos delante el eterno
criador al qual plega de les dar larga vida y
acreçentamiº grāde de mayores reynos
y señorios: y volūtad y disposiçion pa acreçētar
la sancta religiō xrīana asi comō hasta aqui tienē
fecho amen /. oy tire la nao de mōte y me
despacho pa partir el jueves en nōbre de dios e
yr al sueste a buscar del oro y espeçerias y des
cubrir tr̄ra /. estas todas son palabras del almirāte /.
El qual penso partir el jueves: po porq̃ le hizo
el viento contrario: no pudo partir hasta doze
dias de noviembre /.

lunes .12. de noviēbre

Fol. 22
(cont.)
Partio del puᵉrto y rio de mares
al rēdir del quarto de alva: pa yr a vna ysla
q̃ mucho affirmavā los yndios q̃ traya q̃ se lla
mava baveque: adonde segū dizen por
señas q̃ la gente della coge el oro c̄o candelas de
noche

Fol. 22v
en la playa // y despues con martillo diz q̃
hazian vergas dllo /. y pa yr a ella era me
nestr "poner" la proa al leste quarta del sueste /. des
pues de aver andado ocho leguas por la costa delā
te hallo vn rio: y dende andadas otras quatro
hallo otro rio q̃ pareçia m̄y caudaloso y mayor
q̃ ninguº dlos otros q̃ avia hallado /. no se qui
so detener ni entrar en alguº dllos por dos respe
ctos: el vno y principal porq̃l t̄po y viēnto era
bueno pa yr en demāda dla d̄cha isla de babeque
lo otro porq̃ si en el oviera alguᵃ pplosa "o famosa" çiudad
çerca dla mar se pareçiera / y pa yr por el rio
arriba erā menestr navios pequeños: lo q̃ no erā
los q̃ llevava / y asi se pdiera tābiē mūcho t̄po / y los
semejantes rios son cosa pa descobrirse por si /.
toda aq̃lla costa era poblada /mayormēte çerca dl
rio a quiē puso por nōbre el rio del sol /. dixo
q̃l domīgo antes onze de noviēbre le avia pare
çido q̃ fuera biē tomar algunas psonas dlas de aq̃l
rio pa llevar a los reyes: porq̃ aprendierā nr̄a
legua: pa saber lo q̃ ay en la tr̄ra: y porq̃ bolvien
do sean lenguas dlos xrīanos: y tomē nr̄as costū
bres: y las cosas dla fe /. porq̃ yo vi e cognozco (

(dize el almiᵉ) q̃sta gente no tiene secta ninguᵃ ni son
idolatras: salvo m̄y māsos y sin saber q̃ sea mal
ni matar a otros ni prender y sin armas / y tan
temerosos q̃ a vna p̲sona dlos nr̄os fuyen
çiento dllos avnq̃ burlen c̄o ellos /. y credulos
y cognosçedores q̃ ay dios en el çielo: e firmes
q̃ nosotros avemos venido dl çielo: y m̄y pʳsto a
qualquiera oraçion q̃ nos les digamos q̃ digan
y haz̄e el señal dla cruz ✝ /. Asi q̃ dev̄e
vrās altezas determinarse a los hazeʳ xr̄ianos:
q̃ creo q̃ si comiēçan en poco t̄po acabara de los
aver convertido a nr̄a sācta fe multidūbre de
pueblos: y cobrādo grādes señorios y riquezas
y todos sus pueblos dla espāña /. porq̃ sin duda
es en estas tr̄ras grādissima sum̄a de oro q̃ no sin
causa dizen estos yndios q̃ yo traygo q̃ ha ene
stas islas lugares adonde cavan el oro y lo
traen al pescueço / a las orejas / y a los braços / e
a las piernas / y son manillas m̄y gruessas /. y
tābien ha piedras y ha perlas preciosas y in
finita espeçeria /. y en este rio de mares de a
donde parti esta noche sin duda ha grādissima
cantidad de almaçiga / y mayor si mayor se quisie
re hazer /. porq̃ los mismos arboles plantandolos
prenden de ligero: y ha mūchos y mūy grādes y

Fol. 23

tien̄e la hoja como lentisco y el fructo: salvo
q̃ es mayor asi los arboles com̄o la hoja como
dize plinio e yo e visto en la isla de xio en el
arcipielago y māde sangrar
mūchos destos arboles p̲a ver si echaria resina
p̲a la traer y com̄o aya siempʳ llovido el t̄po
q̃ yo e estado en el dcho rio no e podido aver dlla //
salvo m̄y poquita q̃ traygo a .v. al. y tābiē puede
ser q̃ no es el t̄po p̲a los sangrar q̃ esto creo q̃
conviene al t̄po q̃ los arboles comiēçan a salir
dl invierno y quier̄e echar la flor: y aca ya
tien̄e el fruto quasi maduro agora /. y tanbiē
aqui se avria grāde sum̄a de algodon: y creo q̃
se venderia mūy bien aca sin le llevar a espa
ña: salvo a las grādes çiudades del grā Can q
se descubrirā sin duda: y otras mūchas de otros
señores q̃ avran en dicha servir a vrās altezas
y adonde se les darā de otras cosas de espāña
y dlas tr̄ras de oriente: pues estas son a nos
en poniente /. y aqui ha tābien infinito lignaloe

avnq̃ no es cosa p̲a haz^r gr̄a caudal mas del
almaçiga es de ent̄eder bien: porq̃ no la ha sal
vo en la d̄cha ysla de Xio: y creo q̃ sacan dello
bien çinqũeta mill du^{dos} si mal no me acuerdo /
y "ha" aqui en la boca dl d̄cho rio el mejor pu^{er}to q̃
fasta oy vi / limpio e ancho a fondo y bũe
lugar y asiento p̲a haz^{er} vna villa e fuerte e
que qualesquier navios se pũedan llegar
el bordo a los muros: e tr̄ra mũy temperada y
alta y m̄y buenas aguas /. Asi que ayer vino
abordo dla nao vna almadia con seys man
cebos y los çinco entrar̄o en la nao: estos m̄ade
detener e los traygo /. y despues enbie a
vna casa q̃ es de la p̲te del rio dl poniente y tru
xer̄o siete cabeças de mugeres entre "chicas"
e gr̄ades y tres niños /. esto hize porq̃ mejor
se c̄oportan los h̄obres en esp̄aña aviendo mu
geres de su tr̄ra q̃ sin ellas /. porq̃ ya otras mu
chas vezes se acaeçio traer h̄obres de guinea
p̲a q̃ deprendiesen la lengua en portugal
y despues q̃ bolvian y pensav̄a de se aprove
char dllos en su tr̄ra por la buena copañia
q̃ le avīa hecho y dadibas q̃ se les avīa dado:
en lleḡado en tr̄ra jamas parecia /. otros no
lo hazīa asi /. asi que tenīedo sus mugeres

tern̄a gana de negociar lo q̃ se les encargare
y t̄abien estas mugeres mũcho ensen̄ara a los
nr̄os su lengua /. la qual es toda vna en
todas estas islas de yndia / y todos se entien
den y todas las andan c̄o sus almadias: lo
q̃ no han en guinea adonde es mill mañas
de lenguas q̃ la vna no entiende la otra /
Esta noche vino a bordo en vna almadia el
marido de vna destas mugeres y padre de
tres fijos vn macho y dos fenbras: y dixo
q̃ yo le dexase venir c̄o ellos y a mi me aplo
go mũcho: y qued̄a agora todos consolados
con el q̃ deven todos ser parientes y el es ya
h̄obre de .45. años /. todas estas palabras
son formales dl almir̄ate /. dize tambien
arriba q̃ hazia algun frio: y por esto q̃ no le
fuera bũe consejo en invierno navegar al
norte p̲a dscubrir /. Navego este lu
nes hasta el sol puesto .18. leguas al leste
quarta dl sueste hasta vn cabo "a" q̃ puso
por n̄obre el cabo de cuba /.

martes .13. de noviēbre

Fol. 23v
(cont.)

Esta noche toda estuvo a la corda cōmo dizen
los marineros que es andar barlovente
ando y no andar nada: por ver vn abra
q̃ es vn abertura de sierras cōmo entre sier
ra y sierra q̃ le comēço a ver al
poner del sol: a donde se mostra
van dos grandissimas mōtañas: y parecia
q̃ se a.ptavā la tr̄ra de cuba con aq̃lla de
bofio y esto dezian los yndios q̃ consigo lle
vavan / por señas /. venido el dia claro dio
las velas sobre la trra y passo vna punta q̃
le pareçio anoche obra de dos leguas: y entro
en vn grāde golpho çinco "leguas" al sursudueste y le
quedavā otras çinco pa llegar al cabo a donde
en medio de dos grādes mōtes hazia vn degolla
do el qual no pudo determinar si era entrada
de mar /. y porq̃ deseava yr a la isla q̃ llama
vā beneque: adonde tenia nueva segū el entēdia
q̃ avia mucho oro la qual isla le salia al leste: co
mo no vido "alguna" grāde poblaçion pa ponerse al ri
gor del viento q̃ le creçia mas q̃ nūca hasta alli:
acordo de hazerse a la mar y andar al leste con el
viēto q̃ era norte y andava .8. millas cada ora
y desde las diez dl dia q̃ tomo aq̃lla derrota hasta
el poner dl sol anduvo .56. seys millas q̃ son .14.
leguas al leste desde el cabo de cuba . y dla otra
tr̄ra
del bohio q̃ le quedava a sotaviento començando dl
cabo

Fol. 24

dl sobredicho golpho descubrio a su pareçer .80.
millas q̃ son .xx. leguas: y corriase toda aq̃lla
costa lesueste y guesnorueste /.

miercoles .14. de noviēbre

Fol. 24
(cont.)

toda la noche de ayer anduvo al reparo y
barloventeādo (porq̃ dezia q̃ no era razō de
navegar entre "aq̃llas" islas de noche hasta q̃ las
ovie
se descubierto) porq̃ los yndios q̃ traya le
dixerō ayer martes q̃ avria tres jornadas

desde el rio de mares hasta la isla de baneq̃:
q̃ se deve entēder jornadas dsus almadias q̃
pueden andar .7. leguas: y el viento tābiē
le escaseava y aviendo de yr al leste: no podia
sino a la quarta dl sueste y por otros inconvi
nientes q̃ alli refiere: se ovo detener
hasta la mañana /. al salir dl sol determino
de yr a buscar puerto: porq̃ de norte se avia
mudado el viento al nordeste: y si puerto
no hallara: fuera le neçessario bolver
atras a los pueʳtos q̃ dexava en la isla de
cuba /. llego a tr̄ra aviendo andado aq̃lla
noche .24. millas al leste quarta dl sueste
anduvo al sur . . millas hasta tr̄ra: a dōde
vio mūchas entradas y muchas isletas y
pueʳtos: y porq̃l viento era mūcho y la mar
mȳ alterada: no oso acometer a entrar: an
tes corrio por la costa al norueste quarta dl
gueste mirādo si avia puerto y vido q̃ avia
muchos po no mȳ claros /. despues de
aver andado asi .64. millas: hallo vna en
trada mȳ hōda ancha vn quarto de mi
lla y buē pueʳto y rio: donde entro y puso
la proa al sursudueste y dspues al sur hasta
llegar al sueste / todo de buena anchura y
mȳ fondo /. donde vido tantas islas q̃ no las
pudo contar todas de buena gradeza y
mȳ altas tierras llenas de diversos ar
boles de mill mār̄as e infinitas palmas /.
maravillose en grā mār̄a ver tantas islas
y tan altas y çertifica a los reyes q̃
las mōtañas q̃ dsde antier a visto por estas
costas y las dstas islas: q̃ le pareçe q̃ no
las ay mas altas en el mūdo / ni tan her
mosas y claras sin niebla ni nieve: y
al pie dllas grādissimo fondo /. y dize q̃
cree q̃ estas islas son aq̃llas innumera
bles q̃ en los mapanūdos en fin de oriēte
se ponen /. y dixo q̃ creia q̃ avia grādissimas
riquezas y piedras preçiosas y espeçeria en e
llas: y q̃ durā mȳ mucho al sur y se ensanchan
a toda parte /. puso les nōbre la mar de nr̄a
señora /. "y al puerto que esta çerca dla boca
dla entrada de las dchas islas: puso puerto del
prinçipe / en el qual no entro mas de velle dsde
fuera hasta otra buelta q̃ dio el sabado dla

semana venidera como alli parecera /."

dize tantas y tales cosas de la fer
tilidad y hermosura y altura destas islas q̃
hallo en este puerto: q̃ dize a los reyes q̃ no se
maravillen de encareçellas tanto: porq̃ los
certifica: q̃ cree q̃ no dize la çentissima parte
algunas dellas q̃ pareçia q̃ llegā al çielo y he
chas cõmo puntas de diamātes: otras
q̃ sobre su grā altura tienē ençima
cõmo vna mesa: y al pie dllas fondo gran
dissimo q̃ podra llegar a ellas vna grādissima
carraca: todas llenas de arboledas y sin peñas /.

Jueves .15. de noviembre

acordo de andallas estas islas con las barcas
dlos navios y dize maravillas dllas: y q̃
hallo almaçiga e infinito lignaloe: y algunas
dllas erā labradas dlas rayzes de q̃ hazen su
pan los yndios / y hallo aver encēdido huegos
en algunos lugares /. "agua dulce no vido /."
gente avia
alguna y huyerō: en todo lo q̃ anduvo ha
llo hōdo de quinze y diez seys braças y todo
basa q̃ quiere dezir q̃l suelo de abaxo es are
na y no peñas: lo q̃ q̃ mucho dsean los ma
rineros / porq̃ las peñas cortan los cables
dlas anclas dlas naos /.

viernes .16. de noviēbre

porq̃ en todas las ptes islas y trras donde entra
va dexava siempre puesta vna cruz:
entro en la barca y fue a la boca de aq̃llos puertos
y en vna punta dla tierra hallo dos maderos
mȳ grādes vno mas largo q̃ el otro
y el vno sobre el otro hechos cruz q̃ dizque
vn carpintero no los pudiera poner mas
proporçionados /. y adorada aq̃lla cruz mādo hazer
de los mismos
maderos / vna mȳ grāde y alta cruz /. hallo
cañas por aq̃lla playa q̃ no sabia donde na
çian: y creya q̃ las traeria algun rio y las

echava a la playa y tenia en esto razō /. fue
a vna cala dentro dla entrada dl pu^{er}to dla pte
[dl?] sueste: (cala es vna entrada angosta q̃ entra el

agua dl mar en la tierra) alli hazia vn alto
de piedra y pēna comō cabo: y al pie dl era
mȳ fondo q̃ la may[or] carraca dl mūdo pu
piera poner el bordo en tr̄ra y avia vn lugar
(o rincon donde podian estar seys navios sin
anclas comō en vna sala /. pareçiole q̃ se podia
hazer alli vna fortaleza a poca costa: si en algun
tpō en aq̃lla mar de islas resultase algu resga
te famoso /. bolviendose a la nao hallo los
yndios q̃ cōsigo traya q̃ pescavan caracoles
mȳ grādes q̃ en aq̃llas mares ay: y
hizo entrar la gente alli e buscar si avia na
caras q̃ son las hostras donde crian las per
las: y hallarō mūchas / po no perlas
y atribuyolo a q̃ no devia de ser el
tpō dllas q̃ creya el q̃ era por mayo y junio
hallarō los marineros vn animal q̃ parecia taso
/o taxo: pescarō tābien con redes y hallaro
vn pece entre otros muchos q̃ pareçia proprio
puerco no comō tonina /. el qual diz q̃ era todo
concha mȳ tiesta: y no tenia cosa blanda sino la
cola y los ojos y vn agujero debaxo "della" pa expe
ler sus supfluydades mandolo salar pa llevar q̃
lo viesen los reyes /.

sabado .17. de noviēbre

Entro en la barca por la maña y fue
a ver las yslas q̃ no avia visto por la vanda
del sudueste vido mūchas otras y my fertiles
y mȳ graçiosas y entre medio dellas mȳ
grā fondo/. algunas dellas diuidian arroyos
de agua dulçe: y creya q̃ aq̃lla agua
y arroyos salian de algunas fuentes q̃
manavā en los altos de las sierras de
las islas /. de aqui yendo adelante hallo vna
ribera dagua mȳ hermosa y dulçe y salia my
fria por lo enxuto della avia vn prado my
lindo y palmas muchas y altissimas mas
q̃ las q̃ avia visto /. hallo nuezes grades dlas
de yndia creo q̃ dize / y ratones grādes

211

dlos de yndia tabien / y cangrejos gradissi
mos /. aves vido m̄uchas y olor vehemete de
almizque y creyo q̃ lo debia de aver alli Este
dia de seys m̄acebos q̃ tomo en el rio de mares q̃
m̄ado q̃ fuesen en la caravela niña: se huyero los
dos mas viejos /

domingo ~~Sabado~~ .~~18~~. de noviēbre

Fol. 25v

salio en las barcas otra vez con m̄ucha gente de
los navios
y fue a poner la grā cruz
q̃ avia m̄adado hazer dlos dchos
dos maderos a la boca dla entra
da dl dcho puerto dl prinçipe en vn lugar visto
so y descubierto de arboles: ella mȳ alta y my
hermosa vista /. dize q̃ la mar creçe y descreçe
alli mucho mas q̃ en otro puerto dlo q̃ por aq̃lla
tr̄ra aya visto y q̃ no es mas maravilla por las
m̄uchas islas: y q̃ la marea es al reves dlas
nr̄as / porq̃ alli la luna al sudueste quarta del
sur es baxa mar en aq̃l pue[r?]to / no partio d[e]
aqui por ser domīgo /

lunes .19. de noviēbre

Fol. 25v
(cont.)

Partio antes q̃l sol saliese y cō calma: y despues
al medio dia
vento algo al leste y navego al nornordeste
al poner dl sol le quedava el pueᵉrto dl prinçipe
al sursudueste y estaria dl siete leguas /. vido
la isla de baneque al leste justo dla qual estaria
60 millas /. navego toda esta noche al nordeste ,
escasso andaria .60. millas y hasta las diez
dl dia martes otras doze q̃ son por todas .18.
leguas / y al nordeste q̃rta dl norte /

martes .20. de noviēbre

Fol. 25v
(cont.)

Quedavāle el baneque o las islas dl baneque
al lesueste de donde salia el viēto q̃ lle

212

vava contrario: y viendo q̃ no se mudava y la
mar se alterava: determino de dar la buel
ta al pu^{er}to dl p^rncipe de donde avia salido q̃ le
quedava .xxv. leguas /. no quiso yr a la isleta
q̃ llamo isabela q̃ le estava .12. lueguas q̃ pudie
ra yr a surgir aq̃l dia: por dos razones /. la
vna porq̃ vido dos islas al sur las queria ver /.
la otra porq̃ los yndios q̃ traya q̃ avia tomado
en guanahani q̃ llamo san salvador q̃ estava ocho
leguas de aq̃lla isabela: no se le fuesen / dlos qua
les diz q̃ tiene necessidad y por traellos a castilla
etc̄. tenian dizque entēdido q̃ en hallādo
oro los avia el almi^e de dexar tornar a su
tr̄r̄a / llego en paraje dl puerto dl p^rn
cipe / p̣o no lo pudo tomar porq̃ era de noche y porq̃
lo decayerō las corrientes al norueste /. torno a
dar la buelta y puso la proa al nordeste con
viento rezio: amāso y mudose el viento al terçero
quarto dla noche puso la proa en el leste quarta
dl nordeste: el viento era susueste: y mudose al
alva de todo en sur y tocava enl sueste /. salido a
marco el puerto dl principe y quedavale al sudueste
y quasi a la quarta del gueste y estaria dl .48.
                                        millas
que son .12. leguas /.

miercoles 21. de noviēbre

Fol. 26

al sol salido navego al leste con viento sur
anduvo poco por la mar contraria hasta oras de
bisperas ovo andado .24. millas /. dspues se
mudo el viento al leste y anduvo al sur q̃rta del su
ste y al poner dl sol avia andado .12. millas /
Aqui se hallo el almi^e en .42. grados dla linea
equinoçial a la p̣te del norte com̄o en el pu^{er}to de
mares /. p̣o aqui dize q̃ tiene suspenso el quadra
te hasta llegar a tr̄r̄a q̃ lo adobe / por mar̄a q̃
le pareçia q̃ no devia distar tanto y tenia ra
zon porq̃ no era possible comō no esten
estas yslas sino en   grados /. p̣a creer q̄uel
quadrante andava bueno le movia ver diz q̃ el
norte tan alto comō en castilla / y si esto es ver
dad mūcho allegado y alto andava cō la florida /.
p̣o donde estan luego agora estas islas q̃ entre
manos traya ? ayudava a esto q̃ hazia dizque

213

grā calor: p̱o claro es q̃ si estuviera en la costa
dla florida q̃ no oviera calor sino frio: y es
tābien manifiesto q̃ en quarēta y dos grados en
ninguᵃ p̱te dla tr̄ra se cree hazer calor /. sino fue
se por alguᵃ causa de per acçidens: lo q̃ hasta oy
no creyo yo q̃ se sabe /. por este calor q̃ alli el
almi.ᵉ dize q̃ padecia / arguye q̃ en estas yndias
y por alli donde andava devia de aver mucho oro /
Este dia se aparto martin aloso pincon cō la carave
la pinta: sin obediençia y volutad dl almíᵉ
por cudiçia dizq̃ pensando q̃ vn yndio q̃ el
almi.ᵉ avia mādado poner en aq̃lla caravela le
avia de dar mucho oro /. y asi se fue "sin
                        esperar"
sin causa de mal tp̄o sino porq̃ quiso /. y dize a
qui el almi.ᵉ otras mūchas me tiene hecho y
                        dicho /.

Jueves .22.

Fol. 26
(cont.)
miercoles en la noche navego al sur quarta del
sueste cō el viento leste y era quasi calma /. al ter
çero quarto vēto nornordeste todavia iva al sur por
ver aq̃lla tr̄ra q̃ por alli le quedava / y quādo salio
el sol se hallo tā lexos como el dia passado por las
corriētes contrarias y quedavale la tr̄ra quarēta
                        millas
esta noche martin alonso siguio el camino dl leste p̱a
yr a la isla de vaneque donde dizē los yndios q̃ ay
mucho oro /. el qual yva a
vista dl almiᵉ y avria hasta el .16. millas / andu
vo el almi.ᵉ toda la noche la buelta de tr̄ra y hizo
                        tomar

Fol. 26v
algunas dlas velas y tener farol toda la noche
porq̃ le pareçio q̃ venia hazia el / y la noche hizo mȳ
clara y el ventezillo bueno p̱a venir a el si qui
siera /.

viernes .23. de noviēbre

Fol. 26v
(cont.)
navego el almi.ᵉ todo el dia hazia la tr̄ra al sur
siemp̱ʳ con poco viento y la corriente nūca le dexo

214

llegar a ella antes estava oy tā lexos dlla
al poner dl sol: como en la maña /. El viento era
lesnordeste y razonable p̱a yr al sur sino q̃ era
poco /. y sobre este
cabo encavalga otra tr̄ra /o cabo q̃ va tābiēn al
leste a quiē aq̃llos yndios q̃ l·levava llamava
bohio /. la qual dezian q̃ era mȳ grande y q̃ avia
en ella gente q̃ tenia vn ojo en la frente: y otros
q̃ se llamavā canibales: a quien mostravā tener grā
miedo /. y desq̃ vierō q̃ lleva este camino dizque no
podian hablar: porq̃ los comian: y q̃ son gente
mȳ armada /. el almiᵉ dize q̃ bien cree q̃
avia algo dllo: mas q̃ pues erā armados se
ria gente de razō: y creya q̃ avrian captivado al
gunos y q̃ porq̃ no bolvian a sus tr̄ras: di
rian q̃ los comian /. lo mismo creyan dlos xr̄ịa
nos y dl almiᵉ al prinçipio q̃ algunos los vieron /.

Sabado .24. de noviembre

Fol. 26v
(cont.)

Navego aq̃lla noche toda y a la ora de terçia
del dia
tomo la tr̄ra sobre la isla llana en aq̃l mismo
lugar: donde avia arribado la semana passada quā
do "yva" a la isla de baneque /. al principio no oso
llegar
a la tr̄ra porq̃ le pareçio q̃ aq̃lla abra de sierras
rom
pia la mar mucho en ella /. y en fin llego a la mar
de nr̄a señora donde avia las m̄uchas islas: y entro
en el puerto q̃sta junto a la boca dla entrada dlas
islas /. y dize q̃ si el antes supiera este puerto:
y no no se ocupara en ver las islas dla mar de nr̄a
señora: no le fuera neçessario volver atras /. avnq̃
dize q̃ lo da por bien empleado por aver visto las
dchas islas /. asi q̃ llegā́do a tr̄ra en
bio la barca y tēto el puᵉʳto y hallo mȳ buena bar
ra hōda de seys braças y hasta veynte y limpio
todo basa: entro en el poniendo la proa al sudueste
y dspues bolviendo al gueste / quedā́do la isla
llana dla
p̧te dl norte: la qual con otra su vezina hazē vna
laguna de mar en q̃ cabrian todas las naos dspaña
y podrian estar seguras sin amarras de todos las

215

vientos / y esta entrada dla parte dl sueste
q̃ se entra poniendo la proa al susudueste
tiene la salida al gueste mūy hōda y muy an
cha /. asi q̃ se puede passar entremedio dlas
dchas islas :. y por cognoscimiᵒ dllas::a quien
vinie
se dla mar dla ͵pte dl norte q̃s su travesia dsta

costa /. estan las dchas islas al pie de vna grāde
mōtaña q̃s su lōgura de leste gueste y es
harto luēga y mas alta y luēga q̃ ninguna
de todas las otras que estan en esta costa
adonde ay
infinitas /. y haze fuera vna restinga
al luēgo dla dcha mōtaña como vn banco
q̃ llega hasta la entrada /. todo esto dla ͵pte del
sueste: y tambien dla ͵pte dla isla llana: ha
ze otra restinga avnq̃sta es pequeña /. y asi en
tremedias de ambas ay grāde anchura y fondo
grande como dcho es /.
luego a la entrada a la par
te dl sueste dentro eñl mismo
puerto vierō vn rio grāde y mȳ hermoso
y de mas agua q̃ hasta entōçes avian visto y q̃
bevia el agua dulçe hasta la mar / a la entrada
tiene vn banco: mas despues de entro es my
hōdo de ocho y nueve braças /. esta todo lle
no de palmas y de muchas arboledas como
los otros /.

Domingo .25. de noviēbre

Antes dl sol salido entro en la barca y fue a ver
vn cabo /o punta de tr̄ra al sueste dla isleta llana
obra de vna legua y media: porq̃ le parecia
q̃ devia de aVr algū rio bueno /. luego a la entra
da dl cabo dla ͵pte dl sueste andādo dos tiros
de ballesta: vio venir vn grāde arroyo de my
linda agua q̃ desçendia de vna mōtaña abaxo
y hazia grā ruydo /. fue al rio y vio en el
vnas piedras reluzir con vnas māchas en e
llas de color de oro: y acordose q̃ en el rio
tejo q̃ al pie del junto a la mar se halla oro y
pareçiole q̃ çierto devia de tener oro /. y mādo co
ger çiertas de aq̃llas piedras . ͵pa llevar a los re
yes /. estando asi dan dozes los moços grume

tes diziendo q̃ vian pinales .. miro por la sierra
y vido los tan grādes y tan maravillosos: q̃ no [le?] po
dia encareçer su altura y derechura como husos
gordos y delgado / donde cognoscio q̃ se podian
hazer navios e infinita tablazon y masteles p̃a las

Fol. 27v

mayores naos dspaña . vido robles y ma
droños y "vn buē rio y" aparejo p̃a hazer sierras de
agua /. la tr̄ra y los ayres mas templa
dos q̃ hasta alli: por la altura y hermosura
dlas sierras /. vido por la playa mūchas otras
piedras de color de hierro: y otras que dezian
algunos q̃ erā de minas de plata todas las
quales trae el rio . alli cojo vna entena y mastel
p̃a la mezana dla caravela niña /. llego a la
boca dl rio y entro en vna cala al pie de aq̃l cabo
dla p̃te dl sueste mȳ hōda y grande en q̃ cabri
an çient naos sin alguna amarra ni anclas /.
y el puerto q̃ los ojos otro tal nūca vieron /.
lasierras altissimas de las quales descendian
mūchas aguas lindissimas: todos las sierras
llenas de pinos y por todo aq̃llo diversissi
mas y hermosissimas florestas de arboles /.
otros dos /o tres rios le quedavā atras /. enca
reçe todo esto en grā mār̃a a los reyes: y mue
stra aver resçibido de verlo y mayormēte
los pinos inextimable alegria y gozo /. "y
        porq̃ se podian hazer alli quantos navios
        desearen / trayendo los adereços si no
        fuera madera y pez q̃ alli se ha harta /"
afirma no encareçello la çentissima p̃te dlo
q̃ es: y q̃ plugo a nr̄o señor de le mostrar
siempre vna cosa mejor q̃ otra: y siempʳ
en lo q̃ hasta alli avia descubierto yva de biē
en mejor /. ansi en las tr̄ras y arboledas
y yervas y frutos y flores: como en las
gentes: y siempʳ de diversa mār̃a: y asi en
vn lugar cōmo en otro /. lo mismo en los
puertos y en las aguas /. y finalmete dize
q̃ quādo el q̃ lo vee le es tan grāde admiraçion: qua
to mas sera a quie[n] lo oyere: y q̃ nadie lo podra creer
si no lo viere /.

lunes .26. de noviembre

Fol. 27
(cont.)

Al salir dl sol levāto las anclas dl puerto
de sancta cathalina adonde estava dentro dla isla

217

llana: y navego de luengo dla costa con poco
viento "sudueste" al camino dl cabo dl pico q̃ era
al sueste /. llego al cabo tarde porq̃ le calmo el
viento: y llegado vido al sueste q̃rta dl leste otro
cabo q̃staria del .60. millas: y de alli vido otro
cabo q̃ estaria hazia el navio al sueste q̃rta del
sur :. y pareciole q̃staria del .20. millas al
qual puso nōbre el cabo de campana al qual
no pudo llegar de dia porq̃ le torno a calmar
dl todo el viento / andaria en todo aq̃l dia .32.

Fol. 28   millas q̃ son .8. leguas /. dentro dlas
quales noto y marco nueve
puertos mȳ señalados los quales todos
los marineros hazian maravillas / y cin
co rios grādes porq̃ yva siempre jū
to cō tr̄ra / pa ver lo bien todo /. todo aq̃lla
tr̄ra es mōtañas altissimas mȳ hermosas
y no secas ni de peñas: sino todas andables
y valles hermosissimos /. y asi los valles como las
mōtañas erā llenos de arboles altos y frescos
q̃ era gloria mirarlos y pareçia q̃ erā mūchos
pinales /. y tabien detras dl dcho cabo dl pico dla
parte dl sueste: estan dos isletas q̃ terna cada vna
en çerco dos leguas: y dentro dllas tres mara
villosos puertos y dos grādes rios /. en toda
esta costa no vido poblado ninguº dsde la mar
podria ser averlo y ay señales dllo /. porq̃ don
de quiera q̃ saltavā en tr̄ra hallavā señales
de aver gente y huegos mūchos /. estimava q̃
la tr̄ra q̃ oy vido dla pte dl sueste del cabo de can
pana: era la isla q̃ llamavā los yndios bohio
y pareçe "lo" porq̃l dcho cabo esta apartado de aq̃lla
tr̄ra /. toda la gēte q̃ hasta oy a hallado dizque
tiene grādissimo temor dlos de caniba /o canima
y dizē q̃ biven en esta isla de bohio: la qual debe
de ser mȳ grāde segū le pareçe /. y cree
q̃ van a tomar a aq̃llos a sus tr̄ras y casas
como sean mȳ cobardes: y no saben de ar
mas /. y a esta causa "le parece q̃" aq̃llos yndios
                    q̃ traya: no
suelen poblarse a la costa dla mar por ser vezi
nos a esta tr̄ra /. los quales dizq̃ dspues q̃ le
                    vierō
tomar la buelta desta tr̄ra no podian hablar
temiendo q̃ los avian de

comer / y no les podia quitar el temor /. y deziā
q̃ no tenian sino vn ojo y la cara de perro: y cre
ya el almi͞e q̃ me͞tian: y sentia el almi͞e q̃ deviā
de ser dl señorio del gran Can que los captiva
v[an?] /.

Martes 27. de noviembre

Fol. 28
(cont.)
ayer al poner dl sol llego çerca de vn cabo
q̃ llamo campana y porq̃l çielo
claro y el viento poco: no quiso yr a trra a
surgir avnq̃ tenia de sotaviento çinco /o seys
puertos maravillosos: porq̃ se detenia mas dlo q̃

Fol. 28v
queria por el apetito y delectaçion q̃
tenia y resçebia de ver y mirar la hermosu
ra y frescura de aq̃llas t͞rras donde quiera
q̃ entrava: y por no se tardar en proseguir lo
q̃ pretendia /. por estas razones se tuvo aq̃lla
noche a la corda y tem
porejar hasta el dia /. y porq̃ los aguajes y cor
rientes lo avian echado aq̃lla noche mas de
çinco /o seys leguas al sueste adelante de donde
avia anocheçido: y le avia pareçido la t͞rra de
campana: y allende aq̃l
cabo pareçia vna gra͞de entrada q̃ mostrava
dividir vna t͞rra de otra y hazia comō isla en
medio: acordo bolver atras con viento su
dueste y vino adonde le avia pareçido el aber
tura: y hallo q̃ no era sino vna gra͞de baya
y al cabo dlla dla ͜pte del sueste vn cabo
en el qual ay vna mo͞taña alta y quadrada q̃
pareçia isla /. salto el viento en el norte y
torno a tomar la buelta del sueste por correr
la costa y dscubrir todo lo q̃ por alli oviese /. y
vido luego al pie "de aq̃l" cabo de campana vn
puerto maravilloso y vn gra͞ rio: y de a vn
quarto de legua otro rio: y de alli a media legua
otro rio: y de͞de a otra media legua otro rio: y
dende a vna legua otro rio; y dende a otra
otro rio: y dende a otro quarto otro rio: y
dende a otra legua otro rio gra͞de / dsde el qual
hasta el cabo de campana avria .20. millas
y le queda͞ al sueste /. y los mas destos rios
tenian gra͞des entradas y anchas y limpias

219

con sus puertos maravillosos p̲a̲ naos grā
dissimas: sin bancos de arena ni de pedras ni
restringas /. viniendo asi por la costa a la parte
dl sueste dl dc̄ho postrero rio: hallo vna grāde
poblaçion la mayor q̃ hasta oy aya hallado: y
vido venir infinita gente a la ribera dla mar dā
do grādes bozes todos dsnudos con sus azagayas
en la mano /. deseo de hablar c̄o ellos y amay
no las velas y surgio: y enbio las barcas
dla nao y dla caravela por mār̄a ordenados
q̃ no hiziesen daño alguno a los yndios ni lo
resçibiesen: mādando q̃ les diesen algunas
cosillas de aq̃llos resgates: los yndios hizie
r̄o ademanes de no los dexar salitar en tr̄r̄a y

Fol. 29

resistillos / y viendo q̃ las barcas se allegava
mas a tr̄r̄a y q̃ no las avian miedo: se aparta
r̄o dla mar /. y creyēdo q̃ saliendo dos /o tres
hobres dlas barcas no temierā: salierō tres
xrīanos diziēdo q̃ no oviesen miedo en su lengua
porq̃ sabian algo dlla por la conversaçion dlos
q̃ traen consigo: en fin dierō todos a huyr [q̃?]
ni grāde ni chico quedo /. fuerō los tres xrīa
nos a las casas q̃ son de paja y dla hechura de
las otras q̃ avian visto: y no hallarō a nadie
ni cosa en alguᵃ dllas /. bolvierōse a los na
vios y alcarō velas "a medio dia" p̲a̲ yr a vn cabo
                                        hermo
so q̃ quedava al leste q̃ avia hasta el ocho leguas.
aviendo andado media legua por la misma baya
vido el almiᵉ a la ꝑte dl sur vn singularissimo
puerto y dla ꝑte dl sueste vnas tr̄r̄as hermosas
a maravilla asi com̄o vna vega mōtuosa dentro
en estas mōtañas: y parecian grādes humos y gra
des poblaçiones en ellas y las tr̄r̄as "mȳ" labradas: por
lo qual determino de se baxar a este puerto y
provar si podia aver lengua o pratica c̄o ellos /.
el qual era tal q̃ si a los otros puᵉʳtos avia alabado
este dize q̃ alabava mas c̄o las tr̄r̄as y tēplança
y comarca dellas y poblaçion / dize maravi
llas dla lindeza dla tr̄r̄a y dlos arboles don
de ay pinos y palmas y dla grāde vega [q̃?] avn
q̃ no el llana "de llano" q̃ va al sursueste: p̲o̲
                                        es llana
de mōtes llanos y baxos la mas hermosa cosa
del mūdo y salen por ella mūchas riberas de

aguas q̃ desçienden destas mõtañas /. despues
de surgida la nao salto el almiͤ en la barca pa
so[n?]dar el pueͬto q̃s comõ vna escodilla y quã
do fue frõtero dla boca al sur hallo vnᵃ entrada
de vn rio q̃ tenia de anchura q̃ podia entrar vna
galera por ella y de tal mãrã q̃ no se via hasta
q̃ se llegase a ella . y entrãdo por ella tanto comõ
[d?]l longura dla barca tenia çinco braças
y de ocho de hõdo ⋅/ andãdo por ella fue cosa
maravillosa y las arboledas y frescuras y el agua
clarissima y las aves y amenidad: q̃ dize q
le parecia q̃ no quisiera salir de alli / yva
                                        diziẽ
do a los hobres q̃ llevava "en su cõpanͭͣ" q̃ pa
                                  hazͤͬ relacion a los
reyes dlas cosas q̃ vian: no bastarã mill lẽguas
a referillo / ni su mano pa lo escrevir q̃ le
                              parecia
q̃stava encantado / deseava q̃ aq̃llo vierã mũchas

Fol. 29v
otras p̃rsonas prudẽtes y de credito dlas quales
dize ser çierto q̃ no encareçiera estas cosas
menos q̃ el /. Dize mas el almiͤ aqui estas palabras
quato sera el benefiçio q̃ de aqui se puede aver
yo no lo escrivo /. es cierto señores prinçipes
q̃ donde ay tales tr̃ras q̃ deve de aver infini
tas cosas de provecho: mas yo no me detẽ
go en ningud puerto porq̃ querria ver to
das las mas tr̃ras q̃ yo pudiese pa hazer re
lacion dellas a vr̃as altezas: y tãbien no se
la lengua y la gente destas tr̃ras no me en
tienden ni yo ni otro q̃ yo tẽga a ellos / y
estos yndios q̃ yo traygo muchas vezes le
entiendo vna cosa por otra al contrario: ni
fio mũcho dllos / porq̃ mũchas vezes an pro
vado a fugir /. mas agora plaziẽdo "a ñro"
señor vere lo mas q̃ yo pudiere y poco a
poco andare entendiendo y cognosçiendo y fa
re enseñar esta lẽgua a p̃rsonas de mi casa
porq̃ veo q̃s toda la lengua vna fasta a
qui /. y dspues se sabrã los benefiçios y se
trabajara de hazer todos "estos" pueblos xr̃ianos /
porq̃ de ligero se hara: porq̃ ellos no tie
nẽ secta ninguᵃ ni son idolatras / y vr̃as
altezas mãdarã hazͤͬ en estas p̃tes çiudad
e fortaleza: y se convertirã estas tr̃ras /. y

221

çertifico a .v.al. q̃ debaxo dl sol no me
pareçe q̃ las puede aver mejores: en fer
tilidad en temperāçia de frio y calor / en
abūdançia de aguas buenas y sanas y no co
m̄o los rios de guinea q̃ son
todos pestilençia /. porq̃ loado n̄ro señor
hasta oy de toda mi gente no a avido p̱rsona
q̃ le aya mal la cabeça ni estado en cama
por dolençia: salvo vn viejo de dolor de
piedra de q̃ el estava toda su vida apassio
nado / y luego sano al cabo de dos dias /.
Esto q̃ digo es en todos tres "los" navios /.
asi que plazera a dios q̃ v̄r̄as altezas enbia
ran aca /o vernā h̄ōbres doctos y veran des
pues la Vrdad de todo /. y porq̃ atras ten
go hablado dl sitio de villa e fortaleza en
el rio de mares por el buē pu^(er)to

Fol. 30

y por la comarca es çierto q̃ todo es Vrdad lo q̃
yo dixe mas no a ningu^a conpaçion de alla
aqui ni dla mar de n̄r̄a señora /. porq aqui
deve aver infra la tierra / grādes poblacio
nes y gente inumerable y cosas a grāde
provecho /. porq̃ aqui y en todo lo otro dscubier
to y tengo esperāça de descubrir antes q̃
yo vaya a castilla: digo q̃ terna toda la xrian
dad negociaçion en ellas / quāto mas la espa
ña a quien deve estar subjecto todo /. y digo
q̃ .v. altezas no deven consentir q̃ aqui trate
ni faga pie ningund estrāgero / salva catholi
cos xr̄ianos: pues esto fue el fin y el comien
ço dl proposito que fuese por acreçēntami°
y gloria dla religion xriana: ni venir a
estas p̱tes ningu° q̃ no sea buē xr̄iano /.
todas son sus palabras /. subio alli
por el rio arriba y hallo vnos braços del rio
y rodeādo el puerto hallo a la boca dl rio estava
vnas arboledas my graciosas como vna my
deleytable gue^rta y alli hallo vna almadia
/o canoa hecha de vn madero tan grāde como
vna fusta de doze bācos mȳ hermosa varada
debaxo de vna "ataraçana /o" ramada hecha de madera [y?]
cubierta de grādes hojas de palma / por mara
q̃ ni el sol ni el agua le podian hazer daño /
y dize q̃ alli era el proprio lugar p̱a hazer vna
villa /o çiudad y fortaleza por el bue puerto

222

buenas aguas / buenas tr̄r̄as / buenas co
marcas y mucha leña /.

miercoles .28. de noviebre

Fol. 30
(cont.)

Estuvose en aq̃l pu^{er}to aq̃l dia porq̃ llovia
y hazia gr̄a çerrazō avnq̃ podia correr toda
la costa c̄o el viento q̃ era sudueste y fuera a
popa / po porq̃ no pudiera ver bien la tr̄r̄a y no
sabiendola es peligroso a los navios no se p̃tio /
salierō a tr̄r̄a la gente dlos navios a lavar su
ropa / entrarō algunos dllos vn rato
por la tr̄r̄a adentro hallarō gr̄ades poblaciones
y las casas vazias porq̃ se avian huydo to
dos: tornarose por otro rio abaxo mayor q̃ aq̃l
donde estavan en el pu^{er}to /

Jueves .29. de noviebre

Fol. 30
(cont.)
Fol. 30v

porq̃ llovia y el çielo estava de la mar̄a çerrado

que ayer no se partio / llegarō algunos
dlos xr̄ianos a otra poblaçion "çerca" dla p̃te de
norueste y no hallarō en las casas a
nadie ni nada: y en el camino toparo c̄o
vn viejo q̃ no les pudo huyr: tomarole
y dixerōle q̃ no le querian haze^r mal: y di
erōle algunas cosillas dl resgate y dexarolo
el almi^e. quisiera vello pa "vestillo y" tomar
lengua dl/.
porq̃ le c̄otentava mucho la felicidad de aq̃lla
tr̄r̄a y disposicion q̃ pa poblar en ella avia y
juzgava q
devia de aver gr̄ades poblaçiones /. hallaron
en vna casa vn pan de çera q̃ truxo a los re
yes / y dize q̃ donde çera ay t̄abiē deve aver
otras mil cosas buenas /. hallarō t̄abien los
marineros en casa: vna cabeça de h̄obre
dentro en vn çestillo cubierto con otro cestillo
y colgado de vn poste dla casa: y dla misma
mar̄a hallarō otra en otra poblaçion /.
creyo el almi^e. que devia ser de algunos
prinçipales dl linaje: porq̃ aq̃llas casas era

de maῆa ᷐ se acojen en ellas mucha gente en
vna sola: y deven ser parientes desçendiētes de vno
solo /.

viernes .30. de noviēbre

No se pudo partir por᷐l viento era levāte mȳ
cōtrario a su camino: envio ocho hōbres bien
armados y "con ellos" dos yndios dlos ᷐ traya pa ᷐
viesen a᷐llos pueblos dla tᷓra dentro y
por aver lengua /. llegarō a mūchas casas
y no hallarō a nadie ni nada ᷐ todos se aviā
huydo /. vierō quatro māçebos ᷐stavā cavā
do en su heredades asi como vierō los xrianos
dierō a huyr / no loṣ pudierō alcançar /. an
duvierō diz᷐ mūcho camino / vierō muchas po
blaçiones y tierra fertilissima y toda labrada
y grādes riberas de agua / y çerca de vna vie
rō vna almadia /o canoa de noventa y çinco
palmos de lōgura de vn solo madero mȳ her
mosa: y ᷐ en ella cabrian y navegarian çien
to y çinquēta ₚrsonas /

Sabado .1.º dia de diziēbre

no se ₚtio por la misma causa dl viento contra
rio y por᷐ llovia mūcho: asento vna cruz gra
de a la entrada de a᷐l puᵉrto ᷐ creo llamo el
puerto sancto sobre vñas peñas bivas /. la punta
es a᷐lla ᷐sta dla parte dl sueste a la entrada dl

puerto /. y quien oviere de entrar en este puerto
se deve llegar mas sobre la ₚte dl norueste
de a᷐lla punta: ᷐ sobre la otra dl sueste /. puesto
᷐ al pie de ambas junto cō la peña ay doze bracas de
hōdo y mȳ limpio /. mas a la entrada dl puᵉrto
sobre la punta dl sueste ay vna baxa ᷐ sobreagua
la qual dista dla punta tanto ᷐ se podria
passar entremedias aviendo neçessidad por᷐ al
pie de la baxa y dl cabo todo es fondo de doze y de
quinze braças y a la entrada se a de poner la proa
al sudueste /.

224

Domingo .2. de diziēbre

todavia fue contrario el viento y no pudo partir
dize q̃ todas las noches dl mūdo vienta terral: y
q̃ todas las naos q̃ alli estuvierō no ayā miedo
de toda la tormēta dl mūdo porq̃ no puede reca
lar dentro por vna baxa q̃ esta al principio dl
puerto etc. En la boca de aq̃l rio dizq̃ hallo vn
grumete çiertas piedras q̃ pareçen tener oro tru
xolas pa mostrar a los reyes /. dize q̃ ay por alli
a tyro de lōbarda grādes rios /.

lunes .3. de diziēbre

por causa de q̃ hazia siemp^r tp̄o contrario no
partia de aq̃l pu^{er}to / y acordo de yr a ver
vn cabo mȳ hermoso vn quarto de legua
dl pu^{er}to dla p̣te dl sueste / fue c̄o las barcas
y alguna gente armada . al pie del cabo avia
vna boca de vn buē r̄ıo puesta la proa al sue
este pa entrar y tenia çiento passos de anchura
tenia vna braça de "fondo" a la entrada /o en
la boca: p̣o dentro avia doze braças y
çinco y quatro y dos: y cabrian en el quātos
navios ay en españa /. dexādo vn braço de
aq̃l rio fue al sueste y hallo vna caleta en
q̃ vido çinco mȳ grādes almadias q̃ los yndios
llamā canoas com̄o fustas mȳ hermosas
y labradas q̃ era dizq̃ era plazer vellas y al
pie dl mōte vido todo labrado /. estavā deba
xo de arboles mȳ espessos /. y yendo por vn
camino q̃ salia a ellas fuerō a dar a vna atara
çana mȳ biē ordenada y cubierta q̃ ni sol ni
agua no les podia haz^{er} dañ̄o / y debaxo dlla
avia otra canoa hecha de vn
madero com̄o las otras com̄o vna fusta de diez
y siete bancos q̃/ era plazer ver las labores q̃ tenia
y su hermosura /. Subio vna mōtaña arriba
y despues hallola toda llana y senbrada de mū
chas cosas dla tr̄ra y calabaças q̃ era gloria vella:
y en medio della estava vna grā poblacion /.

dio de subito sobre la gente dl pueblo
y comō los vierō hobres y mugeres dan
de huyr /. asegurolos el yndio q̃ llevava
cōsigo dlos q̃ traya diziēdo q̃ no oviesen
miedo q̃ gente buena era: hizolos dar el
almi͠e cascavales y sortijas de laton: y
contezuelas de vidro verdes y amarillas: con q̃
fuerō mȳ contētos /. visto q̃ no tenian oro
ni otra cosa preçiosa y q̃ bastava dexallos segu
ros: y q̃ toda la comarca era poblada y huydos
los demas de miedo y certifica el almi͠e a los
reyes q̃ diez hōbres hagā huyr a diez mill .
tan cobardes y medrosos son
q̃ ni traen armas salvo vna varas y enl cabo
dllas vn pallillo agudo tostado: acordo bolverse /.
dize q̃ las varas se las quito todas con buena
mañā: resgatandoselas / de māra q̃ todas las
dierō /. tornados adonde avian dexado las bar
cas: enbio çiertos xr̄ianos al
lugar por donde subierō: porq̃ le avia pareçido
q̃ avia visto vn "grā" colmenar / antes q̃ viniesen los
q̃ avia embiado: ayuntarōse muchos yndios
y vinierō a las barcas donde ya se avia el almi͠e
recogido cō su gente toda: vno dllos se adelanto
en el rio junto cō la popa dla barca: y hizo vna
grāde platica q̃l almi͠e no entēdia: salvo q̃ los
otros yndios de quādo en quādo alçavā las ma
nos al çielo y davā vna grāde boz /. pensava
el almi͠e q̃ lo aseguravan y q̃ les plazia dsu veni
da: pero vido al yndio q̃ consigo traya "de"mu̦
darse la cara y amarillo comō la çera y tem
blava mucho: diziendo por señas q̃ el almi͠e se
fuese fuera dl rio q̃ los querian matar /.
y llegose a vn xr̄iano q̃ tenia vna ballesta ar
mada y mostrola a los yndios y entendio
al almi͠e q̃ les dezia q̃ los matariā todos / por
q̃ aq̃lla ballesta tyrava lexos y matava /. tā
bien̄ tomo vna espada y la saco dla vayna mō
strandosela diziēdo lo mismo /. lo qual oydo por
ellos dierō todos a huyr: quedādo todavia tem
blando el d̄cho yndio de cobardia y poco coraçon
      y "era bōbre de buenā estatura y rezio /."
no quiso el almi͠e salir dl rio antes hizo
remar en tr̄ra hazia donde ellos estavā que
erā mȳ muchos todos tyñidos de colorado
y dsnudos comō sus madres los pario y algu͠os

dllos cō penachos en la cabeça y otras plumas: to
dos con sus manojos de azagayas /. llegueme
a ellos y diles algunos bocados de pan: y demā
deles las azagayas: y davales por ellas: a vnos

vn cascavelito: a otros vna sortijuela de laton
a otros vnas contezuelas . por marā q̃ todos
se apaziguarō y vinierō todos a las barcas
y davā quāto tenian porq̃ quequiera q̃ les da
van /. los marineros aviā
muerto vna tortuga y la cascara estava en la bar
ca en pedacos: y los grumetes davāles della
comō la uña: y los yndios les davā vn ma
nojo de azagayas /. ellos son gente comō los
otros q̃ e hallado (dize el almiᵉ) y dla misma creē
çia y creyan q̃ veniamos dl çielo y dlo q̃ tienē
luego lo dan por qualquiera cosa q̃ les den sin
dezir q̃s poco y creo q̃ asi harian de especeria
y de oro si lo tuviesen /. vide vna casa hermosa
no mȳ grāde y de dos puertas porq̃ asi son todas
y entre en ella y vide vna obra maravillosa co
mō camaras hechas por vna çierta marā q̃
no lo sabria dezir / y colgado al çielo della cara
coles y otras cosas: yo pense q̃ era tēplo y los
llame y dixe por señas si
hazian en ella oracion . dixerō q̃ no . y subio vno
dllos arriba y me dava todo quāto alli avia y
dllo tome algo /.

martes 4ºde diziebre

hizose a la vela con poco viento y salio de aq̃l
puerto q̃ nōbro puᵉʳto santo a las dos leguas
vido vn buē rio de q̃ ayer hablo: fue de
luēgo de costa y corriase toda la trr̄a passado
el dc̄ho cabo lindo q̃sta al cabo dl mōto al
                                    leste quarta
dl sueste y ay de vno a otro çinco leguas /. dl
cabo del mōte a legua y media ay vn grā rio
algo angosto parecio q̃ tenia buena entrada y
era my hōdo y de alli a tres quartos de legua
vido otro grādissimo rio y deve venir de mȳ
lexos en la boca tenia bien çien passos y
en ella ningū banco y en la boca ocho bracas
y buena entrada porq̃ lo enbio a ver y

227

sondar cō la barca y viene el agua dulce hasta
dentro en la mar / y es dlos caudalosos q̃
avia hallado / y deve aver grādes poblacio
nes /. dspues dl cabo lindo ay vna grāde baya
q̃ seria buen pozo por lesnordeste y suest
y sursudueste .

miercoles 5 de diziēbre

Fol. 32
(cont.)
toda esta noche anduvo a la corda sobre el
                              cabo lindo
adonde anochecio por ver la tr̄ra q̃ yva al leste
y al salir dl sol vido otro cabo al leste a dos le

Fol. 32v
guas y media . passado aq̃l vido q̃ la costa bolvia
al sur y tomava dl sudueste y vido luego vn
cabo mȳ hermoso y alto a la dcha derrota: y distava
desotro siete leguas: quisiera yr alla: po por el de
seo q̃ tenia de yr a la isla de baneque q̃ le queda
va segū dexian los yndios q̃ llevava al nordeste
lo dexo: tanpoco pudo yr al baneque porq̃l
viento q̃ llevava era nordeste /. yendo asi
miro al sueste y vido tr̄ra y era vna isla mūy grā
de dla qual ya tenia dizq̃ informaçion de los yndios
a que llama"vā" ellos bohio poblada de gente / desta
gente dizq̃ los de cuba /o juana y de todas esotras
islas tienē grā miedo porq̃ dizq̃ comīan los hō
bres /. otras cosas le contavā los dchos yndios por
señas mȳ maravillosas: mas el almiᵉ no
dizq̃ las creya: sino q̃ devian "tener" mas astuçia
                              y mejor
ingenio los de aq̃lla isla bohio pa los captivar
                   q̃llos
porq̃ erā mȳ flacos de coraçon /. asi que porq̃l tp̄o
era nordeste y tomava dl norte: determino de
dexar a cuba o juana q̃ hasta entonces avia tenido
por tr̄ra firme por su grādeza "porq̃ bien avria"
                              andado
en vn paraje çiento y veynte leguas: y partio al
sueste quarta del leste puesto que la tr̄ra q̃l avia
                         visto
se hazia al sueste dava este reguardo porq̃ siempr
el viento rodea dl norte pa el nordeste y de alli
al leste y sueste /. cargo mucho el viento y llevava
todas sus velas la mar llana y la corriente q̃ le
ayudava por mar̄a q̃ hasta la vna dspues de me

228

dio "dia" dsde la mañana hazia de camino .8.
                              millas por ora
y erā seys oras avn no cōplidas porq̃ dize q̃ alli
erā las noches "çerca" de quinze oras despues anduvo
diez millas por ora y asi andaria hasta el poner
dl sol .88. millas q̃ son .22. leguas todo
al sueste /. y porq̃ se hazia noche mādo a la
                              caravela
niña q̃ se adelantasse pa ver cō dia el pu^{er}to porq̃
era velera: y llegādo a la boca dl puerto q̃ era
cōmo la baya de caliz y porq̃ era ya de noche: en
bio a su barca q̃ sondase el pu^{er}to /. la qual llevo
lūbre de candela: y antes q̃l almi^e. llegasse
adonde la caravela estava barloventeando y esperā
do q̃ la barca le hiziese señas pa entrar en el puer
to apagosele la lūbre a la barca /. la caravela
cōmo no vido lumbre corrio de largo y hizo lūbre
al almi^e. y llegado a ella cōtarō lo q̃ avia acaeçido /.
estado en esto los dla barca hizierō otra lubre: la
caravela fue a ella y el almi^e no pudo y estuvo
toda aq̃lla noche barloventeando /.

Jueves 6 de diziēbre

Fol. 32v
(cont.)
Fol. 33

quādo amanecio se hallo quatro leguas dl puerto

pusole nōbre puerto maria y vido vn cabo
hermoso al sur quarta del sudueste al qual puso
nōbre cabo dl estrella y parecide q̃ era la
postrera tr̄ra de aq̃lla isla hazia el sur y estaria
el almi^e. dl xxviii millas /. pareçiale otra
tr̄ra cōmo isla no grāde al leste y esta
ria del .40. millas /. quedavale otro cabo
mȳ hermoso y bien hecho a quien puso nōbre
cabo del elefante al leste quarta dl sueste y dista
le ya .54. millas /. Quedavale otro cabo al lessueste
al q̃ puso nōbre el cabo de çinquin: estaria dl
.28. millas /. Quedavale vna gran scisura o aber
tura /o abra a la mar q̃ le pareçio ser rio al sueste
y tomava dla quarta dl leste: avria dl a la abra .20
millas /. pareçiale q̃ entre el cabo dl elifante dl
de çinquin avia vna grādissima entrada y algu
nos dlos marineros dezian q̃ era ap̃ta
miento de isla aq̃lla puso por nōbre la isla
dla tortuga /. aq̃lla isla grāde pareçia altissima

trr̄a no çerrada con mōtes: sino rasa comō her
mosas campiñas y pareçe toda labrada /o grāde
parte dlla y parecian las semēteras comō trigo
en el mes de mayo en la cāpiña de cordova /
vierōse mūchos huegos aꝗlla noche: y de dia
mūchos humos comō atalayas ꝗ parecia estar
sobre aviso de alguna gente cō quiē tuviesen guer
ra /. toda la costa desta trr̄a va al leste /. A oras
de bisperas entro en el puerto dicho y puso
le nōbre puerto de san Nicolas porꝗ era dia
de sant nicolas por hōrra suya / y a la entrada dl se
maravillo de su hermosura y bōdad / y avnꝗ
tiene mūcho alabados los puertos de cuba: p̲o̲ sin
duda dize el ꝗ no es menos este: antes los sobre
puja y ninguᵒ le es semejante /. En boca y entra
da tiene legua y media de ancho y se pone la
proa al sursueste puesto ꝗ por la grāde anchura
se puede poner la proa adonde quisierē /. va desta
mar̄a al sursueste dos leguas: y a la entrada del
por la p̲te del sur: se haze comō vna angla y de
alli se sigue asi igual hasta el cabo adonde esta
vna playa mȳ hermosa y vn campo de arboles
de mill mar̄as y todos cargados de frutas ꝗ creya
el almi̧ᵉ ser de especerias y nuezes moscadas:
sino ꝗ no estava maduras y no se cognoscio /
y vn rio en medio dla playa /. El hōdo deste puer
to es maravilloso ꝗ hasta llegar a la trr̄a en longu
ra de vna   no llego la sondaresa o ploma
da al fondo con quareta braças y ay hasta esta lōgura
el hōdo de .xv. bracas y mȳ limpio /. y asi en todo el

dicho puerto de cada cabo hōdo dentro a vna passada
de trr̄a de 15. braças y limpio . y desta mar̄a es
toda la costa mȳ hōdable y limpia ꝗ no pareçe
vna sola baxa /. y al pie dlla tanto comō longura
de vn remo de barca de trr̄a tiene çinco bra
ças /. y dspues dla lōgura del d̄cho puᵉʳto yen
do al sursueste (en la qual lōgura puedē barlovē
tear mil carracas: bojo vn braço dl puerto
al nordeste por la trr̄a dentro vna grāde media
legua y siempre en vna misma anchura comō ꝗ
lo hizierā por vn cordel: el qual queda de ma
nera ꝗstando en aꝗl braço ꝗ sera de anchura de
veynte y çinco passos no se puede ver la
boca dla entrada grāde / de mar̄a ꝗ queda puer
to çerrado: y el fondo deste braço es asi en

el comienço hasta la fin de onze braças y todo
basa /o arena limpia y hasta tr̄ra y poner los
bordos en las yervas tiene ocho braças /. es todo
el puerto mȳ ayroso y desabahado de arboles
raso /. toda esta isla le pareçio "de" mas peñas q̃
ninguᵃ otra q̃ aya hallado /. los arboles mas
pequeños y muchos dllos dla naturaleza de
españa cōmo carrascas y madroños y otros y
lo mismo dlas yervas /. Es tr̄ra mȳ alta y
toda campiña /o rasa y de mȳ buenos ayres
y no se a visto tanto frio cōmo alli avnq̃ no es
de contar por frio mas dixolo al respecto de
las otras trr̄as /. hazia en frente de aq̃l puer
to vna hermosa vega y en medio dlla el rio
suso d̄cho: y en aq̃lla comarca (dize) deve aver
grādes poblaçiones segū se vian las almadias
con q̃ navegan: tantas y tan grādes dllas cōmo vna
fusta de .15. bancos /. todos los yndios
huyerō y huian cōmo vian los navios /. los
q̃ consigno dlas isletas traya tenian tanta gana
de yr a su tr̄ra: q̃ pensava (dize el almiᵉ.) q̃
despues q̃ se ꝑtiese de alli los tenia de llevar
a sus casas: y q̃ ya lo tenian por sospechoso porq̃
no lleva el camino dsu casa /. por lo qual dize
q̃ ni les creya lo q̃ le dezian: ni los entendia
bien ni ellos a el: y dizq̃ avian el mayor
miedo dl mūdo dla gente de aq̃lla isla /. asi q̃
por querer aver lengua c̄o la gente de aq̃lla
isla: le fuera neçessario detenerse algunos dias
en aq̃l puerto: p̲o no lo hazia por ver mūcha
tr̄ra y por dudar q̃l tp̄o le duraria /. esperava en

Fol. 34

nr̄o señor q̃ los yndios q̃ traya sabrian su lēgua
y el la suya y dspues tornaria y hablara
c̄o aq̃lla gente y
plazera a su magᵈ (dize el) q̃ hallara algū buē
resgate de oro antes q̃ buelva /.

231

Louis De Vorsey, Jr., is professor of geography at the University of Georgia, Athens, and past president of The Society for the History of Discoveries. John Parker is curator of the James Ford Bell Library at the University of Minnesota in Minneapolis. He has been both secretary and president of The Society for the History of Discoveries.

The book was designed by Betty Hanson. The typeface for the text and display is Baskerville, designed by John Baskerville in the eighteenth century. The text is printed on 60-lb. Glatfelter text paper. The book is bound in Joanna Mills' B grade cloth over binder's boards.

Manufactured in the United States of America.